BEYOND
BAKER STREET

BEYOND BAKER STREET

A Sherlockian Anthology
edited and annotated by

MICHAEL HARRISON

THE BOBBS-MERRILL COMPANY, INC.
Indianapolis / New York

Published by the Bobbs-Merrill Company, Inc.
Indianapolis   New York

Designed by Jacques Chazaud

Manufactured in the United States of America
First printing

Library of Congress Cataloging in Publication Data
Main entry under title:

Beyond Baker Street.

Includes index.
  1. Doyle, Sir Arthur Conan, 1859–1930—Characters—Sherlock
Holmes.   2. Doyle, Sir Arthur Conan, 1859–1930—Criticism
and interpretation—Addresses, essays, lectures.   I. Harrison,
Michael.
PR4624.B46   823'.9'12   75–33435
ISBN 0–672–52207–1

Thirteen black-and-white drawings, prepared specially for this anthology,
© 1976, Henry Lauritzen.

Witchcraft in Baker Street, © 1976, Frank Allen.

The Dynamics of an Asteroid, © 1976, Isaac Asimov.

The Other Decalogue, © 1976, Jacques Barzun.

What Sherlock Holmes Knew, or The Dreadful Secret of the UFO, © 1976,
  Jacques Bergier.

Contents

✖

Illustrations   ix

Preface: Twenty-five Authors . . . and an Artist   xi

FRANK ALLEN   *Witchcraft in Baker Street*   1

ISAAC ASIMOV   *The Dynamics of an Asteroid*   13

JACQUES BARZUN   *The Other Decalogue*   21

JACQUES BERGIER   *What Sherlock Holmes Knew, or,*
                     The Dreadful Secret of the UFO   33

S. TUPPER BIGELOW   *The Ten Best Canonical Stories*   45

ALAN BRADLEY   *Nothing of Value*   57

PETER COOPER   *Holmesian Chemistry*   67

PHILIP DALTON   *Sherlock Holmes and New*
                     Scotland Yard   75

QUENTIN DOWNES   *Why Did He Call Her "Carfax"?*   87

ANDREW G. FUSCO   *The Case Against Mr. Holmes*   95

JOHN GARDNER   *Moriarty and the Real Underworld*   111

MARTIN GARDNER   *The Irrelevance of Conan Doyle*   123

MICHAEL HARRISON   *Sherlock Holmes and "The King of*
                     Bohemia"   137

BANESH HOFFMANN *Red Faces and "The Red-headed League"* 175

ANTHONY HOWLETT *The Impersonators: Sherlock Holmes on Stage and Screen* 187

NICHOLAS MEYER *Psychological Directions in Holmesian Criticism* 205

DAVID PEARSON *Did Holmes Believe in God?* 211

DONALD A. REDMOND *This Is Not Our Sherlock! (Part I)* 227

KARL KREJCI-GRAF *This Is Not Our Sherlock! (Part II)* 240

SAMUEL ROSENBERG *Some Notes on the Conan Doyle Syndrome and Allegory in "The Adventure of Red Circle"* 245

JOHN BENNETT SHAW *Sherlock and the American Indian* 271

NICHOLAS UTECHIN *The Colonel of the Matter: The Early Career of Colonel Sebastian Moran* 283

EDWARD VAN LIERE *A Critique of the Biologic Plots* 295

ALAN WATKINS *Sherlock Holmes and the Invisible Car Park* 305

COLIN WILSON *The Flawed Superman* 311

Notes on the Contributors 335

List of Illustrations

✄

Thirteen Sherlockian Drawings

✄

HENRY LAURITZEN

✄

The thirteen black-and-white drawings which decorate an equal number of the contributions in this anthology are the work of Henry Lauritzen and were done specially for this book as Lauritzen's contribution to it.

✄

Joyce-Armstrong's sixth flying machine, 1897   41

A blueprint for immortality—Conan Doyle's rough notes for the characters of Holmes and Watson   53

Original Metropolitan Police headquarters, Great Scotland Yard, 1829–1892   78

Norman Shaw's "baronial" New Scotland Yard, 1892   79

London's *new* New Scotland Yard, at the corner of Broadway and Victoria Street   80

Coat-of-arms of the Barons Churchill of Wychwood   92

Sherlock's legal college? The "Holbein" gateway of Lincoln's Inn (1518)   99

The "New Law Courts," opened in the Strand, 1882   102

A notorious London slum of Victorian days: St. Giles's   112

"Antigarotting collar"—spoof of Victorian advertisement   113

An even worse Victorian slum: Field Lane, Clerkenwell   115

A Victorian "loafer" ripe for mischief   119

Victorian "peelers" chasing street musicians   119

"Fairy" photographs (from *Fairies* by Edward L. Gardner)
warmly endorsed by Sir Arthur Conan Doyle   130

Lillie Langtry, the real "Irene Adler"—in a
Victorian Pears' Soap advertisement   146

"Bertie," Prince of Wales, in "Balkan" uniform   154

"Sandro"—Alexander, first sovereign ruler of Bulgaria   154

Queen Victoria at the time of her Golden Jubilee (1887)   155

James Bragington, first British Sherlock Holmes on film, 1914   196

Eille Norwood, 1921, in one of his forty-eight Holmes films   197

Arthur Wontner, *the* film Holmes of his day—1937   200

The most famous filmic Holmes-Watson partnership:
Basil Rathbone and Nigel Bruce, 1939   201

Interior of the Norman priory church of
St. Bartholomew-the-Great   218

The vanished church of St. Paul's Portman Square, Baker
Street   219

A Portuguese translation of a German "Sherlock Holmes"
story not by Doyle   232

A Portuguese plagiarism   233

Holmes in the bull ring in a Spanish plagiarism   234

The Enslaved Conan Doyle—cartoon by Sir Bernard Partridge   253

Sherlockian questions and answers—in Cherokee   275

Sequoya's Cherokee syllabary—a native American script   276

Ted Walker's impression of the Master's solution of a
"three-pipe problem"   278

Holmes and Watson meet for the first time at "Bart's"   297

Queen Elizabeth II passing the "Invisible Car Park"   307

Holmes gazing unmoved at the ruins of a bombed
Strand building   321

Preface
Twenty-five Authors ... and an Artist

✠

This is not the first Sherlock-orientated anthology to have been collected and published. It is, however, the first to have been put together with a larger public in view than the dedicated membership—however large—of the various Sherlock Holmes societies now scattered throughout the world, from the Netherlands to Chile, from Britain to the United States, from Holland to Denmark, from Sweden to Japan.

Two intentions lay behind this collection: the first—to which I shall return presently—was a personal, one might say an emotional, one; the other was to take the analysis of Sherlock Holmes out of the dangerously parochial confinement to which too specialized research and criticism seem (at least to me) to be condemning what should be, since he belongs to the world, a world figure.

The other night, I resigned myself to a whole evening of what was, unhappily for me, average television, though the fact that it was average was one that I welcomed. The periods covered by the various plays and films ranged from Hollywood Medieval, through Pinewood and Shepperton Victorian and Edwardian, to British, French and American Modern Tough.

I also listened to the commercials. On one channel, between 6:00
P.M. and midnight, I heard the name of Sherlock Holmes introduced into the various scripts no fewer than five times. Repeating
the experiment on two other nights, I heard mention of the Baker
Street Master four times on the first night, three times on the
second: he had thus been mentioned, on one channel only, twelve
times in three nights. I have no doubt that tuning in on other
channels would have yielded similar results.

These mentions had nothing to do with the plot, nor were they
"pararelevant" in that they occurred only in films relating to crime
and detection. They were mostly to be heard in such expressions
as "How do I know *where* he is? I'm not a Sherlock Holmes!"
Once, complimenting her husband on having found something for
which he had been searching too long, the young wife said sar-
castically, "Bravo, Sherlock Holmes!" Such expressions, such casual
references to the Master, arise out of the ordinary stuff of aimless
human conversation because now, after nearly ninety years of
existence, Holmes has indeed become part of the ordinary stuff of
human existence. But what is so strange about this literary creation, a fact that sets him apart from all the other household words
of an author's imagining, is that he had become part of the stuff of
human living within a few years of his having first appeared in
Beeton's Christmas Annual for 1887. I turn up a copy of *The Idler*
for the year 1894 and find there this rather grisly joke:

> YOUNG SHERLOCK *(in cemetery, by unmarked grave):* Mamma, that's
> a man buried there.
>
> MOTHER: Why, goodness gracious, how can you tell?
>
> YOUNG SHERLOCK: Look, Mamma, there's the end of his cigar!

I did not introduce this late-Victorian jest for the purpose of
what the Victorians would have called "tickling the risible faculties" of my readers on both sides of the Atlantic, but as proof that
even by the early nineties, Sherlock Holmes, as a character, had
found complete acceptance even in the least highbrow of contemporary periodical literature. References to him, from this period,
abound in the music hall and the theater, in serious and light
novels, and—as I have found—in private correspondence. This acceptance, which is as total today as it was eighty years ago, has

never been fully explained, and I do not intend to attempt the explanation here. I merely mention this acceptance as a fact.

It was not as though there had been no fictional detectives before Holmes appeared in *Beeton's Christmas Annual.* Poe's Dupin, appearing first in April 1841, had become deservedly popular in America, Britain and the British Empire, France, and Germany in the nearly half-century that had passed between his appearance and that of Holmes. Dickens's Inspector Bucket is still a credible police officer; and on the more popular level of reading, Hawkshaw the detective had an immense following, and an immense fame. But Holmes seems to have stepped, as it were, into a place that had been kept reserved for him. He was treated on his appearance as he has been treated ever since: as something unique in the way of detectives; something unique, indeed, in the way of men.

The csarist army authorities considered that the adventures of Sherlock Holmes were good, sound reading for Russian soldiers —the Soviet army authorities concur in the opinion (in this important particular) of their csarist predecessors; and so it is that soldiers of the Red Army still read of Holmes in books bearing the imprimatur of the Red Army Publishing House.

What is important to observe here, and I mention this because it is not mentioned by any of our twenty-five literary contributors, is that this acceptance by the csarist and Soviet authorities in no way implies that Sherlock Holmes is, or may be interpreted as being, a political animal. I recall how astonished I was, some years ago, to find that John Galsworthy—Old Harrovian and Cantab solicitor, comfortably placed inheritor of the old established family legal practice—was a best-seller behind the Iron Curtain because of his "advanced" politico-social views. His literary agent explained to me that it was this interpretation of, principally, *The Forsyte Saga* that accounted for the scrupulous care with which these supporters calculated and paid the royalties on his pirated work (that is to say, work printed without the author's express permission). As a young book reviewer, one day I found John Galsworthy's autobiography among the books to be read for review. Next to that of A. A. Milne, this autobiography was the dullest that I have ever encountered: curiosity made me open the book; only duty carried me through to the end.

The book contained nothing. Nothing at all. It wasn't that Galsworthy's politico-social views were encouragingly radical or hopelessly conservative. The truth is that he had no views at all—and if our friends behind the Iron Curtain may read into this neutrality of opinion a leaning toward the radical, then jolly good luck to them! But the fact is that Galsworthy is popular in the eastern parts of Europe because he is one of the quite numerous band of skilled writers able to present deftly the ambitions and prejudices of bourgeois life—a life having a curious appeal for a newer type of bourgeois.

The adoption or acceptance of Sherlock Holmes has nothing at all in common with the rather patronizing taking-up, on both sides of the Iron Curtain, of such portrayers of middle-class drawing rooms as Galsworthy, Trollope, Henry James, Proust, Thomas Mann, and, of course, Ibsen and Strindberg.

No one, not even the most fervent Marxist, has sought to father views and significances upon Holmes which are not plainly apparent at the first reading of the stories. If, in this anthology, David Pearson attempts to assess Holmes's fundamental religious beliefs, his views are based on what the stories tell him—and tell us, too, for that matter—and not on what Pearson thinks Watson or the Agent either left unsaid or cut out. And when Peter Cooper makes his own assessment of Holmes's chemical knowledge, this assessment goes no further for its evidence than Holmes's words or Watson's descriptions. And the same remark applies to John Bennett Shaw's look at Holmes's relations with the Red Indian: in all these cases, speculation counts for nothing; the written evidence from the Holmesian Saga, for everything.

In this refusal to foist views and political awareness on Holmes, the world, over nearly a century, has paid him a unique compliment. I can think of no other world figure in literature, from Don Quixote to Huckleberry Finn, from Robinson Crusoe to the Count of Monte Cristo, from Lemuel Gulliver to Struwelpeter, who hasn't had his image blurred and distorted by the ever-more-subtle interpretations by which he has been represented to the public. The literary disease of myth interpretation begins with the interpretation of what appears to be myth, and ends with the interpretation of what the interpreter claims is myth. This diversion of an undisciplined scholarship of which such men as Förschhammer, in the last century, were principal practitioners, turned all the characters of Homeric saga into "Nature myths" (especially great play was made with the legend of Jason and the Golden Fleece). Crusoe and Gulliver and Struwelpeter didn't become exactly Nature myths, but one feels that they escaped this interpretive fate by a very narrow margin. Holmes has never been interpreted to demonstrate that he is anything other than what he claimed to be: a private consulting detective.

Holmes is, without doubt, a world figure. People who cannot read a word of English know his name; thousands of people write each year to his supposed address in a big modern building on Baker Street whose owners employ a permanent staff to answer every letter. And the odd thing is that his fame increases in a world which has changed more in thirty years than in the previous three centuries. At a recent London film series of Sherlockian interest, there must have been nearly four hundred people; it is no exaggeration on my part to claim that eighty percent of that number were under thirty. The young who laugh and are encouraged to laugh at anything that has had its origin outside of their own fleeting generation do not laugh at Holmes. They accept Holmes, as their fathers and grandfathers accepted him—though perhaps not always for the same reasons.

Does this make Holmes a hero figure? I would regard that as a most unlikely claim. Holmes has some heroic qualities, but heroic qualities of the sort that are common to most decent, quite ordinary people. He is intensely prejudiced, often bad-tempered, irritable with the people who might look to him for a little kindness, capable of a quite unmerited snub, grossly (and I don't mean the cocaine) self-indulgent, arrogant, self-opinionated, and decidedly touchy about trivialities. (For a prime example of this, the reader is referred to his rebuking of the Austrian Baron Gruner.) There are other faults—all as plain to see—but this small tally will serve us for the present. If Holmes is a hero, then he had legs, not merely feet, of clay.

Is that why Holmes has become a world figure—because he isn't a hero? This may well be the answer—for, if one looks not even closely, the other world figures weren't really heroes, either. Ulysses was a self-indulgent (another one) trickster who usually managed to have his cake and eat it, too; both Gulliver and Crusoe fled domestic lives in which they had taught their wives to prefer their absence to their company; Don Quixote—well, we know what an oddity he was! And as for all the other figures familiar in men's mouths as household words, there's not a King Arthur among them (and even he was cuckolded by his most loyal knight). Perhaps the world appeal of Holmes is the world appeal, not of the hero, but of Everyman; Everyman with all his petty faults making his ordinary courage to face life so much the more splendid. Do not be deceived by the title of Colin Wilson's contribution to this anthology: Holmes was not—nor has anyone ever thought him to be—a Superman. That he had some qualities of the Superman, I shall agree with Wilson, but then, even the lowliest of mankind has some of these qualities; otherwise, as Turgenev said in a slightly different context, he could not continue to live on this earth.

I have given, I suppose, some two dozen radio talks on Holmes; John Bennett Shaw, he tells me, has given over three hundred; the total of Samuel Rosenberg's lectures on Holmes must now be approaching Shaw's handsome achievement. In all these talks—and the combined output of Sherlockian lecturers over the past fifty years must total thousands—some attempt has been made to answer the question which has invariably been put to me: "How do you account for the fascination that Sherlock Holmes exerts over so many people, from so many backgrounds and countries, and over such a length of time?"

I try to answer this question. I never succeed. Like the classic description, in the Poe tale, of one's trying to recall a dream, trying until the dream is on the very verge of recall: I often think that I have found the answer—only to have the knowledge escape me before I can grasp it.

Perhaps the answer may be found in this book. I sincerely hope so.

And now I come to that second intention behind the making of this anthology: that more personal intention to which I referred.

It all began (as they say in novels) in the lounge of the Cumberland Hotel in London nearly two years ago. I was having a drink with an eminent fellow Sherlockian, Dr. Banesh Hoffmann, now Professor of Mathematics at Queens College, New York. In the course of gossip about some other—mostly transatlantic—Sherlockians, Dr. Hoffmann mentioned that Dr. Julian Wolff, Commissionnaire of the Baker Street Irregulars, and hard-working, enviably efficient and editorially brilliant producer of *The Baker Street Journal*, would be completing his third lustrum—a full fifteen years —as editor in 1975. "And that," said Dr. Hoffmann, "will coincide with his seventieth birthday. . . ."

Now, from what we both knew of Dr. Wolff, and from what we both thought of the *Journal* under his inspired management and editorship, it seemed to us that this double anniversary was one calling for the tribute of—at least—one of those collections that the Germans call a *Festschrift:* an album of essays in honor of some eminent person to whom respect is due; a recognition of Dr. Wolff's personality and work from some of his friends.

I asked another Sherlockian "Irregular Shilling"—a detective-novelist of world sales and world fame—if he might recommend a sympathetic publisher. He did—and I got in touch. The publisher *was* sympathetic. As Dr. Hoffmann was fully engaged in teaching mathematics, writing his books, lecturing, and generally living the full academic life, and as I had sat in the editorial chair almost twenty times, I offered to do the actual work of editing the collection and seeing it through the press. The collecting of contributors was to be our joint responsibility. The motive was, of course, to pay tribute to Dr. Wolff, both as an editor and as a great Sherlockian.

The publisher whom I approached was sympathetic to the idea of a Sherlockian anthology, but not in the narrowly restricted form of a *Festschrift*. "I view it with suspicion," said Samuel Butler, "as being academic." The publisher had the same reservations. He wished for an anthology that would proclaim its message *urbi et orbi*—to the greatest number of readers—not merely to the inner circle of *Sherlockismus*.

Well, here is the collection.

It has gaps of course. Among those who were invited to contribute, there were many who had to refuse—unwillingly, it is true, but decisively, nonetheless. Age, the pressure of other work, the inability to say anything new—there were many reasons, almost none of them excuses. And, for purely economic reasons (for we live in an expensive age), the book had to be calculated to a very precise length.

The diversity of talent which has gone to make up this collection reflects, we like to think, the diversity—no less than the talent—which is, perhaps, the most striking characteristic of the Sherlockian movement generally. Within its two principal societies, the Baker Street Irregulars of New York and the Sherlock Holmes Society of London—not forgetting the many scion societies scattered throughout the world—every profession, every vocation and avocation, every creed and every color, join in one of the happiest associations known to history. Judges and scientists, novelists and accountants, Monsignori and rabbis, mathematicians and philosophers, geologists and television engineers, medical practitioners and bank presidents . . . all meet, within this Sherlockian unity, in an unruffled harmony which must be the envy of noisily self-advertising brotherhoods. At least one cardinal and one president of the United States may be found among the Baker Street Irregulars, and if, as a friend pointed out to me, the IQ of the Irregulars "must be as high as that of the Royal Society or the Academy of Sciences in France," then that must be because these other, and older, bodies attract the same type of mind.

What sets the Sherlockian movement (I suppose one may call it that) apart from all other movements is that it is entirely free from that jockeying for the plum jobs which is at once the cause and the result of an understandable human ambition that the rules of other societies license. As there are no plum jobs in Holmesdom, there may be no jockeying to attain them. I feel that in this simple statement there is a recipe for that world peace for which so many noisy others constantly tell us they are striving.

I mention this unifying quality of the Holmes fellowship—bringing persons of every faith, profession, occupation, race, and social standing together in harmony—to call attention to the biographical note on each contributor. Here, in these twenty-six contributions in honor of Dr. Wolff—twenty-five articles and one set of drawings—is, I suggest, the composition and spirit of the Holmesian movement in microcosm. Pharmacists, lawyers (one a judge), librarians, a geologist, university professors, a radio executive, a TV engineer, a minister of religion, a Dean Emeritus of a university medical center, journalists, a Scotland Yard man, a professional artist, a writer of film scripts—all have combined in an effort to present Sherlock Holmes and/or his creator in an entirely new light.

We all hope that this book will give you a new understanding of the Master.

—MICHAEL HARRISON

The case of "Charles Augustus Milverton" has long puzzled—and, in many cases, pained—dedicated Sherlockians. It is a case difficult to explain. It begins easily enough—with a supposed blackmailer's calling at 221B Baker Street; but even before the supposed blackmailer has left "our comfortable rooms," something strange has happened to both Holmes and Watson—something strange that the Watsonian narrative either takes for granted or totally ignores. And, as the case progresses, the strict moral standards of both Holmes and Watson melt, vanish, like snowflakes in the hot sun. Watson, the respectable, the prudish, the absolutely loyal, threatens Holmes with blackmail; Holmes, to get into the blackmailer's (no—not Watson's: the other blackmailer's) house, engages the affections of an innocent servant, and actually becomes engaged to her. And, to cap all this, Holmes and Watson let a lady-murderer escape—nor seek to save her victim. Why this strange behavior out of character? Sherlockians, up to now, have been unhappily resigned to accepting the facts and ignoring the implications on the not very reasonable grounds that "we all behave badly at one time or another." True. We do. But do we do it together—as Holmes and Watson did (and which makes it sound very like a criminal conspiracy)? Do we do it when—and this was January 1889, remember, when Holmes was at the very top of his profession—we stand to lose everything by even one of the several felonious acts upon which we have, it seems, lightheartedly embarked? Is there an explanation for the out-of-character behavior of Holmes and Watson in the matter of Milverton? The author of this article thinks there is. His explanation, though, is an unusual—even a startling—one; no less, in fact, than . . .

Witchcraft in Baker Street

FRANK A. D. ALLEN

Introduction and Synopsis

Sherlock Holmes twice described Charles Augustus Milverton as "the worst man in London." No one has ever disputed that assessment. The eponymous case which culminates in Milverton's assassination continues to be read with satisfaction and to be presented with equal approbation on television.

The outline of the case is as follows:

Charles Augustus Milverton, a late-Victorian blackmailer, living in apparent style at Appledore Towers, beside Hampstead Heath, London, calls at 221B Baker Street to negotiate with Sherlock Holmes, who is acting on behalf of the young and beautiful Lady Eva Brackwell.

The sum demanded by Milverton for the return of some compromising letters written by Lady Eva to an impecunious country squire cannot be met. Her impending marriage to the Earl of Dovercourt is thus put in hazard. There is some forceful altercation, and Milverton departs in his carriage and pair.

During the next few days Holmes, disguised as a plumber, reconnoiters the house and grounds of Appledore Towers. He becomes engaged to Milverton's housemaid and enlists her aid. The maid having agreed to lock up the dangerous guard dog, Holmes, accompanied by Watson, burgles the house by night.

Holmes cracks Milverton's ground floor study safe, but he and Watson are interrupted by Milverton's unexpected approach; he was supposed to have retired to bed in an adjoining room.

Holmes and Watson hide behind the study curtain, from which vantage they witness Milverton's fatal shooting by another late-night visitor, an earlier victim of blackmail. The anonymous lady (for such she is) departs immediately. The alarm is raised. Holmes throws the bulky contents of the safe on the study fire, and he and Watson are chased through the garden but escape over the wall and across Hampstead Heath.

Next day Inspector Lestrade of Scotland Yard seeks but fails to obtain Holmes's assistance in the case.

Later Holmes takes Watson to an Oxford Street photographer's shop window, where he is able to indicate secretly the noble identity of Milverton's executioner in one of the portraits of celebrities and beauties of the day there displayed.

Hampstead's Erring Son
A Reappraisal of Charles Augustus Milverton

"The worst man in London." A subliminal misprint? The worst [treated] man? Even the worst [off] man? Be that as it may, something "absolutely unique" is the term used in the opening paragraph and is the claim made for the case eponymously titled "Charles Augustus Milverton."

It is, indeed, a unique case. Its cavalcade of villainy is almost gothic. The narrative opens and proceeds as if some spell of evil had been cast upon every character. And that is what I think happened.

The first to deviate from his normal behavior and to demonstrate this pervasive wrong influence is Sherlock Holmes himself. Holmes is a man of science. We have been told he has a cold scientific brain. We know him to be an expert herpetologist, recognizing elsewhere, instantly and in poor lighting, the Indian swamp adder. Yet on the very first page of this present case we find Holmes expressing himself with a quite unscientific revulsion against a branch of natural creation. He remarks, comparing them with Milverton, a "creeping, shrinking sensation," whenever he confronts the serpents at the zoo. Finally, he falls into a classic pathetic fallacy when he finds their faces "wicked."

Thenceforward we are surely entitled to question everything. Milverton can certainly not have been a good man. But is he as bad as we are invited to believe—"the worst man in London"? With Holmes's normal scientific detachment dislocated, we must for once be wary here of accepting his judgments uncritically.

Without feeling any prime concern to rehabilitate Milverton, and aware that in any such redressing, other well-established reputations will be endangered, let us not shrink from at least a tentative refocusing of the stated facts. And if some force of evil has caused distortion, then let us reveal its source if we can.

At random, then, let us ask a question. Is this an account of one blackmailer or of two? Despite Holmes's firm declaration that Watson would be redundant to the burglary (and as it turned out Watson almost wrecked the enterprise by nearly getting caught scaling the garden wall), Watson insists on a share in what he regards as a sporting adventure by persuasion, which is nothing less than blackmail. Watson's earnest threat to give Holmes away to the local police unless he accompanies Holmes can be nothing other. The good Watson a blackmailer! There must verily be a vile influence at work!

To return to the beginning, when Milverton called at 221B Baker Street it was at Holmes's invitation. It was a parley between opposing commanders in an engagement later described by Holmes as a "sporting duel." Milverton was to that extent entitled to some degree of formal courteous reception ("Holmes disregarded the outstretched hand") and to free departure. Instead of the latter, Holmes attempted robbery with violence, with Watson brandishing a chair. Such joint failure of proper observances was quite atypical of Holmes and Watson alike. Here again, and as all the way through, we smell something amiss.

The "large revolver" with which Milverton covered his retreat on the above occasion is one of the earlier clues to Milverton's not possessing those "swollen money-bags" with which Holmes credited him. A big, heavy revolver is not the sort of firearm that one would expect of a well-to-do, so to say fashionable, blackmailer. A small pearl-handled automatic, perhaps otherwise a derringer, would have been more in keeping. The revolver in question suggests that Milverton had to have had recourse to some late-Victorian equivalent of army surplus stores for the very tools of his trade. Even some of his wardrobe may have been picked up from the same seedy source: "a semi-military smoking jacket, claret colored, with a black velvet collar."

Poor Milverton's wardrobe! If there is one fur that is never "shaggy" except in its ultimate decrepitude, it is astrakhan. Yet, and surely a sight to make a furrier flinch, this is how Watson noted

Milverton's arrival: "a small, stout man in a *shaggy* astrakhan." No wonder Milverton wore at that cold season of the year a "perpetual frozen smile"—of embarrassment if not of positive chill. It becomes all the more touching then to observe the way the poor chap is cherishing his decrepit fur coat by folding it "with great deliberation over the back of a chair"; or maybe by so placing it— lining outward—he is trying to hide its disgraceful shagginess.

So there are two blackmailers in the story. Can there also be two sufferers from impecuniosity—Lady Eva's cast-off country squire and, also, Milverton? A small but possibly significant sign preceded Milverton's first appearance. His calling card economized quite penuriously on letters of the alphabet. The address closed at "Hampstead," which saved, at so much a letter, on "London" and "N.W."

Further clues to Milverton's chronic shortage of money proliferate throughout the case. The "several coats" hanging in the passage outside Milverton's study could hardly have been his. It would not have been worth his, or indeed anyone's, while to preserve spare overcoats still further down the rag-bag scale than that uncurling astrakhan. Equally, had Milverton possessed better ones than the overcoat he wore to the parley in Baker Street, then surely he would have sought to dominate an important occasion with one such. I suggest that the overcoats in the passage belonged to members of Milverton's household other than the servants. The domestics' cloakroom would have been elsewhere, in their quarters. One of the garments might have belonged to the daytime secretary. For the rest we may conclude that to eke out the expensive upkeep of his big house, Milverton had had to take in lodgers. (The fellow who raised the view hulloo in the garden sounds like a countryman from the hunting shires lured like a moth to the extravagance of Appledore Towers' metropolitan electrical lighting.) Occupancy of the upper floors by these presumptive lodgers seems to have driven Milverton to make his own bedroom on the ground floor. It could hardly have been for reasons of security that he slept alongside his study, for Milverton could not have been unaware of his plethoric sleeping or of the standing joke in the servants' quarters: "It's impossible to wake the master." Anyhow, the main security against nocturnal intrusion was the loose guard dog. After that there was the safe.

The safe. It seems that even here Milverton had had to pinch and scrape. For all its size and brass knobs, the safe could not have been an expensive one. Its cladding must have been pathetically thin to have resisted Holmes's drill for only half an hour. Acknowledging Holmes's "concentrated energy," his drills were not powered and he evidently cut out the lock by a semicircle of holes. The easier screwman approach is from the rear, drilling out the rivets and then levering off the back with a jimmy. Only thirty minutes for the more resistant front argues a pretty cheap safe even if one too heavy in the base to turn around. Poor Milverton. An inelegant but serviceable pistol is one thing, but a weak safe is quite another when it comes to economizing on professional equipment.

As one looks around Milverton's study, it seems for the period to have been uncommonly short on marble busts. One (of Athene) is hardly adequately in period for a large bookcase. The *mise en scène* down to the single bust (also of Pallas Athene) recalls something of the depressed accommodation that Poe's poet shared with a raven.

And where was the ormolu clock customary to studies? Milverton kept consulting only his watch. We face the possibility of his clock's having been in pawn.

The study air was heavy with tobacco smoke. But what tobacco? That "pungently reeking, long, black cigar" argues more a cheap Burmese rat's tail than a decent Havana.

There was no sign of a decanter. Despite Holmes's view of Milverton as a "little man who does himself well," there was no sign at all of an evening glass or nightcap. The very boundaries of Milverton's demesne echoed this economy in the broken-down *chevaux de frise*. Milverton's consumption of wine and spirits was simply too meager to produce a sufficiency of empty bottles for the repair of his boundary walls' glass-strewn coping. Otherwise Watson's heavy scramble over it would have been a lacerating affair, which evidently it was not. Not only, then, was Milverton's wardrobe sinking into disrepair but his property also.

That the trees in Appledore Towers were expressly described as a plantation of small ones suggests that that classic act preceding Carey Street had already taken place—cutting the timber on the estate.

Of course Milverton's expenses were necessarily fearfully high.

"It is a long drive to Hampstead," Milverton said in Baker Street. In terms of mileage it is not a long drive. Here is a cry from the heart of a man still attempting a brave professional show while anticipating the livery stable bill for the stately carriage and pair of matched chestnuts with which he arrived—all hired, to be sure, by the hour; footman extra.

How could Milverton have been so overtaken by impecuniosity? The several armfuls of letters in his safe could well have been what is known elsewhere in business as dead stock or bad debts. At the time of his death Milverton admitted to having no more than eight or ten cases maturing. Now, if the profession of "agent" on Milverton's calling card were to connote "commission agent," then some of the papers in the safe could be dishonored racing debts or IOU's. The sad road from putting pressure on an aristocratic bilker to actual blackmail becomes discernible.

Unfortunately for Milverton, he does not seem to have been any better at blackmailing than at the presumptive original bookmaking. He was not made for it. Watson noted that "there was something of Mr. Pickwick's benevolence in his appearance," and that, for all their ultimate hardness, "his eyes twinkled humorously." Almost his last words were to declare that he wouldn't hurt a fly on his own accord, and that his terms were not exorbitant. It was Holmes who gave him that "heart of marble." Milverton's natural generosity is revealed in the admitted liberality, the "no niggard hand," with which he paid, probably overpaid, his own agents, valets and ladies' maids—as much as "seven hundred pounds to a footman for a note two lines in length."

It seems that Milverton just did not have what it takes. A lack of drive is suggested by the "indolent fashion" with which he pursued his homework, perusing with no more than "languid interest" some legal document that fatal night in his study.

Milverton's crowning misfortune was to fall foul of the beautiful Lady Eva Brackwell. This drew in Holmes and Watson, whose burglaring exploit at Appledore Towers threw Milverton's household off the line of his murderess, so that his death has remained unavenged and his reputation has stayed blackened beyond its deserts.

The time has come to reveal Holmes's illustrious client, Lady Eva Brackwell, as the great evil genius of this case. Incredible to reflect that because she was the most beautiful debutante of the previous season (and was also piteous), the hardheaded Holmes (Watson we would allow) permitted himself to be recruited as her hired bravo. And this was solely to advance the lady's disreputable enterprise, which was, in essence, to be rid of some inconvenient mementoes of an earlier unprofitable sweetheart and go on to make a career (Holmes: "ruin this woman's career") out of marrying a narrow-minded and evidently unforgiving earl. In deviating to serve Lady Eva, Holmes came near to destroying himself—and Watson, too.

Holmes was never a snob—we remember his liberal attitude toward board schools and his ease of manner in any society—and he was never a cad. Nevertheless, on behalf of Lady Eva's squalidly profitable, loveless but aristocratic nuptials, Holmes trifled most cynically with the affections of Agatha, the servant girl at Appledore Towers, even to their becoming engaged. This attitude, that the *affaires du cœur* of the lower orders are as expendable as they are comic, quite shocked his friend Watson, as it does us.

With such dubious goings on in the marriage market of those days, there almost emerges a tincture of justification for operators like Milverton to move in for pickings.

Lady Eva's evil influence goes to the limit. Through her, both Holmes and Watson become passive accessories to murder. We shall never know which particular shot of the six hit a vital part. Certainly Milverton did not die instantly. Having fallen, Milverton staggered to his feet between the penultimate and the final shot. Holmes and Watson certainly had time to emerge from behind the curtain and at least seek to save Milverton. Watson's claim that interference would have been fruitless cannot at all excuse their inaction. Anyhow, Holmes had already indicated by his "cold, strong grip" on Watson's wrist that "their own objects were not to be lost sight of," come what may. Holmes later coolly admitted to Inspector Lestrade of Scotland Yard that his sympathies were identified with the criminal's private revenge. In France Holmes's inaction could have visited him with a capital charge. What do Holmes's gallic Vernet ghosts on his maternal side make of that?

Holmes's personal catalogue of criminality (and again he pulled Watson into it) concluded by his concealing from the processes of law the identity of the murderess after he had recognized her likeness in the Oxford Street photographer's shop window. Here again our sympathies are invoked through *ultra vires* considerations of her social position and nobility of aspect. In response to this, it is fair to point out that the lady could not have been keeping totally good company in the photographer's shop window. The euphemism "celebrities and beauties of the day" has some very equivocal overtones of meaning.

How can it have come about that Holmes's, also Watson's, behavior falls in this absolutely unique case so far below their customary high standards?

We must prepare ourselves for a shock.

Holmes and Watson were bewitched! This was, to quote Dr. Watson, the "absolutely unique experience in the career of both Mr. Sherlock Holmes and myself."

The clue to this revelation resides in the pseudonymous family name that is given to Holmes's beautiful client by Watson's literary agent. "Brackwell" indicates in cipher Lady Eva's tainted blood. She was a witch.

Her descent from a line of hereditary guardians of an ancient pagan sacred spring—a saline one, hence "brack"—is laid bare. In such occupations stand the primeval origin of witches. And she was one.

The source of the evil that directs, permeates and consumes the principals of this most bizarre case is thus revealed.

The influence reached a peak on that ill-starred night on Friday, 13 January. After scaling the garden wall, Holmes and Watson are reported to have run two miles across Hampstead Heath. Despite Watson's old war wound it would seem that our heroes were running in a thaumaturgic circle, for the Heath is little more than a mile across at its widest point.

§

NOTE BY THE EDITOR

This brief addition to Frank Allen's article is printed here at the invitation of the author: its substance represents the contents of two letters I wrote to Mr. Allen after having received his article, which I considered—and still do consider—one of the most original writings in the Sherlockian context that I have ever seen. I was so struck by what may or may not be a piece of pure coincidence that I wrote to him immediately (10 December 1974), following that letter with another four days later. The two letters pointed out that, in lightly crediting Lady Eva Brackwell with having been a witch, Allen had fortuitously selected a character whose name appears to belong to witchcraft—or, at any rate, to have a meaning explicable in terms of the old witch language.

In my book, *The Roots of Witchcraft* (London: Muller, 1973; New York: Citadel, 1974), I showed that the language of the witches of Western Europe, as used in the rituals or noted as evidence in the witch trials of the fifteenth to eighteenth centuries, was, in fact, Basque; the Basque language being to witchcraft (or ritual magic) what Latin used to be to the Roman Catholic Church, and what Old Slavonic still is to the Russian Orthodox Church.

Basque, I should explain, uses (as do the Scandinavian and Rumanian languages, and as did proto-Latin) an enclitic postpositional definite article: Danish -*en (klubben,* the club); Rumanian, -*ul (domnul,* the master); Basque, -*ac (emakumeac,* the women).

In all languages, ancient and modern, the sounds of *L* and *R* are very often interchangeable,* especially in proper nouns. That Conan Doyle or Watson, or whoever supplied the names for the stories, was undecided whether it should be *Blackwell* or *Brackwell* is shown by the appearance, elsewhere in the Canon, of the variant forms *Blackwater, Brackenstall, Bradley,* and *Breckenridge.* Lady Eva's name, then, might well be written, "Bl/rackwell."

As I wrote to Mr. Allen: "So just look at this, and lightly dismiss it as coincidence!"

Basque: *birau*   = curse, malediction, witch's spell
    -*ac*   = definite article, plural: the
    birauac = (the) curses, (the) witch's spells

—which looks as though "Brack" is an only slightly modified form of the original Basque *birauac,* which, in any case, is pronounced by present-day Basques *brauac,* with the last vowel very lightly stressed, so that the word sounds almost like *brauc.*

---

* To take an everyday example, consider English *marble* or French *marbre,* both from Latin *marmor.*

Again it's curious, but *eba* forms the stem of the Basque word *ebaki (eba-ki),* in which the final part, *-ki,* is one of the endings of the infinitive. *Ebaki,* verb transitive, means to cut, to cut off, to curtail; to separate, to hew, to chop; to cut off part of the enemy's army; to cut (at cards), to interrupt; to abridge (Milverton's life?). Isn't this all rather odd?

And what follows now I find odder still.

Basque *ohil* (pronounced *o'il,* almost exactly like our "will" or even "well") means savage, ferocious, etc. So that *birauac ohil (b'rau'c o'il =* Brack-well) means "the witch's savage curses."

Of course, all this may be the purest coincidence. But, you know, it's still odd that Frank Allen doesn't know a word of Basque, that he had never read my book (so was completely uninfluenced by my theories), and that he didn't know, when he attributed witch's powers to Lady Eva, that he was selecting a female character already appropriately bearing a witch name.

Every reader of the Holmes stories knows that Professor Moriarty was as imaginatively learned as he was imaginatively evil. At twenty-one he wrote a treatise on the binomial theorem "which enjoyed a European vogue," and, only a little later, the very much more impressive "The Dynamics of an Asteroid," "which ascends," Holmes told Watson, "to such rarefied heights of pure mathematics that it is said that there was no man in the scientific press capable of criticizing it."* Both these publications are now lost, and because many would gladly know what Moriarty had to say in the latter treatise, we invited Dr. Asimov to reconstruct the lost Moriarty paper. In accepting our invitation, our distinguished contributor assured us that his reconstruction is absolutely authentic. *"All the scientists mentioned are real ones, who did exactly what I say they did, and in the year that I say they did it. The reasoning is correct, and every astronomical statement that I make is correct (insofar as we know at present)." Here, then, is the masterly reconstruction of Moriarty's most famous scientific essay . . .*

---

* *The Valley of Fear.*

The Dynamics
of an Asteroid

❧

ISAAC ASIMOV

❧

The Moriarty who was the monster of evil and the mastermind of crime, we all know well, thanks to the gifted pen of Dr. Watson. The Moriarty who was one of the great mathematicians of all time, we know only glancingly. Watson mentions the titles of two of the treatises that astonished the scientists of the world. Unfortunately, he gives us no details of their content.

This is a blow to scholarship, for none of the works of Moriarty is to be found in the annals of science. Undoubtedly, the rigid morals of the late-Victorian era have found Moriarty's work too incompatible with the purity and lofty ideals of science to leave, in its archives, the products of that evil man. But how can pure mathematics be evil?

I believe we can answer that question if we consider the famous "The Dynamics of an Asteroid" which Moriarty published about 1875. Of that great work we have only the title, and yet I maintain that from that title we can deduce the contents and even discover why the work was suppressed.

By "dynamics" is meant the study of the motion of a body and the changes induced in that motion. At first glance, it would seem that there would be very little that anyone could write, in 1875, about the dynamics of an asteroid that would be a useful addition to the body of knowledge on the subject.

The motion of an asteroid is governed entirely by the gravitational influences to which it is subjected. First and foremost is the gravitational influence of the Sun, which impels the asteroid to take on an elliptical orbit about that luminary. This orbit is modified by the considerably smaller gravitational influences (perturbations) of the various planets, particularly the influence of Jupiter.

The theory of universal gravitation was worked out quite satisfactorily (for its time) by the English physicist Newton some two centuries before the date of Moriarty's treatise.

Thus, the first asteroid was discovered in 1801 and was almost instantly lost when its position in the sky drew too near to the solar disc. Fortunately, the German mathematician Gauss found that he could work out its orbit from the few observations already made, by the method of least squares (which he had invented), and the asteroid was indeed found again. The method was based on the assumption that Newton's theory of gravitation was correct, and its success was a powerful demonstration of the worth of that theory.

The most important refinement in connection with planetary perturbations of asteroidal orbits began in 1857, when the American astronomer Daniel Kirkwood showed that the asteroidal orbits were not spread evenly through the space between the orbits of the planets Mars and Jupiter. There were gaps in which no asteroidal orbits were to be found. By 1866, he had demonstrated that any asteroid circling the Sun in those gaps would have a period of revolution some simple fraction of that of Jupiter. He showed that this would entail a repeated pull from Jupiter either forward or backward, the effect building up with time. This would force the asteroid into a farther orbit or a nearer orbit, but would make it impossible for it to remain in the gap. These are called "Kirkwood gaps" to this day.

To be sure, American astronomical achievements were sometimes overlooked and neglected in Europe in the nineteenth century. Was it possible that Moriarty in 1875 had repeated the work

of Kirkwood in 1866 and that it was his demonstration of the existence of "Moriarty gaps" that astonished Europe?

No, that cannot be. Kirkwood's achievements were properly publicized, and the accomplishment, though a worthy one, was beneath
the level of Moriarty's ability.

But what is left?

Can we conceive that Moriarty had looked forward forty years
and anticipated the general theory of relativity which the German
physicist Einstein gave to the world in 1916 and which served to
correct and complete the Newtonian picture of the gravitational
effect?

It is conceivable, certainly. That Moriarty could have anticipated Einstein no sane man can doubt. However, had Moriarty
done so he would have found that relativistic calculations added
little to the dynamics of the asteroid. Such calculations would, on
the other hand, produce a much more noticeable correction in the
motion of Mercury.

As long before as 1843, the French astronomer Leverrier had
pointed out that Mercury's perihelion was advancing by a tiny
amount (to a nonastronomer, a totally insignificant amount) beyond that which would be predicted by gravitational theory, even
if all known gravitational influences were taken into account. General relativity would have accounted for that tiny discrepancy, and
Moriarty would, in that case, beyond any shadow of doubt, have
titled his treatise, "The Dynamics of Mercury."

Are we then at a dead end? Is there no way we can imagine what
it was that Moriarty did that was worthy of the world's attention?
That he did something is, after all, certain, for Dr. Watson is a
model of rectitude, and we may take whatever he says as gospel.

Let us pass on then and consider the fact that the title refers to
"an Asteroid."

Good heavens, *an* asteroid. Even in 1875, there were already a
couple of score of the small bodies known, and there was every
indication that many more remained to be discovered. (Some seventeen hundred are known well enough today to have had their
orbits calculated.) Why, then, *an* asteroid?

Did Moriarty by any chance intend to imply that it was only
necessary to work out the dynamics of one asteroid, to understand
them all? That might well be, but in that case it is customary to
refer to the principle in general terms. The title would undoubtedly have been "The Dynamics of Asteroids."

Did Moriarty, then, mean to refer to one particular asteroid
whose dynamics were markedly different from the rest, perhaps because that one approached some planetary body that the others
did not?

Actually, all the asteroids known in 1875 had their orbits between those of Mars and Jupiter, and, at least from the orbital
standpoint, none was particularly more remarkable than the rest.
The first asteroid to be discovered that possessed an unusual orbit
was Eros—which was spotted in 1898 by the German astronomer

Witt. Its orbit carried it within that of Mars to a point within fourteen million miles of Earth, an astonishing discovery. Might Moriarty have anticipated Witt's discovery?

Yes, certainly, but then surely the title would have been "The Dynamics of an Intra-Martian Asteroid," thus giving some indication as to why the author of the treatise should be dealing with a single asteroid.

What is left? One strong, overwhelmingly probable alternative.

When the first asteroid was discovered in 1801, there was some surprise over its small size of less than five hundred miles diameter. That, however, was nothing compared to the surprise over the fact that three more asteroids, smaller still, and moving in similar orbits, were discovered by 1804.

The German astronomer Olbers, who had discovered two of the first four, speculated at once that in the space between the orbits of Mars and Jupiter, a full-sized planet had once existed, but that it had blown up in some cosmic catastrophe and that it had, in this way, produced the asteroidal fragments that now exist.

Others took up this rather attractive hypothesis, and surely it is that to which Moriarty was alluding. His "*an* asteroid" must refer to the single asteroid planet that existed between the orbits of Mars and Jupiter prior to the catastrophe, and his study is that of the mathematical treatment (exorbitantly complex) of the effects of that explosion, and how the fragments under the influence of gravitational attractions took up the asteroidal orbits of today.

Not only would the mathematical problem have been worthy of Moriarty's brain; not only would it have represented the first attempt of any scientist to take up so complicated an astronomical problem; but think how the very nature of the problem would have appealed to Moriarty. The destruction of a world!

To a master criminal whose diseased genius strove to produce chaos on Earth, to disrupt and corrupt the world's economy and society, there must have been something utterly fascinating in the vision of the actual *physical* destruction of a world.

Could Moriarty have imagined that on that original asteroid, another like himself had existed, one who had tapped not only the vicious currents of the human soul, but even the dangerous forces of the planet's interior? Could he have supposed that this super-Moriarty of the original asteroid deliberately destroyed his world, leaving the asteroids that now exist as the various tombstones that commemorate the action? Could he have envied the deed and tried to work out the necessary action that would have done the same to Earth? It is no wonder, if that were so, that a horrified scientific community suppressed the work.

After Moriarty's time, the concept of an exploded asteroid lost its appeal. About half a century after the great treatise, the Japanese astronomer Kiyotsugu Hirayama showed that no single explosion could have created the asteroidal orbits that now exist, but that five separate explosions of five separate (smaller) worlds might have done it.

To imagine five explosions is considerably less attractive than to imagine one, and modern astronomers generally suppose the asteroids to have been small fragments from the start—fragments that never coalesced into a planet because of the disturbing influence of Jupiter's gravitational field.

The Moriarty theory has been rejected with horror, and in all likelihood will never be revived.

"Since countless examples of successful pastiche have enlivened modern literature . . . are we to conclude," asks the author of this most topical article, "that only Sherlock Holmes and his congeners, seeming perhaps too easy, have defeated—or escaped—the skillful?" It is because the pasticheur—*"we are in the full tide of* pasticherie" *—has made Holmes his or her favorite target (or model) that Professor Barzun begins by specifically examining the attempts to imitate the Holmes stories, and from the particular goes on to the general: to a study of what constitutes parody, pastiche, and plagiarism, and a clear definition of the points at which these three main types of imitation differ. To help the* pasticheur *to do a little better in future, Professor Barzun thoughtfully provides ten rules, ten commandments, for the would-be* pasticheur *(whether of Sherlock Holmes or any other of the great literary characters), presenting them here as . . .*

The Other Decalogue

JACQUES BARZUN

To the memory of Vincent Starrett

Parody, pastiche, and forgery depend on a common element without which the special pleasure of each is denied. I mean a high degree of resemblance to the model. In forgery, this requirement is obvious: the signature on that large check must be good enough to pass for an original, or the pleasure anticipated from the proceeds turns into a dull sojourn behind the bars. In parody, success depends on the reader's sustained recognition of a style he knows extremely well—otherwise he will not find pleasure in the parodist's exaggeration of significant traits: the fun begins when the likeness is seen, as in caricature. There can be no parody—or caricature—of a little known author. It is in pastiche that this principle of fidelity tends to be forgotten or imperfectly followed, because a pastiche could conceivably please independently of what it imitates. Since humor through comparison is not the aim, the piece may be in itself a good story or poem or essay which an innocent person might take at face value, not suspecting that a famous original determined the form and manner. But if the audience is expected to enjoy both the contents and the aping, then the mimicry must be first-rate.

Now among all the subjects of pastiche and parody, it is fair to say that the Sherlock Holmes stories are pre-eminent. They surely outnumber all others put together and outdo them in the literary standing of their authors. And new efforts keep appearing, as all Sherlockians know. The reason for this glut is obviously that the originals, besides being universally known, possess features that look easy to copy. The catchwords, attitudes, and stage props in the Holmes stories impress themselves on the least analytical mind.* When such a mind is visited by a likely plot, it seems the simplest thing in the world to sprinkle the narrative with the familiar points and thus achieve a colorable imitation—an acceptable pastiche, or the sound basis of a parody.

That is the great fallacy. By far the larger number of would-be Sherlock Holmes stories are not acceptable but painful. They suffer from the same error as that which spoils most historical novels: the belief, namely, that the addition of "Zounds!" "By'r lady!" "Sirrah!" to an indifferent tale will supply all the atmosphere needed. The truth is that all this "tushery," as Stevenson called it, only makes plainer the defects of, precisely, atmosphere. We as readers know that to create the authentic mood, the right tone is more important than correct facts. We readily swallow factual error and falsification—an imaginary meeting between historical figures who never met, or a reasonable alteration of their ages to make their meeting possible. But we balk at their talking like you and me if they lived in the days of Queen Anne.

The genuine Holmes stories are themselves full of factual impossibilities, as the critical literature has proved, blaming Watson's memory or bad handwriting. But the atmosphere, at least up to *The Case Book,* is perfection itself. Conan Doyle cannot have hobnobbed with many dukes, but his aristocrats talk as they should —and so do his urchins and poultrymen. His imitators hobnob freely with Holmes and Watson but do not make *them* talk as they should. Atmosphere, it is clear, comes out of diction; hence the first law of pastiche is a great negative from which there is no appeal: allow no word or phrase that could not have been used. What

* One cause is that these points were necessarily "plugged" by Conan Doyle. It was his idea, accepted by the *Strand Magazine,* to undertake consecutive monthly publication without writing a serial. He therefore could not help repeating each time the setting and peculiarities of his continuing characters.

ruined a splendid forgery of love letters from Chopin some years ago was the pianist-lover's reference to "an inferiority complex."

Elementary, one would suppose; a caution not hard to observe; since, after all, the writer of pastiche advertises by his purpose that he wants to show off his literary skill and that he has studied his model with devotion. But the role of words as words is evidently ill-understood, and storytellers who would be ashamed to set down a wrong date or to misstate a material fact are content to palm off verbal impossibilities. The late August Derleth wrote some half dozen collections of stories about Solar Pons as an avatar of Sherlock Holmes, in which he shows a certain awareness that the language of his original (even in 1919, when the pastiche adventures began) is not that of Sauk City, Wisconsin; Pons's style aims at formality in vocabulary and syntax. But the oversights and fallings off are deplorably frequent. Again and again they annoy not merely by breaking the spell, but also by betraying ignorance of the very scene we are to believe in.

For the wrong word often carries with it a second error involving fact and likelihood. For example, on the first page of the first Solar Pons adventure ("The Frightened Baronet"), Pons remarks that "horse-drawn carriages are uncommon indeed within the city." Now what Londoner says "the City" to denote anything other than the northeasterly district, one mile square, which is to Greater London what Wall Street is to New York? All the rest is *town, in town.* Again, any reader of English novels knows that the English say *cater for,* not *cater to,* as in the United States. In a pastiche this unimportant difference stands out as a blunder. Conversely, to have Pons say: "He cried out when he was *slain,*" is to put in his mouth a piece of American journalese.

I said that the wrong words make one doubt whether the writer knows what he is talking about. This suspicion can go so far as to interfere with the plot. In Pons's next adventure ("The Late Mr. Faversham") we are told that "Professor F. V. Faversham of Merk College" is "on six months' leave." The president (head) of his college is a Dr. Dunnel, who coughs and says: "Professor Faversham, of our faculty . . ." Here are three indications close together that the events are surely not taking place in England: the leave of absence (for a *semester,* at that), the title *Dr.* ("President" is rare but will pass), and "our faculty." We are pushed still further from reality when people refer to their and other people's *homes*. The last blow to credibility comes when a young constable joins the proceedings: first, Pons had "previously worked with him" (what Lestrade would say to that constable!); next, speaking to Pons, the constable refers to the missing man as Faversham, without "Mr." or other title; finally, he relates that when he saw another elderly academic on the *stoop* of the house, he "instructed him to wait." By that time, we *are* in Sauk City, where any young cop standing on a stoop would call any man Joe and order him about. But in Sauk City the other phrases that Pons and his Parker have uttered would sound affected and would get them run out of town.

I have stressed these points to show that there are worlds apart in geography and society which express themselves in differences of usage. The contrasts are as clear as those between the language of 1700 and that of 1900. That is why a sense of time and place *in words* is the first prerequisite of the accomplished *pasticheur*. But there is more to it than that, as I hope to show by turning now to what is perhaps the best known and—one would think—most authoritative series of Holmes sequels. I refer of course to *The Exploits of Sherlock Holmes,* which were put together by Adrian Conan Doyle and John Dickson Carr in varying degrees of collaboration.*

On the appearance of these tales in 1954 it was reasonable to expect the old thrill, heightened by the thought that reverent forgery inspired the two minds at work. One of the authors was English, the other a seasoned writer of detective fiction who had lived in England for a number of years. Adrian, son of Conan, had been reared in an atmosphere close to that which he was trying to re-create—indeed, as we were told, he was writing not just at his father's desk, but at his *very* desk.

Alas! this unusual accumulation of favoring chances did not avail. *The Exploits* turned out to be an indigestible mixture of clever ideas and absurd ones, of occasionally good dialogue and persistently amateurish writing. It will not do simply to say that

---

* There being little to choose stylistically between the two halves of the set of twelve, I shall mark no difference in discussing their shortcomings. I find it hard to believe on the evidence that the first six were written jointly and the last six by A. C. Doyle alone. The plots perhaps were separate products.

the work is flawed. There would be nothing to discuss here if
human imperfection were the only thing to complain of. Any sensible critic would note the flaws in passing and receive the rest with
gratitude. What he cannot accept is the failure to carry out, despite
some futile gestures, a stated purpose of the most definite, measur-
able kind. In *The Exploits* hardly a page but administers a shock
to the sense of place, time, and reality. Remember the great model
and then consider a few excerpts, illustrative of long series; to begin with, plain malaprops totally at variance with Holmes's and
Watson's practice:

—Sherlock Holmes was moody and distraught. (distrait)
—Shall I raise the house? (rouse)
—I beg that you will spare me my delusion. (illusion)
—Her cry became a shriek which ran through the house. (rang)

The sense of period is no better observed. We come upon: "a
great whitewashed *home*" / "This is *not too* surprising" / "They
employed an imaginative *approach*" / "retired ostensibly to *drink
a port*," and other modernisms that would have made Holmes
wince. Had he kept on reading his friend's prose, he could have
culled materials for a trifling monograph on strange idioms:
"upped and died" / "bronzed men flocking the streets" / "amid
the magic of *Manon Lescaut*" / "the calm of a man who waits
upon an inescapable destiny" / "grey eyes encircled with black
lashes" / "a copy of a marriage certificate between H . . . and
F . . ." He would doubtless have objected also to the tiresome repetition of *morose* and *moody* to characterize him and *monstrous* to
characterize the recurrent occasions of his livelihood.

In a moment of lucid thought and expression, Holmes is made
to say: "We live in an age of propriety, Watson; and I confess I
prefer it so." But this sentiment is not borne out in action when
he is "pausing to knock out his pipe in the nearest teacup" or when
he wants Watson to "ask Mrs. Hudson to whistle a cab." (One
would enjoy seeing Mrs. Hudson's face at this request.) Nor do
the gentry that visit 221B seem to know any better how to behave.
A young lady says: "Lady Mayo in turn presented me to Charles"
(a young man). The said Charles, wearing a long coat and top hat,
carries a malacca stick described as heavy. (Another such stick appears in a later tale.) But malacca is light in both color and weight,

being a Malayan rattan palm; it does not go with formal attire, and it would not shatter the clock as in the story, but would itself be shattered. Thus do wrong words raise inapt images.

Yet, it would be a mistake to infer from these examples that the atmospheric use of words has been neglected throughout. Side by side with carelessness killing illusion is contortion attempting to strike the right note:

—Oh? sets the wind in that quarter? asks Holmes.
—this marriage must be even more unhappy than are most.
—Now suppose I were first softly to spread on the face of the victim a thin film of such ointment as this . . .
—though little he suspects I followed him.
—I may be much shallower, and you far more deep, than customarily I am wont to believe. . . . Otherwise, I know not why I should have rushed. . . . (says Watson).

Fiddling with normal word order is apparently the formula for faking late-Victorian prose. A more elaborate plan underlies remarks like these: "You place a higher value on the ascetic rarities of Nature than on the intrinsic treasures of man's handiwork."/ "You do me less than justice, Holmes, should I become accessory after the fact in a good cause."/ "I can recommend heartily the rarity of this vintage." In short, we are to be fooled by the sort of mindless utterance that only melodrama will get away with on the stage. This notion is confirmed when we hear a damsel in distress cry out, "Oh, horror unthinkable!" and when Holmes hopes to "catch up in my studies of Oriental plant poisons on the organic blood stream." After such nonsense it does no good to drag in the well-worn props—the haze of tobacco smoke or the "old and beloved Stradivarius"*—for our wish to believe has died within us.

Does it follow from these reflections that no Sherlock Holmes pastiches or parodies can be written by a modern in the English or American of today? Must the sedulous ape be an antiquarian linguist? By no means. Pastiche is always possible. Its negative against what clashes with the original leaves open a large free territory, as the Holmes Canon itself indicates. For was it not because some ex-

---

* A *new* Stradivarius would be a prime suspect.—*J.B.* (And an *inorganic* blood stream would be a real medical curiosity—*Ed.*)

pressions and attitudes in *The Case Book* did clash with those remembered from earlier adventures that scholarly doubts were raised about the genuineness of those postwar stories? Yet several of Holmes's finest effects are to be found in that volume. So the principle of success is simply to keep the diction *neutral* as regards the things that matter. Neither purism nor archaism is the point. The point is to be artful enough, artist enough, to offer the reader a consistent whole.* It will be acceptable if it nowhere violates our informed recollection of its model; it will be a triumph if it captures the authentic tone, the *Ur-Watsohnische Sprache,* especially as it issues from Holmes—studied without pedantry, ranging from didactic clarity to courteous reserve, saved from pomposity by impatience and light sarcasm, the utterance of a man who sees farther and quicker than his neighbors but does not look down on them unless their pretensions outrun their performance. In a devotee's eager reading of Pons or any pseudo-Holmes, it is not purposeful fault-finding that uncovers the errors; it is this same impulse to see if a promise has been fulfilled.

These remarks apply to all the writers who have lately been drawn by the increasing fame of the classic authors of detection to borrow their plumes and ride on their coattails. Christie, Sayers, Rex Stout, and others have had their heroes used in the rough-and-ready manner here deprecated, as if reproducing their names and a few mannerisms would renew the spell that made them heroes to begin with. The proposition that this subterfuge will never work is, if one may say so, the Pons *asinorum* which seems unexpectedly hard to cross. Shakespeare himself has been brought before us in blank verse without showing cause why his modest detective cleverness could not have filled an ordinary short story without Elizabethan poetical trimmings.

Since countless examples of successful pastiche have enlivened modern literature, from Max Beerbohm's *Christmas Garland* to Joyce's series in *Ulysses,* are we to conclude that only Sherlock Holmes and his congeners, seeming perhaps too easy, have defeated —or escaped—the skillful? Thirty years ago, as all Conanical stu-

---

* Borrowing the philological distinction between the *langue d'oc* which led to Provençal and the *langue d'oil* which led to modern French, one might say that the *langue D'oyle* is broad enough to include everything not in some way *provincial,* which is to say off-key.

dents are aware, Ellery Queen published as *The Misadventures of Sherlock Holmes* a collection of all the imitations he could find. Of these thirty-three tales or skits, I think fewer than a dozen give anything like the required double pleasure of fiction and fictiveness.* The best of these, in my opinion, is Vincent Starrett's "straight" story, "The Unique Hamlet." Except for the inveterate use of *home* for *house* and one or two other Americanisms, it is virtually perfect. It contains a neat *Sherlockismus*, good characters, a very fair plot, and the true atmosphere. And by a refinement of method, the author manages some subdued touches of humor at the expense of his heroes and his model—who could ask for more than this blend of satisfactions?

I know of no other work that compares with it on its own theme. It stands on a level with Cyril Connolly's parody of James Bond in *Previous Convictions* and with the serious imitations of Poe's Dupin by Michael Harrison, which are truly beyond compare— the final demonstration that language can be modern and yet sustain the illusion that the events and the recital go back a century and a quarter. It might seem as if 1895 should be easier to imitate than 1845, being nearer. But nearness will not help the incapable. The 1920s were still nearer to 1895 than we are, and it was then that a fellow-journalist of Starrett's perpetrated a Holmes pastiche which later deceived not only Conan Doyle's biographer, but also Doyle's son Denis and the editor of *Cosmopolitan,* who published it, warts and all, as a genuine production of the late Sir Arthur's.† That none of the three men was stopped short by such details as: Baker Street, London, *S.W.,* or Holmes's saying: ". . . If only you would have looked at this blotter"—two blunders among a score— is hard to believe, or would be, if what we saw earlier did not prove how easily the pipe and the dressing gown obscure bad workmanship from the impercipient. One is reminded of Holmes's simple disguises in a world of Watsons.

---

* In a somewhat different realm of imitation, the works of Andrew Garve have shown that it is possible for a writer to give the impression of familiarity with a subject when in fact he has worked it up from books. Mr. Garve is not a small-boat sailor, has never been to Australia, etc., etc., but he is a master of plausibility who has repeatedly deceived the experts.

† "The Case of the Man Who Was Wanted," by Sir Arthur Conan Doyle (actually by Arthur Whitaker), *Cosmopolitan,* August 1943.

In truth, the evidence would incline one to think that when a Holmes pastiche turns out convincing, it is not workmanship at all but the product of instinct, refined by good reading habits. Thus when J. C. Masterman, the author of *An Oxford Tragedy*, takes off Holmes from the point of view of Lestrade in "The Case of the Gifted Amateur," he seems to pull off this mild parody without strain—and without a hitch.* Likewise the detective stories by Lillian de la Torre portraying Boswell and Dr. Johnson, and the reconstructions by Peter Lovesy of London life and crime between 1870 and 1900; whereas the comparable attempts by J. G. Jeffreys to do a late eighteenth-century Bow Street runner are marred by the noisy, jovial bawdiness which is one form of tushery.

Though talent is of course decisive, some warnings to intending mimics might be set down here, in the same spirit of self-defense that prompted Father Ronald Knox to issue his famous decalogue on detection in 1929. He foresaw the coming flood of detective stories; we are in the full tide of *pasticherie*. Like his, the suggestions that follow aim at securing fairness to the reader as well as to the great masters. Anybody is free to write in any style about the detectives, crooks, tough guys, lawyers, and cops of his own creation. But if a writer borrows the name of Holmes, Wimsey, Poirot, Dupin, or Nero Wolfe, he makes a contract with the reader which decency compels him to fulfill. *Noblesse oblige:* an imitation must imitate. Satire, farce, lunacy are allowed, but likeness and fitness must prevail, in the very interests of caricature and fun. For the serious pastiche, the debt of honor is all the more compelling. Here are its dictates:

1. No shilly-shallying between pastiche and parody. The work must be one or the other, because belief in a criminal hunt excludes easy laughter and high jinks. Any satirical intention must be fleeting and well-concealed, as in the Starrett example.

2. Whether in pastiche or parody, no fancy writing; plain language is safest. The passages where the work comes close to the original, for verisimilitude or caricature, must be so adroitly wrought that the remainder is best kept neutral, both to heighten the effect and to avoid breaking the mood.

---

* The tale will be found in the author's *Bits and Pieces* (London, 1962).

3. No recourse merely to the well-known tricks of speech and action in the original. They will not by themselves produce a good, much less an amusing, likeness. Though occasionally direct quoting is allowable, it is necessary to invent *parallels,* new sayings and gestures that fit so naturally as to delight the reader by enlarging his experience of the favorite figures.

4. No incessant effort to squeeze comedy out of every remark or incident. It is tiresome and it obscures the development of the story, which is the only thing that keeps the reader going. The supreme model in this respect is "Scruts" in Beerbohm's *Christmas Garland.*

5. No gross or grotesque proper names. On the contrary, a good choice of names is essential; they recur and will help plausibility— with or without satiric overtones—only if kept in the original key. To transform *Sherlock* into *Schlock* is not good slapstick, but pointless defacement. As for *Solar Pons,* the awkward sound and the flavor of the anatomy class disqualify it. Better Holmlock Shears and Shamrock Jolnes or even Picklock Holes.

6. No expressions of recent coinage, high or low. They come under the head of anachronism, which destroys with one hand what is being fashioned by the other. And the wrong overtones of certain expressions also matter. The real Holmes cannot be made to say "put them *someplace,*" as the author of "The Man Who Was Wanted" did not hesitate to make him do.

7. No technical terms thrown about needlessly. The conscientious plagiarist also respects words that may not seem technical but are: August Derleth assumed that the usages of an American college held throughout the universe, when they were in fact local technicalities. Even that useful book *British Self-Taught* will not solve all the difficulties, just as no American book will help the English parodist with the language of Nero Wolfe and Archie Goodwin.

8. No pastiche of Sherlock Holmes without the Holmes touch. What that touch is can be learned by ascertaining what gives style to such remarks as: "My charges are upon a fixed scale; I do not alter them save when I remit them altogether."/ "It is too much of a coincidence . . . that a promiscuous iconoclast should chance

to begin upon three specimens of the same bust."/ "Also . . . if page 534 finds us only in the second chapter, the length of the first one must have been really intolerable."

For good measure, ponder the marvelous aptness of naming the headmaster of the Priory School Thorneycroft Huxtable and making him the author of *Huxtable's Sidelights on Horace*—sidelights!

9. No Sherlock Holmes pastiche that degrades him through any piece of feeble or patently false reasoning. In a parody the "deduction" may be absurd, a mad semblance of reason, but it must not be inept, for no true artist caricatures a dolt or a halfwit. In short, the imitation, comic or serious, requires a solid basis in plot and incident.

10. No Sherlock Holmes pastiche without at least one *Sherlockismus,* the equivalent of one truffle in each *pâté de foie gras.* That famous turn of thought was first defined by Father Knox in *Essays and Satire* and is best exemplified in the curious incident of the dog in the nighttime, which Vincent Starrett adapted to the actions of "the taller servant engaged in the assault"—neither dog nor servant did anything: that was the curious incident.

Though I may have seemed hard on the imitative effort so far lavished on Holmes and Watson, my temper is hopeful and welcoming. I have accused not in order to hurt but to stimulate, and like another accuser in a far greater cause, I close by saying simply: "I am waiting."

Much of modern science is concerned with the "investigation of the science of the Ancient World"—a patronizing euphemism which really means the (often difficult) task of accepting that our forefathers knew a lot about this world, while, at the same time, pretending that nothing at all was known until—at least—the end of the last century. The author of this article, himself a scientist, knows that what we know today was known ages ago, and that we do not need to prove the validity of ancient knowledge by sophisticated modern scientific apparatus. The existence of such taken-for-granted things—so far as the Ancient World is concerned—as the parallel electromagnetic body, multidimensional creation, multiphyle creation, and the rest of what, until this very present, has been called the supernatural or (grudgingly) paranormal is accepted by the author without reservation and without needing the proof of modern scientific instruments. Of Holmes in this dimension, the many articles in this anthology provide ample material for discussion. But what of Holmes in a dimension—or dimensions —different from that which is called, by us, reality? That such dimensions exist is implicit in all modern scientific cosmologies and cosmogonies—but implicit, too, in the Canon and its allied writings, is the fact that Holmes not only became aware of these other dimensions, but even ventured to explore them. Why he did so, and what he may have found is told here in . . .

What Sherlock Holmes Knew,
or, The Dreadful Secret of the UFO

❈

JACQUES BERGIER

❈

> To one man in a million, dreadful knowledge is revealed . . .
>
> —Robert Bloch

The chilling intimation of sinister extraterrestrial influences may have come first to Sherlock Holmes in the bizarre and terrifying matter of the Giant Rat of Sumatra, a case, Watson remarked as late as 1922, "for which the world is not yet ready." Why . . . ? The case of the *Matilda Briggs* and the Giant Rat of Sumatra had come to shock Holmes into a fearful recognition of Otherness as early in his career as the latter part of 1880.* Watson, referring obliquely to this case in 1922—still resolutely maintaining that it must remain unchronicled for what we may only accept as what are now called security reasons—is writing of events that happened over forty years before. What, in the name of Heaven—or, here, of the Devil, rather—could be the secret which, in the enlightened post–World War I years, three years after Rutherford, at Cambridge, had effected the first transmutation of an element in modern times, could still not be revealed?

We have a hint—and perhaps more than a mere hint—in the

---

* I adopt here the late William Baring-Gould's dating of this case, but other Sherlockian chronologists' adduced dates do not differ by much.

fact that Watson uses the adjective *giant* to convey some intimation
of the horrific. Many rats must have been giants among their kin;
what was so unusual, so alarming, so horrific, about the giantness
of this particular Giant Rat that it becomes a matter so important
that it must be concealed from public knowledge? The answer can
be only that this gigantism was no isolated genetic aberration, but
the emergence of a new species and, more frightening still, that
the mutation had been induced by Influences which could never
mean but harm to mankind. Eight years or so after the success of
the experiments that had produced the Giant Rat, equally successful experiments found their literally diabolical results in the production of a breed of human mutants, of which the most successful
was to be a weedy son born to Herr Schickelgruber, a petty Austrian customs official.

Sherlock Holmes lived, as we now realize, two completely separate lives, though it often happened that those two lives came
together. In one life, he was the puzzle-solver of unchallenged
efficiency, but always working well within the dimensions of conventional social ideas and ideals; in the other, he was working
secretly to combat hideous forces of Evil whose existence and almost plenary powers were unsuspected by the ordinary man, and
known to only a few inspired adepts scattered in remote places
throughout the world. It was to learn wisdom from some of the
more advanced of these inspired persons that Holmes, some ten
years after his first intimation of Malign Otherness in the matter
of the Giant Rat, staged his disappearance in the Reichenbach
Falls. (And we may note here the symbolism of that name: Baron
Karl von Reichenbach was the first to risk public opprobrium
by investigating that aura known now as the life-field, and the
present subject of intense research under the name of The Kirlian
Effect.) Not only did Holmes spend two years among the adepts of
then completely cut-off Tibet, but—something here revealed for
the first time—in Armenia also, where he met and studied under
the now famous sage Georges Ivanovitch Gurdjieff, and healed the
long breach between himself and Arsène Lupin, who was in Armenia at that period. The long months of special instruction in
Tibet have been mentioned by Watson; the months in Armenia,
studying under Gurdjieff, have not.

Was there a reason for Watson's reticence here? Or was Watson never told of Gurdjieff? If the latter, we may venture an explanation. Gurdjieff, like so many—perhaps the majority—of the more successful soul-adjusters of the past (here St. Bernard and St. Theresa of Avila spring to mind), laid the greatest stress on the importance to the soul of heavy work for the body. Gurdjieff, in conversation with Ouspensky, stated his opinion that a man who could make a good pair of boots had the potential to become a better student of the Gurdjieff teaching than some intellectual who had written a dozen books but who had never done a day's physical labor. A woman novelist wrote to Gurdjieff that she always felt more conscious when writing. The sharp, almost brutal, but essentially truthful reply was: "You live in dreams, and you write about your dreams. How much better it would be for you that you scrubbed one floor *consciously* than that you wrote an hundred books."

There is no space here to describe Gurdjieff's essentially practical teaching, but, like all intellectual/emotional disciplines which set out to correct the psychical-physical imbalance, one of its inevitable results was a broadening of the mind, to exclude petty considerations of self, and to make the fortunate subject of the teaching vividly aware of the sensitivities of others. (That Holmes returned from The Great Hiatus, as Sherlockians call it, a better and wiser man, the chronicles make clear.) And now we may suggest that Holmes might well, out of charity, have refrained from mentioning a work-based spiritual discipline to a man whose two war wounds and generally impaired vitality would have prevented his ever joining Gurdjieff's band of disciples. The Holmes of former days would have had no hesitation in saying, "Wouldn't have been any good to *you*, Doctor—you simply couldn't have met the *physical* demands . . ." The new Gurdjieff-conditioned Holmes would have suppressed the Gurdjieff episode, rather than hurt his old friend. And it was this same acquired charitableness which prevented Holmes's leaving Armenia without having fully reconciled himself with his old rival, the French detective Arsène Lupin.

As the years passed, and Holmes's awareness of Otherness forced itself upon him through the apparent oddity of so many of his

experiences—the loss of the British barque, *Sophy Anderson,* in
that notorious "Bermuda Triangle," which has absorbed, without
trace, so many ships and, in the latter years, airplanes also; the
death of Mrs. Stewart of Lauder (a repetition of that grave-robbing
case chronicled by Watson under the title, "The Dreadful Business
of the Abernetty Family"); the disappearance of Mr. James Phillimore, who, "stepping back into his own house to get his umbrella,
was never more seen in this world"; the Abbas Parva tragedy—
Holmes came to the very modern view (perhaps the only respect
in which modern man may claim to have an edge on his fathers!)
that the supernatural simply does not, cannot, exist. That all phenomena, however mysterious, however uncanny, however startling,
are all phenomena within the total aspect of Nature. Holmes was
not irreligious; far less was he an atheist; "The ways of Fate," he
once said, "are indeed hard to understand. If there is not some
compensation hereafter, then the world is a cruel jest." But to him
there was nothing supernatural about even the hereafter—it was
merely a second stage in a progress of existence. He could become
most indignant, even with Watson, when it seemed that the supernatural was about to be evoked for an explanation.

"Now, let us calmly define our position, Watson . . . I take it, in the first
place, that neither of us is prepared to admit diabolical intrusions into
the affairs of men. Let us begin by ruling that entirely out of our
minds."

One feels that, without his unambiguous guidance, Watson
might well have been prepared to admit diabolical intrusions into
the affairs of men; this was said in the case of "The Devil's Foot"
(March 1897). But Holmes peremptorily brushed aside this recourse, for an explanation, to Satan.

In view of what I am about to write on Holmes's combating of
Malign Forces from Otherwhere, it may strike the reader as somewhat contradictory that Holmes should deny diabolical intrusions
into the affairs of men, for that, the average person would say, was
just what was happening. But to Holmes—and especially after his
meetings with Gurdjieff and the Tibetan adepts—the dark forces
ranging up to attack mankind, though to be described loosely as
diabolical, were not Satan and not supernatural. They were no

more (though, alas! no less) than phenomena of a different aspect of Nature.

After his return from what may properly be called his initiation, Holmes was to meet many more examples of a sinister intrusion into human affairs; but with his new knowledge, he was able to recognize and to protect himself from the presence of Otherlife. Operating through their power to mutate existing life forms, these antihuman entities continued to introduce new and ever more frightening species into Holmes's—and others'—experience: there was the remarkable case of the Venomous Lizard referred to in "The Adventure of the Sussex Vampire"; The Mortal Terror of Old Abrahams; The Repulsive Story of the Red Leech and The Terrible Death of Crosby the Banker; and there was, of course, The Case of Isadora Persano, the well-known journalist and duelist. The reader may recall that Persano was found staring at a matchbox containing a "worm" completely unknown to science; and that Persano was stark mad. . . .

I think that this undescribed case has attracted far too little attention. In the first place, it is always assumed that Persano was a man (presumably because the word journalist may be taken generally as of the masculine gender); but, if so, why does the well-known journalist and duelist use the feminine form of the name, Isadora? That Watson was familiar with the feminine form is shown by his use of it in finding a pseudonym for a well-known adventuress (as they called them in those more euphemistic days), Isadora Klein.

But perhaps people have always attributed male sex to Isadora Persano because they have not been able to imagine a well-known *lady* duelist—but that must lead us to consider that word "duelist" more closely. It seems such an odd title for anyone. One doesn't make a profession, surely, of fighting duels; one claims mastery of foil or épée as a recognized *maître d'escrime*. I think that the amanuensis who was taking down Watson's narrative to dictation did not know the word that Watson actually used, and so guessed that he had said "duelist," when Watson had said "dualist"—in other words, an androgynous creature, a hermaphrodite: the product of a terrible mutational technique. The "worm" unknown to science might well have terrified Persano—let us think of it as the calling card of Malignancy—but it was the knowledge of what he would become, what he had already begun to change into, which drove Persano into hopeless insanity.

It is not by coincidence that the case of Isadore/Isadora Persano is among the last to be handled by Holmes before his "official" retirement in late October 1903, for it was the case of Persano, among others, which convinced Holmes that the time had come to devote all his energies and capabilities to the combating of those paranormal forces which held such a threat for mankind and his world. Nor should Holmes's declared intention to retire to bee-keeping be misinterpreted: it was against the forces of a dangerous group mind that Holmes was now about to fight, and the essential study of a group mind's mentality could not be better begun than in the study of a hive of bees.

A word is needed here about the alias that Holmes adopted for his undercover work in respect of what is commonly thought to be anti-German activities but that we now know to have been desperately urgent combatting of a newer and more serious menace than Kaiser Wilhelm II could ever present—the menace of The People of the UFO. The alias that Holmes adopted was, as is well known, "Altamont."

In the book, *In the Footsteps of Sherlock Holmes,* by Michael Harrison, it is pointed out that the name Altamont was the same as that of the beggar-by-day/gentleman-by-night in that story of Thackeray's which so resembles the actual happenings of "The Man with the Twisted Lip." The coincidence of plot was surely not lost upon Holmes, but he adopted the name Altamont because it seemed to him to echo a Latin phrase most apposite at the time: *supra altum montem*—"above the high mountain"—where, in fact, those intelligences lurked and gathered to wreak the world harm.

And now let me call attention to a date: 1903. We shall see the significance of this date later, but for the moment let us bear it well in mind.

From 1903 to 1912, as may be read in the most minute detail in the books of Charles Fort, an all-out attack on cosmic sanity (if we may be permitted here to coin an expressive phrase) was launched

from above. UFOs of every description went flashing and whistling
and booming and shrieking through the sky; lights glowed in the
heavens; innocent spinsters burst into flames; animals, of known
or unknown species, appeared where natural law ordained they
should never have appeared . . . the cosmos (and the people in it)
seemed to have been hit with a spontaneous madness. A joint committee was organized to investigate and, if possible, to destroy the
forces that were controlling this attack on terrestrial natural law.
Even today, the members of that committee are not known,
with the exception of three: Sherlock Holmes; Augustus Joyce-
Armstrong, the pioneer aeronaut; and Dr. J. H. Atherton of Hartfield, to whom came eventually that document of vital importance
known as "The Joyce-Armstrong Fragment." It has been impossible to ascertain whether or not Watson was a member of this secret
committee, but it is possible that the inventor of the airplane used
by Joyce-Armstrong to make his final—both successful and fatal—
attempt to reach the heights may have been a member. His name
is given in the published accounts as Paul Veroner. In the history
of aeronautical design this man is unknown, but if we may (and I
think we may) accept this name as a misprint for Paul Verner, then
we see that we are dealing with a cousin of Holmes and thus, possibly, with a member of the committee.

In the nine years which had elapsed between Holmes's official retirement and the disappearance of Mr. Joyce-Armstrong and his
Veroner monoplane at a height of 43,000 feet, Holmes's investi-
gations, both practical and arcane, established the presence of
something—perhaps we should spell it with a capital letter: Something—hovering at no great distance above the Earth; Something
that was possessed of tremendous powers, but whose intentions
could not, as yet, be specifically determined. There was only one
way of discovering, in those days, what lurked above, sending out
its UFOs and lights and hysteria-inducing impulses—and that was
to send someone up, in an airplane, to find out.
    The first attempts took place in the latter part of 1909 and the
early part of 1910; an aircraft based on the Dunne annular-wing
design being among the types used. Intrepid aviators, all sworn to
secrecy, went up and failed to return. Pieces of their planes fell;
sometimes the men themselves returned, but not alive. Hay Con-

nor died of what was diagnosed as heart failure, with the word "Monsters!" on his cyanosed lips. A young naval officer, Lieutenant Myrtle, R. N., returned to Earth minus his head. Joyce-Armstrong, undeterred by these strange total or partial disappearances, set out in his Veroner monoplane to seek out and identify whatever Hay Connor had seen, and whatever had taken off Lieutenant Myrtle's head. Joyce-Armstrong made two flights, from the second of which he did not return. However, he had made an account of his first flight and what he had seen then; on the second flight, he had taken his notebook with him to add to the account. We know that he reached a height of more than eight miles; that, on both occasions, he had seen the Beasts which inhabit the spaces above the Earth—creatures like huge jellyfish, with bells as big as the dome of St. Paul's, of an incredibly beautiful pastel color; and Things of infinite menace, huge and flat, with bulges above (the classic UFO pattern, as photographed since). It was a creature of this latter type which nearly killed Joyce-Armstrong on his first exploratory flight; it was a ganging-up of three or more which, so it is obvious from his notebook, killed him on his second.

This notebook, dropped into a field and found by a farm laborer, was taken immediately to Dr. Atherton at Hartfield; Holmes analyzed the bloodstains on it and discovered that already Joyce-Armstrong's blood had begun to show an aberrant character.

The time had come, Holmes now decided, for a partial revelation of the menace facing the world. Either after taking advice or, perhaps, on instructions from his masters, Holmes commissioned his literary agent—Watson's, rather—to prepare and publish an account of the Joyce-Armstrong investigation. This was published in 1912 under the title of "The Horror of the Heights."

There is one small but curious passage in "The Horror of the Heights" which has, up to now, not been noticed even by the most dedicated Sherlockian scholars. It is that passage from Mr. Joyce-Armstrong's notebook (of which the last frantically scrawled entry was on 15 September 1911) which begins: "Aeroplaning has been with us now for more than twenty years . . ."

Twenty years back from 1911 takes us to 1891: eight years before the first officially recorded man-carrying flight by a powered lighter-than-air craft—17 December 1903, by the brothers Orville and Wilbur Wright.

Now, in 1891 Holmes had voluntarily disappeared. We know that he was in Tibet, Armenia, Persia, the Sudan and France, "conducting researches into the coal-tar derivatives at a laboratory in Montpellier." What were the real experiments in which he was engaged? Had they to do with aviation? And if so, were they in France, where they have always claimed to have anticipated (in Clément Ader's *Avion*) the Wright Brothers' success by at least seven years? Or did Holmes, from nearby Armenia, get in secret touch with the Russian aircraft designer Tsiolkovsy, then in banishment in Siberia? Certainly, when Holmes heard that another aeronautical designer had been successful at the end of 1903, he determined to watch progress in the U.S.A.—and promptly retired.

The fearful decision that Holmes had to make in the first quarter of this century was: How much to reveal, and when?

Leaf from Joyce-Armstrong's notebook. The note reads: 'My sixth machine—Jubilee Year [1897]—Harry and V aboard. H died." (The reference is to Harry Hay Conner and Percival Venables, Joyce-Armstrong's co-experimenters.) *Contrad Research Library.*

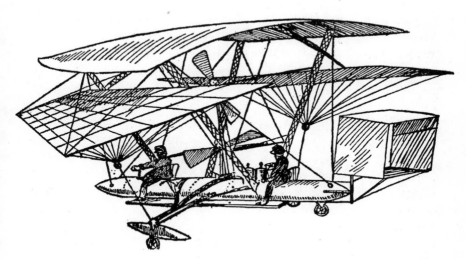

My sixth machine — Jubilee Year —
Harry and V aboard. H died.

Even before the revelations in Joyce-Armstrong's notebook, Holmes had equated the forces which seized ships with those which seized airplanes and, of course (as in the case of Mr. James Phillimore, and so many others), men and women. The revelation that Holmes authorized in 1912 contained the first accurate description of a UFO, half a century before the first of the present waves.

But the revelation was only a partial one. The logic of Sherlock Holmes drew him to a terrible conclusion which was never published: "If there are Beasts in the Stratosphere, why not Intelligences?" Intelligences as powerful as, or more powerful than, ours. Intelligences which experiment, not only on animal life, but on human, too; producing mutations such as the Giant Rat of Sumatra and . . . Adolf Hitler.

The UFO does not seem to belong to—or, rather, exist in—our world.

But there are other worlds, and, among them, the world in which Sherlock Holmes now dwells forever. It is a world both better and more real than ours; a world in which justice is done and truth revealed. It was in visiting this Other World that Sherlock Holmes had his first intimation of the dreadful secret of the UFO.

The time has now come, I think, when what was revealed to Holmes long ago is to be revealed to us. Our world is not truly menaced . . . but what of that parallel world in which Holmes still lives?

Time will tell. . . .

Even in the ideally equal world of the near future, George Orwell pointed out, it was possible for some to be more equal than others. And in the sixty-tale collection of Sherlockian adventures, though all (this is a matter of faith) equally good, some must be—it's now freely admitted—more equally good than some others. So where does that leave us? Obviously, with the need to see exactly how this unequal equality affects the rating of the stories. And rating obviously involves an assessment of value. And value obviously may never be immutably anchored to some absolute of worth. Many people read the stories for their entertainment value; others for their power to instruct, and so on. How does one assess the inequality of merit of the Canonical stories? How, in fact, does one define merit? No task seems so difficult but that an intrepid Sherlockian is ready to spring forward to tackle it. And here, to judge the stories—or, at any rate, to tell us how he and others have judged them (those others including Sir Arthur Conan Doyle himself)— is a judge who may well have heard more important evidence, but hardly any evidence more interesting than that here summed up in . . .

An Assessment and Valuation of the Ten Best Canonical Stories, with Some Observations on Those Somewhat Less Deserving of Praise

S. T U P P E R   B I G E L O W

This paltry monograph, let it be said at once, is no original contribution to Sherlockian scholarship. Rather it is an attempt, by
lavish use of paste and scissors, to set out what has happened over
the years in attempts by worshipers of the Master to determine if
they could say which are the ten best stories in the Canon, and in
so doing, which are, not the ten worst, because no Sherlockian tale
could ever be bad, but which are the least appealing to worshipers
of the Master.

Sir Arthur himself started the ball rolling.

In the March 1927 issue of the *Strand Magazine,* Sir Arthur contributed an article entitled, "Mr. Sherlock Holmes to His Readers," which was later shortened and amended to take its place as an
introduction to some editions of *The Case Book.* In the article, Sir
Arthur announced that he had prepared a list of what he considered to be the twelve best Sherlockian stories, and challenged his
readers to duplicate his list. But as *The Case Book* had not at that
time been published in book form, the stories in it were left out of
consideration. First prize was £100, and there were one hundred

consolation prizes: autographed copies of Sir Arthur's *Memories and Adventures*.

Sir Arthur's choices were, in order of merit, "The Speckled Band," "The Red-headed League," "The Dancing Men," "The Final Problem," "A Scandal in Bohemia," "The Empty House," "The Five Orange Pips," "The Second Stain," "The Devil's Foot," "The Priory School," "The Musgrave Ritual," and "The Reigate Squires."

As reported in the *Sherlock Holmes Journal*, II, 4, the winner of the first prize was R. T. Norman, Spring Hill, Wellingborough, Northants, wherever that may be.*

Although Norman was not reported as saying anything about his uncanny win (presumably he had all twelve correct and in order), the *Sherlock Holmes Journal* reported that two winners of the consolation prizes were available for interviews or perhaps written comments. Each had nine right.

Humphrey Morton, a member of the Sherlock Holmes Society, said: "Mine included 'A Scandal in Bohemia,' 'The Red-headed League' and 'The Speckled Band,' but my error was including 'The Six Napoleons.' This should have been 'The Priory School.' "

William George Dalliba, of the Musgrave Ritualists of New York, wrote: "Sir Arthur's list did not include 'The Abbey Grange,' but I have always been of the opinion, shared by quite a few of my friends, that this story never received full recognition. It contains one of the cleverest bits of deduction in any one of the tales. Take, for instance, the following quotation:

'But the glasses do puzzle me, I confess. Lady Brackenstall actually saw the three men drinking, did she not?'
'Yes, she is clear about that.'
'Then there is an end of it. What more is to be said? And yet you must admit that the three glasses are very remarkable? Well, well, let it pass.'

"We know, however, that Holmes could not let it pass, and pulled Watson out of their train at a suburban station as they were on their way back to London. Then they took the next train

---

* A busy boot-and-shoe-manufacturing town, 68 miles NNE of London; map reference, on the British National Grid: SP86.—*Ed.*

back and revisited the scene of the crime, and Holmes soon found
out the true solution."

Sir Arthur must have repented of his original list of the twelve
best, probably because of the thousands of entries in the *Strand*
competition that included "Silver Blaze." How could any ten-best
list possibly exclude "Silver Blaze"? the meanest Sherlockian dilettante might ask. The curious incident of the dog in the nighttime
that did not bark? Once read, never forgotten.

Let me offer my solution. In *Memories and Adventures,* Sir
Arthur recalls:

Some times I have got on dangerous ground where I have taken risks
through my own want of knowledge of the correct atmosphere. I have,
for example, never been a racing man, and yet I ventured to write
"Silver Blaze" in which the mystery depends upon the laws [*sic*] of
training and racing. The story is all right, and Holmes may have been at
the top of his form, but my ignorance cried aloud to heaven. I read an
excellent and very disparaging criticism of the story in some sporting
paper [Could this have been the newspaper in which Red Smith, BSI,
published his coruscating and diabolical attack on the Master as a crook
of the highest order?]* written clearly by a man who *did* know [that fits
Smith], in which he explained the exact penalties which would [have]
come upon everyone concerned if they had acted as I described. Half
would have been sent to gaol and the other half ruled off the turf forever. However, I have never been nervous about details, and one must
be masterful some times.

At any rate, according to the *Baker Street Journal,* I, 4, 458, Sir
Arthur added another seven to his first list of twelve, again in order
of merit. They were "Silver Blaze," "The Bruce-Partington Plans,"
"The Crooked Man," "The Man with the Twisted Lip," "The
Greek Intepreter," "The Resident Patient," and "The Naval
Treaty." And in the same issue of the *BSJ,* the editor wrote:

On January 14, 1944, despite the regard in which they held Dr Doyle's
judgment, the Baker Street Irregulars decided to poll their own membership with a view to establishing an official aggregate expression of
opinion regarding the respective merits of the tales which might stand
for all time or at least another seventeen years. The BSI's first twelve

---

* Certainly not. Red Smith wasn't even thought of, let alone born, when Sir
   Arthur wrote his *Memories and Adventures.* Our contributor appears to be
   no chronologist!—*Ed.*

showed a remarkable correspondence to Dr Doyle's; they omitted *The Priory School* from their chosen dozen (which they placed 18th) and *The Reigate Squires* (which they placed 19th) and included in their places Dr Doyle's 13th and 14th choices, *Silver Blaze* and *The Bruce-Partington Plans*.

The twelve best of the Baker Street Irregulars' choices, in order of merit, were *The Speckled Band, A Scandal in Bohemia, The Red-headed League, Silver Blaze, The Dancing Men, The Musgrave Ritual, The Five Orange Pips, The Final Problem, The Empty House, The Bruce-Partington Plans, The Second Stain* and *The Devil's Foot.*

In *BSJ*, III, 3, Edgar Smith, its erudite editor, referring to the BSI choices, wrote in 1933:

It is not these tales about which we are thinking today—it is, rather, these others, however few, which might be best described as the "least magnificent" of the lot: that come only occasionally to the mind: the stars that are dimmed and paled, as it were, by the brilliance of the total galaxy in which they are set. By the very definition of the term, we must stop to think what tales these are before we can name them. Perhaps *The Crooked Man, Abbey Grange, The Three Garridebs* could be so classified; but for our own part, at the very bottom of the list, the almost forgotten adventure of *The Three Garridebs.*

Nearly a year later, one of Edgar Smith's editorials said: "As an adjunct to the BSI 100th Anniversary dinner (of the Master's birth, of course; not the society's), a poll was conducted to determine the consensus as to the 'ten best' and the 'ten least.' "

And so a poll was taken at the 100th Anniversary dinner—on the basis of ten points for first choice, nine for second, and so on, down to one point for tenth choice. The total number of entries was, quite appropriately, 56, and the following ratings were assessed:

"The Speckled Band"	355
"The Red-headed League"	259
"A Scandal in Bohemia"	256
"Silver Blaze"	253
"The Musgrave Ritual"	163
"The Blue Carbuncle"	145
"The Bruce-Partington Plans"	128
"The Priory School"	93
"The Empty House"	92
"The Dancing Men"	92

In *Leaves From the Copper Beeches* (1959), Frank J. Eustace, Jr., reported a poll he had taken of the members of what is probably the most learned and sophisticated scion Sherlockian society. Their scholarship is so profound on all matters dealing with the Master that when I attended one of their dinners in Philadelphia, I actually won second prize in their quiz, with a mark of 69 out of a possible 120. The winner was a university professor with more initials after his name than Thorneycroft Huxtable, but all the lout could score was a paltry 74. I may say that I thought the question, "Where did Sherlock Holmes keep his tobacco?" was a trick question, because any half-wit knows that he kept it in his Persian slipper, but it was so obvious that I tried to think of some other place he might have kept it in some other story, and the judge called "Time" before I could write the simple answer. It appeared that there was no appeal available to me.

Well, that is digressing. Mr. Eustace's method of assessing the stories (and now we have the long stories in the poll, as well as the short ones in *The Case Book*) was to canvass ten members of the Sons of the Copper Beeches, asking them to assess the 60 stories with 4, 3, 2, 1, or 0. Quite obviously, Mr. Eustace must have selected the ten most scholarly Sherlockians in the Sons to participate in his experiment. Some serious Sherlockians will quarrel with his results:

40	*The Hound of the Baskervilles*
39	"The Red-headed League"
38	"The Speckled Band"
37	——
36	"The Blue Carbuncle," "Silver Blaze"
35	"The Bruce-Partington Plans," "The Naval Treaty," *The Sign of Four*
34	——
33	"The Priory School," "The Musgrave Ritual," *A Study in Scarlet*
32	——
31	"A Scandal in Bohemia," "The Final Problem"
30	"The Six Napoleons," "The Five Orange Pips"
29	"The Man with the Twisted Lip," "The Devil's Foot," "The Stockbroker's Clerk"
28	"A Case of Identity," "The Empty House," "The Second Stain," "The Golden Pince-Nez," "The Boscombe Valley Mystery," "The *Gloria Scott*"

27   "The Copper Beeches," "Black Peter," "The Dancing Men,"
         "Abbey Grange," "The Reigate Squires"
26   "The Noble Bachelor," "The Norwood Builder,"
         "Charles Augustus Milverton," "Wisteria Lodge,"
         The Valley of Fear
25   "His Last Bow," "The Solitary Cyclist"
24   "The Cardboard Box," "The Three Garridebs,"
         "The Lion's Mane"
23   "The Engineer's Thumb," "The Greek Interpreter,"
         "The Beryl Coronet," "The Resident Patient,"
         "Thor Bridge," "Shoscombe Old Place"
22   "Lady Frances Carfax"
21   "The Illustrious Client," "The Crooked Man,"
         "The Retired Colourman"
20   "The Dying Detective," "The Three Students,"
         "The Red Circle," "The Creeping Man"
19   "The Blanched Soldier," "The Sussex Vampire"
18   ——
17   "The Missing Three-Quarter"
16   ——
15   "The Three Gables"
14   "The Yellow Face," "The Veiled Lodger"
13   "The Mazarin Stone"

In the same year (1959), the *Baker Street Journal* announced another "Ten Best" Contest in its April issue, but again, this contest
specified only the short stories, although competitors were asked
to rate the four long stories, of which there could not be much
doubt. The long stories, to no one's surprise, rated:

HOUN	126	*(The Hound of the Baskervilles)*
SIGN	93	*(The Sign of Four)*
STUD	70	*(A Study in Scarlet)*
VALL	61	*(The Valley of Fear)*

Using the same ratings as in the 1954 poll, the results were:

SPEC	278	("The Speckled Band")
REDH	234	("The Red-headed League")
BLUE	199	("The Blue Carbuncle")
SILV	199	("Silver Blaze")
SCAN	172	("A Scandal in Bohemia")
MUSG	149	("The Musgrave Ritual")

BRUC 114   ("The Bruce-Partington Plans")
SIXN 101   ("The Six Napoleons")
DANC 88   ("The Dancing Men")
EMPT 79   ("The Empty House")

So now, for the benefit of our readers who haven't been paying attention, here are the results of all the competitions,* so far as the short stories are concerned:

1927 Sir Arthur	1944 BSI	1954 BSJ	1959 SOCB	1959 BSJ
SPEC	SPEC	SPEC	REDH	SPEC
REDH	SCAN	SILV	SPEC	REDH
DANC	REDH	SCAN	BLUE	BLUE
FINA	SILV	REDH	SILV	SILV
SCAN	DANC	MUSG	BRUC	SCAN
EMPT	MUSG	BLUE	NAVA	MUSG
FIVE	FIVE	BRUC	PRIO	BRUC
SECO	FINA	EMPT	MUSG	SIXN
DEVI	EMPT	PRIO	SCAN	DANC
PRIO	BRUC	DANC	FINA	EMPT

An analysis of these polls could be a fascinating exercise for anyone who has abundant spare time at his disposal. For example, regard the pre-eminence of "The Blue Carbuncle" in the 1950s, omitted by Sir Arthur even in his first nineteen choices; possibly because, being somewhat ashamed of his racing errors in "Silver Blaze," he was appalled by the many egregious errors in "The Blue Carbuncle." But Sherlockians do not seem to care much about errors in the stories; the errors of dating in "The Red-headed League" have caused chronologists, after solving the dating problems as best they could, to consult the nearest psychiatrist. "Silver Blaze," of course, rates high in any poll except Sir Arthur's, and so it should. Not all Sherlockians are racing aficionados, and they remain perfectly indifferent to the subtle nuances involving breaches of the rules of racing.

"The Devil's Foot" is alone in Sir Arthur's list. "The Dancing Men," Sir Arthur's third choice, is largely ignored in the polls of

---

* Recorded in the established Sherlockian 4-letter code, interpreted by reference to the lists above.—*Ed.*

the 1950s, possibly because Sherlockians were quick to detect that it was too reminiscent of Edgar Allan Poe's *"The Gold Bug."*

"The Five Orange Pips" is omitted from the last three polls, and I think any serious Sherlockian would admit that it simply does not belong in the first ten, or even twenty, *pace* Sir Arthur. But why go on? Be my guest and try to make some sense out of the many polls and the competitors' consensuses.

The Ten Less Deserving of Praise

Let us admit, first of all, that there is no bad Sherlock Holmes story. In this connection, it is always fashionable to recall Sir Arthur's own words in "Some Personalia About Sherlock Holmes," published in the *Strand Magazine* in its issue of December 1917.

Sir Arthur recalls, "The most trenchant criticism of the stories as a series came from a Cornish boatman who remarked to me: 'When Mr. Holmes had that fall, he may not have been killed, but he was certainly injured, for he was never the same man afterwards.' "

And of course discussions about the proto- and deutero-Holmes have been with us since the founding of the Sherlock Holmes Society and the Baker Street Irregulars in 1934, and probably before that. Criticism of the stories in *The Case Book* has been abundant in the writings upon the writings, and yet—and yet, I can well recall my horror on first reading "The Blanched Soldier"; the plot in "Thor Bridge" I have always thought excellent, even though it has been said that Sir Arthur borrowed it from an actual case mentioned in *System Der Kriminalistik* by Herr Dr. Hans Gross. I read it in German and in English, and whoever said Gross mentioned such a thing is a liar.

"Shoscombe Old Place," another story I like, deals with racing, as well as does "Silver Blaze," and there is no error in it I have been able to discover about racing or, indeed, anything else. Furthermore, as in "Silver Blaze," the dénouement owed a good deal to a dog. Quite likely, Sir Arthur had picked up a few pointers about racing since he wrote "Silver Blaze" in 1892; "Shoscombe Old Place" was published in 1927.

Well, enough of my personal opinions, which have no validity in this *parvum opus.* Suffice it to say that no story in *The Case Book* ranks in the first ten of any list.

A Study in Scarlet

Ormond Sacker - ~~from Soudan~~ from Afghanistan
    Lived at 221 B Upper Baker Street

with

    I Sherrinford Holmes -

        The Laws of Evidence

  Reserved -

Sleepy eyed young man - philosopher - Collector of rare Violins
An Amati -   Chemical laboratory

     I have four hundred a year -

I am a Consulting detective -

What rot this is" I cried - throwing the volume
petulantly aside " I must say that I have no
patience with people who build up fine theories in their
own armchairs which can never be reduced to
practice -.   Lecoq was a bungler -
Dupin was better. Dupin was decidedly smart -
His trick of following a train of thought was more
sensational than clever but still he had analytical genius.

A blueprint for immortality! From these rough notes emerged, not
"I. Sherrinford Holmes" and "Ormond Sacker," but Sherlock Holmes
and Dr. John H. Watson—not of *Upper* Baker Street, either! The late
Mr. Adrian Conan Doyle, son of Sir Arthur, accepted your Editor's
suggestion that the initial "I." of "Sherrinford Holmes" was almost
certainly intended to stand for "Innes," the name of Sir Arthur's
younger brother, later killed in the first World War. *Copy reproduced
by written permission, given personally to Michael Harrison by the
late Adrian Conan Doyle.*

So now let us look at the polls once again, this time to determine, if we can, those stories least deserving of praise:

1944 BSI	1954 BSJ		1959 SOCB		1959 BSJ	
CROO	3GAB	177	MAZA	13	MAZA	208
RESI	YELL	177	YELL	14	VEIL	201
IDEN	MAZA	172	VEIL	14	YELL	193
NOBL	VEIL	157	3GAB	15	BLAN	168
YELL	BLAN	135	MISS	17	3GAB	139
STOC	LION	103	BLAN	19	CREE	117
MISS	REDC	99	MISS	19	RETI	101
LADY	MISS	87	DYIN	20	LION	86
(No votes)	3GAR	82	3STU	20	SUSS	83
	RETI	73	REDC	20	MISS	69
			CREE	20		

All polls, of course, used the same marking system they used for the ten best.

I just now notice, with some embarrassment, that my dear and beloved "The Blanched Soldier" is placed pretty high in the ten worst list. Some of these alleged Sherlockian scholars are not a bit perceptive, I am sore afraid. And too many of my choices, for my liking, are in *The Case Book*.

But I don't see "Thor Bridge" or "Shoscombe Old Place" in any of the lists. Of course, I didn't see them in any of the ten best lists, either. Oh, well, as I always say, *de gustibus non est disputandum.* Or nearly always. Sometimes I say *chacun à son goût.*

And another thought for my readers, if any of them are still with me and think that the series in *The Case Book* are unworthy of Sir Arthur. From 1921 to 1927 inclusive, Sir Arthur sold his stories in *The Case Book* to three different publications: the *Strand Magazine* in the United Kingdom; and *Collier's* and *Liberty* in the United States, each for $8 thousand. Captious critics, could you do as well?

Can a treasure be a treasure when the finder is unaware of what it is that he has found? We had intended to classify this account of a lonely Canadian's bored night in London as the only piece of fiction in our collection. But is it? Hasn't what happened to Parker —and to what Parker found—happened a thousand times in the past? Fact or fiction? Judge for yourselves as you chill in the realization of how Parker disposed of . . .

Nothing of Value

❦

ALAN BRADLEY

❦

London, March 4

Dear Frank,

I arrived last night in London in the rain. Your much touted English countryside was hidden in the darkness and drizzle. After the formalities at the airport had been concluded, I was whisked away by a representative of the University of London, which is to be the location of my lecture in four days' time, and left at this hotel.

As you warned me, this damned country is damp, and as I slid between the sodden sheets last night, I roundly cursed the country and the climate.

Today the rain continues, and as I sit looking out into the street, I find myself curiously homesick; a feeling I haven't experienced in the twenty years since, as a boy, I was sent away to a miserable camp in northern Ontario.

Enough of this for now; I have wasted the day and must put the final touch on my paper. Tomorrow I will take your advice and look for a room in a private home.

As always,
Parker

London, March 5

Dear Frank,

As promised, I am writing you each day to keep you up to date on my doings, and to supply you with my impressions of the country. This, then, is my second letter. I must apologize for the brevity of yesterday's communication, but I was too damned tired, damp and depressed to write more. Although the rain continues, I set out early this morning in search of a place to stay. After an abortive attempt to strike up a conversation with the hotel desk-clerk, I did manage to acquire some information from a bystander: an elderly, military-looking gentleman with a smooth ruddy face who informed me that I should seek out an estate agent, rather than a real estate dealer, and that he had once spent several months in Montreal during the last war; something to do with the British Intelligence, or so he implied.

Having taken leave of the hotel and my informant, I took a taxi to the nearest estate agent's office, where I was introduced to another old gentleman, who seemed pleased that I wanted to learn something of British life by staying in other than a hotel.

Having brought out assorted listings for my inspection and consideration, he offered me a cup of tea as we viewed his wares. Most of the places he had listed were too expensive or too far away. Only two seemed satisfactory, and we set out to see them.

Both residences were on Baker Street, or as they say here, in Baker Street. By the time we arrived, the first flat had already been taken, and so, a short walk up the street, I first saw what has come to be my temporary London residence. It is a suite located on the second floor, which the agent referred to as the first floor, and consists of one large room overlooking the street, two small bedrooms, and a bath.

The terms are reasonable and I am content, except for a constant chill which I cannot seem to shake. At least the larger room has a fireplace and will, if I can scare up some fuel, warm my bones and make things almost as comfortable as being back home. Sitting at one of the front windows and writing keeps my hands warm, but my legs, feet and shoulders continue to deny the sparse warmth generated by an ancient steam radiator. I have wrapped myself in a soggy quilt from the bed, but it doesn't help greatly.

I still have a few hours of revision left to do on my paper, and must get at it. Will write tomorrow.

Regards,
Parker

London, March 6

Dear Frank,

Last evening, having mailed off your letter, I set out on foot to locate some food. In this I was successful, and found a small shop where I was able to obtain some buns, butter, bread and tea; no great meal, but enough for an evening snack. I will not begin my sightseeing in earnest until after the presentation of my paper.

Back at the flat, and having feasted, I finished off the last details of my paper, which will no doubt create quite a stir in certain academic circles.

I find myself strangely tired these evenings, and had decided to go to bed and catch up on my sleep. I suppose I wasn't as tired as I thought, for I became distressfully aware of the moisture in the sheets, the traffic outside, the sound of the rain beating at the windows, and finally of little noises which sounded like mice scurrying and scratching in the room overhead. The more I tried to sleep, the more awake and annoyed I became, until finally it struck me: I was worried. Worried about reading that damned paper and worried about its reception.

Once the source of my sleeplessness was identified, I relaxed and began to laugh. Not out loud, mind you; just a silent chuckle at myself for being such a fool. Then, having chuckled myself into a wide-awake state, I got up out of bed and finished off the last of the buttered buns while pacing around the front room to keep warm.

By this time it was late, and most of the traffic noises had stopped, and even the rain seemed to have degenerated to a drifting mist. In the comparative silence I could hear only the mice, still rummaging about somewhere overhead.

Suddenly remembering that I needed my sleep, I became terribly tired again and went back to bed.

But I couldn't sleep. Those damned mice sounded like a football squad somewhere above. If I didn't silence them I would get no sleep.

I arose, dressed, and went out onto the landing, where a shaky-looking staircase led upward to a smaller landing whose two closed doors were scarcely visible by the light of a dim hall lamp below me.

The first door I reached, on my right, was unlocked, and I struck a match and stepped in.

The floor groaned with my weight as a quick look showed the room to be completely empty.

The door on the left was also unlocked and, although somewhat stiff on its hinges, yielded to pressure and swung inward.

The light of a second match showed clearly the origin of the noises I had heard downstairs. At least a dozen mice stared unblinkingly at me, their eyes showing red in the flickering light. They did not appear to be overly alarmed, although one or two of them jumped to a better vantage point on the piled-up furniture which filled one end of the room.

Another match, and I stepped closer. The mice broke for cover.

Now, Frank, this is the part that will interest you. I am not much of an antique buff, as you are, but I do know that you will cheerfully give up an afternoon of golf to root through someone's attic in search of treasure, so I will try to fill in a bit more detail.

The far end of the room, as I have said, was piled high with junk and old furniture which must have been there for fifty years or longer, judging by the thick accumulation of dust. An old wooden table, two big overstuffed couches, a couple of wicker chairs (like the one in your study, though these weren't painted), a coat rack, and an old tin trunk.

These were certainly not all viewed by the light of a single match; in fact, it took quite a few, and more than one burned finger, to get that far in my survey.

As you well know, I am not ordinarily a curious person, but I found myself wondering about the contents of that trunk. You never know in this country; we're always reading about bodies being stuffed in trunks and stored away somewhere, and not being discovered for years. Not that I believed for a moment there would be a body in the trunk, but I must admit that the thought did cross my mind.

I was now running out of matches, the room was bitterly cold and damp, and the smell, which I neglected to mention before,

seemed to be that of mildewed dust, which I found most unpleasant, as I am allergic to dust and had already begun to display
the symptoms.

Deciding that the best way to satisfy my sudden curiosity would
be to get the trunk out into the light, I grasped its leather loop
handle protruding from one end, and pulled. The handle disinte-
grated in my hand.

I then placed myself behind the trunk and began to push; the
trunk, being much lighter than I had judged it to be, moved
rapidly across the wooden floor with a metallic squealing sound.

At the landing, I found that I could lift the trunk without un-
due effort, and so came back down to my own rooms and deposited
it in the center of the floor. An overwhelming odor of decay filled
the room, and I began to doubt the wisdom of bringing that filthy,
reeking object down here. You know how I hate to soil my hands,
but that strange outbreak of curiosity had the better of me.

The trunk had two metal clasps on the front which popped up
immediately upon being pressed, and I lifted the lid.

The trunk was about half filled with rubbish. Before going any
further, I decided to wash up and have a cup of tea, as I was
feeling the cold more than ever. The smell emanating from the
trunk removed from my mind any idea I might have entertained
about food, and so I returned to the repellent task I had set
myself.

At the top of the trunk were a number of old scrapbooks whose
spines were hand-lettered in indication of some sort of alphabetic
arrangement—much like the sequence of letters and names found
on the back of a set of encyclopedias. I glanced through one or
two of them, the stiff old paper as often as not crumbling and
disintegrating in my hands.

As near as I could figure, it was some sort of collection of newspaper clippings, all referring to crimes, most of them reported in
horrible detail, and all seemingly having occurred in the 1880s and
1890s.

Placing these aside, I next discovered four stacks of paper tied
with string, which also tended to crumble at a touch. These were
covered with handwriting, the words being in a brownish sort of
ink and very difficult to read, as the penmanship was of the very
old-fashioned sort.

I did, however, jot down what appeared to be a title on one of them, remembering that you are always urging me to pay more attention to these things. As closely as I could decipher it, it read: "The Singular Affair of the Aluminium Crutch."

It seemed likely that this somehow referred to the lurid news clippings in the scrapbooks. As I have already mentioned, there were more of these tied parcels of paper, but they were in such poor condition, all of them turning brown and spotted with mildew, that I laid them aside with the scrapbooks.

Next came an old wooden cigar box which contained not only a handful of petrified cigars, but also an old-fashioned pipe, still half-stuffed with burned-out tobacco ash, and stinking to high heaven. I dropped this with the rest and washed my hands again before gingerly picking out a revolver which was so rusted as to be utterly useless. Flakes of it came away on my hands. I was beginning to regret having started this whole thing.

And that was the lot. Nothing of value, as you can see.

I hope you will appreciate my mucking about in all this trash, so that I can safely assure you that I have missed no old timepieces for your collection; have overlooked no silver plate, no family jewels. As I said before, nothing of value.

Oh yes, I nearly forgot . . . lest you should later accuse me of being less than thorough, I must report that in the bottom of the trunk was a filthy old rag which I almost overlooked. Upon inspection it turned out to be some sort of hat with a peak in front and another in back, with flaps up over the side and tied across the top with the remnants of a ribbon.

Somewhat disappointed at not finding a body after all, I piled this sorry lot back into the trunk, removed it to the landing, and retired, exhausted.

I will report further tomorrow.

Regards,
Parker

London, March 7

Dear Frank,

This will be brief. I learned today that my talk has been canceled, due to a severe outbreak of influenza which seems to have stricken more than half of my proposed audience. Tomorrow I leave for home. It is raining again and cold, and, if possible, damper than before.

When I returned to the suite, the heat was off, due to some mal-function in the boiler system. Having had the foresight to stock up once more with food, I have spent the better part of the day in front of the fireplace. That trunk of rubbish proved to be of value after all.

I will call you as soon as I am home again.

Regards,
Parker

The carping nature of some of the modern Sherlockian criticism has generated, in an understandable reaction to the mean-minded sniping at (usually) Watson or (less often) Holmes, that the trend of present-day criticism is toward a much more tolerant examination of what seem to be the inconsistencies and contradictions of the Canon. Whereas it has been a fairly widespread fashion to find Watson's chronology wrong and necessary to be corrected in almost all the stories, it is being found that Watson's correct dating may be accepted—and that that correct dating will confirm (as one of our contributors points out) the historic validity of the adventure. The narrower-minded critics have usually chosen, as their favorite targets, errors in date and place (which includes route): ". . . it is not possible to get to Bedfordshire from Euston." A more fatuous criticism, solemnly pronounced and set up in type, would be hard to imagine! Watson's medical knowledge and Holmes's chemical expertise: Here a professional chemist examines not only Holmes's chemical knowledge, but also the attacks upon it, and comes to what even Holmes's passionately loyal defenders will find a startling conclusion. In Colin Wilson's article, he refers to Holmes as a "flawed Superman"; here we learn, on the highest authority, that Holmes was "a farseeing chemist." That, at any rate, is what the author maintains in . . .

Holmesian Chemistry

PETER COOPER

Many a Sherlockian pilgrim—the majority of such reverent travelers from overseas—have asked their way through the seemingly haphazard congeries of buildings and rooms which is present-day St. Bartholomew's Hospital, to seek out the famous Path. Lab., and there to gaze on a bronze plaque fastened to a (generally dingy) wall. This plaque commemorates what is possibly the most momentous encounter in all literary history: the first meeting of Sherlock Holmes and the old boy of Bart's—Dr. John H. Watson, M.D.

The metal plaque, commissioned and erected on this historic spot by the Baker Street Irregulars, through its scion society, The Amateur Mendicants at the Caucus Club, has been in position since 21 January 1954; there is some alarming talk of their pulling down the old Path. Lab., but if this barbarism should come to pass, one need not fear that the bronze plaque will be lost in the rebuilding. It will still be on the newer wall to commemorate, as it does today, that meeting on 1 January 1881, when Holmes greeted Watson with the deathless words now eternalized on the plaque: "You have been in Afghanistan, I perceive!"

On that New Year's Day, now nearly a century ago, the historic meeting took place in "a lofty chamber, lined and littered with countless bottles. Broad, low tables were scattered about, which bristled with retorts, test-tubes and little Bunsen lamps, with their blue flickering flames. . . ."

Thus Watson, from memory: the place hasn't changed much since.

It was an enthusiastic, excited Holmes whom Watson met for the first time on that bitterly cold January day. Holmes, we may recall, had just—so he told Watson and young Stamford, who had brought the ex-military medico along—discovered (or perfected) "an infallible test for bloodstains." "As he spoke, he threw into the vessel a few white crystals, and then added some drops of a transparent fluid. In an instant the contents assumed a dull mahogany colour, and a brownish dust was precipitated to the bottom of the glass jar." Watson, as Holmes had evidently intended him to be, was suitably impressed by this chemical expertise.

Who was this Sherlock Holmes, and what were the qualities by which we may judge the sort of chemist that he was? Guessing, as Holmes himself has told us, destroys the logical faculty, and "it is a capital mistake, my dear Watson, to theorize before one has the facts." Holmes was born probably in January 1854, a century before the bronze plaque was erected. Modern astrologers— if we may place any reliance on them—have calculated that on 6 January 1854 Scorpio was in the ascendant, and that Holmes therefore ranks by nativity among those who instinctively dabble in poisons and chemicals.

The Holmes family apparently wandered during Holmes's youth, giving him a passing acquaintance with the continent of Europe. In all probability he studied at Oxford, for he afterward remarked to Watson that he considered Cambridge "inhospitable," as it would have seemed to an Oxford man recognized as such.* As a graduate, he came to rooms in Montague Street, Bloomsbury, "filling in my too abundant leisure time by studying all those

---

* *Tot homines, tot sententiae* must be the rule with Sherlock, when it comes to the consideration of Holmes's university.

branches of science which might make me more efficient." It was
during this period that he set his sights on a promising lodging at
221B Baker Street, for which he needed a roommate. Thus, young
Stamford of Bart's, running into the invalided Watson in the
Criterion bar, drew two lone stars into a new constellation.

Stamford, it is obvious, believed that Holmes was a first-class chemist, though his studies were desultory and eccentric, and he had not
studied medicine—or anything else but the new faculty he was
creating. Watson's assessment in "The Five Orange Pips" was
"Chemistry eccentric," though in earlier days it had been "Chemistry profound." It has been deduced by A. N. Griffith that Holmes
may have been one of the two private students of Augustus Mattiesson, who lectured in chemistry at Bart's from 1870. This so-
far-unnamed student helped Mattiesson in the investigation of

opium alkaloids and is reputed to have been a keen experimenter.

We may hope that it was not Mattiesson who was responsible for Holmes's rather slapdash methods. Throwing a few white crystals into a liter-measure, and adding a few drops of liquid, is not careful chemistry. Nor is using one pipette for several reagents a praiseworthy habit, as Watson describes it in "The Naval Treaty." "A large curved retort was boiling furiously in the bluish flame of the Bunsen burner, and the distilled drops were condensing into a two litre-measure. . . . He dipped into this bottle or that, drawing out a few drops of each with his glass pipette. . . ." It is noteworthy that Holmes seems to have a penchant for macrochemistry: he deals with liters, large retorts, and, one presumes, the regulation $\frac{5}{8}$-inch test tube. Moreover, the operation described by Watson is carried out in Holmes's dressing gown.

It is apparent, too, that Holmes became careless as time passed. Early in the partnership Watson remarks that Holmes "was possessed of remarkable delicacy of touch, as I frequently had occasion to observe when I watched him manipulating his frail philosophical instruments." Yet the first draft of "The Resident Patient" in 1893 tells us that Holmes spent a day in some abstruse experiment, but that, toward evening, "the breaking of a test tube brought his research to a premature ending, and he sprang up from his chair with an exclamation of impatience and a clouded brow. 'A day's work ruined, Watson,' said he, striding across to the window." Yet a chemist who keeps all his sample in one test tube is, to say the least, unwise.

What sort of lines did Holmes follow in his private researches? we may ask. Time and time again Watson finds him before a formidable array of reagent bottles and test tubes, sometimes eked out with those incredibly fragile retorts which used to be all the rage, surrounded by a malodorous reek or "the pungently clean smell of hydrochloric acid."

Sometimes the research took all day, often all night. "Well," Watson asked in "A Case of Identity," "have you solved it?" "Yes, it was the bisulphate of baryta."

A chemical curiosity, this one!

Partington remarks that barium acid sulphate may be made by the action of concentrated hot sulphuric acid on barium sulphate. It would hardly crop up in the course of a toxicological analysis such as Holmes was wont to revel in. One cannot but wonder whether Holmes undertook a certain amount of consultant analytical work, and had been asked to report on a wandering museum specimen; indeed, a subsidiary case of identity.

Then there are the acetones—plural. In "The Adventure of the Copper Beeches," Watson tells us of an all-night chemistry session which was put off. ". . . Perhaps I had better postpone my analysis of the acetones, as we may need to be at our best in the morning," says Holmes. Was he speaking carelessly? Critics have suggested that perhaps he meant the acetone bodies of blood in metabolic disorders. Ure's *Dictionary of Arts, Manufactures, and Mines,* in its 1861 edition, remarks: "It has been found that a great number of organic acids, when distilled under similar circumstances, yield bodies bearing the same relation to the parent acid that acetone does to acetic acid: this fact has caused the word acetone to be used of late in a more extended sense than formerly." Holmes, then, was quite in order in his day, in calling ketones "acetones."

Then there are the hydrocarbons, the coal-tar derivatives, and the creosote of Pondicherry Lodge, chronicled by Watson in *The Sign of Four.* Holmes followed Gladstone's dictum that a change of work is the best rest: "When I had succeeded in dissolving the hydrocarbon which I was at work at," he says, "I came back to the problem of the Sholtos."

Despite the cavilers who claim that any fool can dissolve a hydrocarbon, it is evident that Holmes was really characterizing a specific hydrocarbon by its physical constants. There are few ways, since he had no gas chromatograph, apart from solubility and boiling point, which would have served him.

It is a pity, though, that he did not speculate on the strange hobby of Bartholomew Sholto, whose room had a double row of glass-stoppered bottles on the wall, a table littered with the habitual Bunsen burners, test tubes, and retorts, and—strange phenomenon—carboys in wicker baskets, with a trickle of creosote issuing from one of them. Can the unfortunate Bartholomew have been doing pilot-scale tests for a manufacturer? Certainly he did not teach chemistry, to require all those carboys of acid. And what of all that creosote? It would be a capital mistake, as Holmes has warned us, to attempt to theorize without facts.

Holmes himself assures us, in "The Adventure of the Empty House," that after his presumed death in the Reichenbach affair, he "spent some months in a research into the coal-tar derivatives" in a laboratory at Montpellier. From their modern standpoint, the critics have cried out at so grandiose a statement, coal-tar derivatives being virtually unlimited.

Yet in Holmes's day coal tar was in the news. Ure, in 1860, could write: "There is not perhaps any waste article of our manufacturing industry which has been so singularly neglected as coal tar, and yet there can be but very few which offer so fair a field of remuneration for the exercise of skill and ingenuity."

In Holmes's time, in fact, the gas from coal was valued, but the tar was still largely a drug on the market. Mischerlich had nitrated benzene in 1834; Zinin had reduced nitrobenzene to aniline in 1841; Perkin produced his mauveine in 1856. The first coal-tar dye factory in England was opened in 1857. Things, then, were not yet so advanced that research might not cash in on coal tar. Holmes, it would appear, was a farseeing chemist, not the braggart that some have painted.

Lack of time alone prevented Holmes from developing new microchemical techniques. With his low-power microscope, described in "Shoscombe Old Place," he distinguished fibers and glue, zinc and copper filings. To apply reagents dropwise on the slide must surely have been his next step. In deciphering his palimpsests under a powerful lens, as Watson describes in "The Golden Pince-Nez," he must surely have applied developing reagents tentatively, as his creator did by proxy to those mysterious blank sheets which were posted to a publisher from Canada (*Memories and Adventures*, 1924).

Perhaps Holmes suffered from the frustration of those abortive chemical demonstrations that Arthur Conan Doyle witnessed in his Edinburgh University days. "There was kindly Crum Brown, the chemist," he tells us in *Memories and Adventures,* "who sheltered himself carefully before exploding some mixture, which usually failed to ignite, so that the loud 'Boom!' uttered by the class was the only resulting sound."

For, in many respects, Sherlock Holmes was a frustrated chemist, hamstrung by the laboratory conventions of his day.

We asked the author of this article to describe for us the impact that the new *New Scotland Yard would make on Sherlock Holmes were he to revisit the Yard today. It is fitting that the author should be not only a distinguished Sherlockian, but also a member of the staff at New Scotland Yard—able, thus, to talk as authoritatively of Holmes in Holmes's heyday as to talk of the mechanized, computerized, streamlined Yard that the old Metropolitan Police Office of Lestrade and Gregson and Athelney Jones has become over the past ninety years. Yet, for all its startling changes, would the new Yard be quite the shock for Holmes that we might assume? Might one not argue that a fully scientific Yard was the sort toward which Holmes was already working in the 1880s; that the highly sophisticated crime detection and crime prevention organization of today is merely the logical and inevitable development of a pattern that Holmes initiated by his own example? . . .*

Sherlock Holmes
and New Scotland Yard

✖

PHILIP DALTON

✖

Very early in his career as a consulting detective, Sherlock Holmes said to Watson: "It is a capital mistake to theorize before one has data. Insensibly one begins to twist facts to suit theories, instead of theories to suit facts."

With those words ringing in my ears, I am going to attempt to answer a question I was asked by the Editor of this book: "What would be Sherlock Holmes's reactions if he were to be restored to us, and could see Scotland Yard today?"

I was asked the question because, aside from looking after the Sherlock Holmes Society of London's modest funds, I am employed by the Commissioner of Metropolitan Police as an Information Officer at New Scotland Yard. I hope that what follows will not be judged as an effort to twist theories to suit facts.

Sherlock Holmes's working life as a consulting detective covers the years 1871 to 1914—forty-three years of first-hand dealings with criminals of all kinds, and forty-three years of dealings of one sort or another with police officers, mostly Scotland Yarders. However, the great majority of the sixty adventures took place between 1880 and 1900, so I think it is fair to compare Scotland

Yard today with Scotland Yard in 1890 in order to put the theorizing into some kind of factual perspective.

The Report of the Commissioner of Police of the Metropolis for 1890 reveals that 15,264 police officers were available to police an area of 688.31 square miles, and that the total of serious offenses (down the scale from murder to forgery and counterfeiting) was 18,815.

Provisional figures for 1974 show that 20,055 police officers were available to police an area of 788 square miles, and that the total number of indictable crimes (fairly comparable with the serious crimes of 1890) was 413,516.

In 1890, the Metropolitan Police dealt with 67 cases of murder, manslaughter and infanticide. In 1974, the MPD dealt with 142 cases of homicide (again, fairly comparable).

The present Commissioner of Police of the metropolis, Sir Robert Mark, was the guest of honor of the Sherlock Holmes Society at their Annual Dinner in January 1974, and he had this to say about the difference in policing London in 1890, compared with policing the Capital in 1974: "Holmes fulfilled the need for a folk hero against a believable background . . . a cosily domestic setting against which one brilliant individual could shine, especially in comparison with an illiterate police force with a music hall tradition of relieving intoxicated gentlemen of their watches and chains."

In the sixty adventures recorded for us, Holmes had dealings with thirteen police officers, eleven of them Metropolitan Police officers. The two we hear of most are Inspectors Lestrade and Gregson. Lestrade is described by Holmes, when he first met him, as "a sallow, rat-faced, dark-eyed fellow," but in spite of that, Holmes had considerable respect for Lestrade: "I have been down to see friend Lestrade at the Yard," he tells Watson one day; "there may be an occasional want of imaginative intuition down there, but they lead the world for thoroughness and method." Inspector Gregson was considered by Holmes to be "the smartest of the Scotland Yarders," and he and Lestrade, in Holmes's opinion, were "the pick of a bad lot." In spite of that, there is no record of either Gregson's or Lestrade's ever being promoted; they remained among the ranks of the 858 inspectors, which was the authorized strength in 1890.

Holmes's view of Scotland Yard, then, was somewhat jaundiced, but one might be justified in thinking that Holmes's low opinion of the official force might be partly due to his high opinion of himself: "There is no one who knows the higher criminal world of London so well as I do. . . ."

Presumably some of Holmes's visits to the Yard, early in his career, would have been to No. 4 Whitehall Place, where the Police Office was until 1890. In that year came the move down Whitehall to the Embankment building, partly built with granite quarried by Dartmoor convicts. "This change," wrote the Commissioner in his 1890 Report, "has resulted in a very great increase of convenience, and the work is now carried on under more favorable conditions than was formerly the case, especially with regard to space, light and ventilation, in all of which essentials the old headquarters was lamentably deficient."

The Criminal Investigation Department of the Yard had been set up in 1878, and it was during the ten years from 1890 to 1900 that the CID built up a world-wide reputation for efficiency in crime detection. That is a fact too easily lost sight of, if you accept Holmes's view of the Yard in his day.

What might now be his view if he were to be restored to us and shown the workings of the Metropolitan Police force today?

There are four basic inventions, all being discussed in Holmes's time, which he would quickly recognize as having completely altered the method of policing the metropolis since 1890; radio, telephone, photography, and the internal combustion engine are essential ingredients of police work today, as Holmes would appreciate. He would also appreciate the irony in the fact that the internal combustion engine has presented the Metropolitan Police with a massive problem; how massive can be gauged from the fact that of 1974's indictable crime total of 413,516, no fewer than 134,836 concern autocrime—taking and driving away or theft from motor vehicles. To that, one might point out to Holmes, can be added more than 600 road deaths and some 53,000 injuries in London, compared with 144 deaths and 5,500 injuries in 1890. Although it might seem that the road accident problem was relatively small in 1890, it was in fact causing the Commissioner much concern, especially since many of the casualties were children riding illegally on the backs of carts.

[SCOTLAND-YARD, THE HEAD-QUARTERS OF THE METROPOLITAN POLICE.]

The original headquarters of the Metropolitan Police,
in Scotland Yard and Whitehall Court. The Clarence
public house, seen in this old *Illustrated London News*
engraving, was badly damaged by the Dynamiters in
1884. *Contrad Research Library.*

New Scotland Yard, as Holmes knew it well. Built to
the designs of Norman Shaw on the foundations of the
never-realized National Opera House, it was extended
from Derby Gate to the Thames Embankment in 1912.
To many, this will always be *the* Scotland Yard.
Copyright: Commissioner of Metropolitan Police.

The *new* New Scotland Yard of which the author writes. The building dominates the important corner site formed by Broadway (LEFT) and Victoria Street (RIGHT). The dome in the center of the photograph is not a pretentious architectural feature of the new "Yard" but belongs to the distant Central (Methodist) Hall. *Copyright: Commissioner of Metropolitan Police.*

Holmes would instantly recognize the value of radio, and especially the way in which the walkie-talkie has transformed the beat situation. One wonders for how long Professor Moriarty and his minions would have eluded justice if the Serious Crime Squad had existed in 1890; but Marconi didn't patent his invention until 1896.

The telephone presents us with something of a puzzle. Bell had invented it in 1876,* but it does not appear at 221B Baker Street until July 1898. The telephone was certainly installed in New Scotland Yard in 1890, but Holmes seems to have had a preference for telegrams, although in "The Adventure of the Retired Colourman" there is a tantalizing reference to the telephone: in conversation with Watson, Holmes says: "Thanks to the telephone and the help of the Yard, I can usually get my essentials without leaving this room." So although this is the first reference to the telephone in the adventures, perhaps it had been installed in Baker Street for some time, but neither Holmes nor Watson bothered to mention it. Even if Holmes was one of those people who don't like the telephone—and there are still plenty of them—he would appreciate its use in the Yard today: the Information Room alone receives a million and a quarter telephone messages in the course of a year.

In Holmes's time, photography was, in the words of Christopher Pulling, Senior Assistant Secretary at Scotland Yard for a period during the 1950s, "a cumbrous art, strictly limited in the uses which could be made of it." Nevertheless, the Commissioner in his 1890 Report refers to "an extension of the work of the CID in relation to habitual criminals," and he mentions the building up of albums of photographs of habitual criminals. Here we have the genesis of the Criminal Record Office (CRO), and Holmes would rub his hands with glee if he were to see the operation of this arm of the Yard's criminal intelligence system. He would probably agree that the greatest tribute paid to its efficiency is the venom

---

* The electromagnetic telephone was actually invented by Johann Philipp Reis in 1861, an event which, on my representations, was celebrated in Germany by the issue of a postage stamp and several big exhibitions organized by the principal electrical manufacturing companies of West Germany. The modern (carbon-diaphragm) telephone was really the joint achievement of Bell, Gray, and Edison—the last-named opening London's first telephone exchange in Lombard Street in 1879.—*Ed.*

with which it is attacked by those who would like to see the disbandment of the Metropolitan Police force.

Another branch at the Yard, the Fingerprint Branch, would be sure to interest Holmes. In 1890, fingerprints were being written and talked about in the scientific world, but it was not until 1901 that they were officially adopted as a legal method of identification. For some years before that, the Yard used the Bertillon method, which involved the measurement of certain bony structures of the body, and especially the head. Holmes would probably be glad to know that the Bertillon method was discarded: he bitterly resented it when someone spoke of Bertillon as "a rival expert." Today, the Fingerprint Branch adds about a quarter of a million new criminal records annually to the National Fingerprint Collection, which is now approaching the three-million mark. Again, this arm of the Yard's offensive against crime comes under attack from certain quarters, and this would interest Holmes very much.

What other changes would Holmes observe?

He would certainly be interested in the work of the Drug Squad —though, to be fair, we know that Dr. Watson successfully weaned him from his mild addiction to a seven percent solution of cocaine. He would be startled to learn that he and Watson required firearms certificates for their revolvers, and, indeed, would probably be running the risk of committing an offense if they carried firearms in the course of their adventures.*

Holmes was very much of a scientific bent of mind (despite his apparent ignorance of the talk about fingerprints current in 1890), and an important part of the domestic scene at 221B Baker Street was "the chemical corner and the acid-stained deal-topped table" over which Watson sometimes found Holmes crouched. Thus he would be sure to be fascinated to visit the Forensic Science Laboratory, now newly installed at Lambeth. Here he would surely be very much at home, remembering his interest in (and his promised monograph on) 140 different varieties of pipe, cigar and cigarette tobacco, thumbnails, bootlaces, typewriters, battered old hats, bones, bicycle tire impressions, and so on.

Here, at Lambeth, he would have much common ground with

---

* The reader may care to ponder this remark in relation to Andrew Fusco's article in this collection.—*Ed.*

the chemists and technicans working there: perhaps, by now, he has completed his "little monograph . . . on the typewriter and its relation to crime." One thinks of forged documents and ransom notes, of which some of the latter are put together from headlines cut from newspapers, and one remembers that Holmes once said: "The detection of types [in newspapers] is one of the most elementary branches of knowledge to the special expert in crime, though I confess that once when I was very young I confused the *Leeds Mercury* with the *Western Morning News*." (As a complete aside, Holmes would today appreciate the fact that, so far as possible, the Sherlock Holmes Society of London specifies Baskerville typeface for its printed communications—even though we also have to resort to the typewriter.)

At Lambeth, one can imagine an interesting conversation between Holmes and the chemists on the "seventy-five perfumes, which it is very necessary that a criminal expert should be able to distinguish from each other." He would be able to enlarge on the tantalizing words he uttered just before he was introduced to young Stamford in the chemical laboratory at St. Bartholomew's Hospital in 1881: "I've found it! . . . I have found a reagent which is precipitated by hemoglobin and nothing else . . . it is the most practical medico-legal discovery for years . . . it gives us an infallible test for bloodstains. Come over here now!"

From that moment on, after what some hold to be the most momentous meeting in literary history, Dr. Watson was in it up to his neck, as Holmes's biographer, comrade in arms and, occasionally, accessory after the fact.

Holmes would notice with interest, but probably without amazement, such advances as air surveillance by helicopter, hounds trained to sniff out drugs and explosives, closed circuit television for surveillance and traffic control, the infrared camera, and firearms training for certain selected police officers—quite unknown in 1890, and regrettably accepted as a necessity in a more violent 1975.

Perhaps what would interest him most is a marked increase in quality of man and woman in the Metropolitan Police service in 1975 compared with his day. Perhaps the stereotype of the stolid Bobby in his size ten boots, pounding the beat, clipping street urchins round the ear with his cape, unimaginative but brave as a lion, does not reflect the whole truth, but it is not entirely myth. Today's Metropolitan Police officer and, for that matter, a police officer in any force in the country, has to be highly intelligent, able to work on his own initiative when required, capable of operating highly sophisticated equipment, willing to be involved in community relations and all the allied problems that this involves. He or she has to be steady under fire from many quarters, whether it be a rain of spittle from football hooligans or obscenities shouted by demonstrators, a bomb incident, a highway pile-up, or a lost child.

This is not to say that the police officer of Holmes's time could not have coped with such situations, but I am in no doubt that the Metropolitan Police Officer of today, from the beat upward, is of a caliber that would impress Holmes.

Holmes said he was going to devote his declining years "to the composition of a textbook which shall focus the whole art of detection into one volume. . . ."

It is not to be found in the Commissioner's Library at New Scotland Yard, so perhaps he never completed it. Let our present Commissioner, Sir Robert Mark, have the last word: ". . . there is not an English-speaking country in which the words Scotland Yard and Sherlock Holmes require any explanation at all. They are two of the comparatively few symbols which bring to all minds the London which produced both."

If "The Disappearance of Lady Frances Carfax" is one of the less important stories, the name "Carfax" is one of the most important in the entire Sherlockian Canon. Its use, by Watson or the Agent, has been cited as proof that Holmes was an Oxonian rather than a Cantab; and from this unusual name many other conclusions have been drawn, too. The author of this article believes that the choice was deliberate, and that the name was intended to provide a clue to the lady's real identity. He clears up, once and for all, a very old Sherlockian mystery in answering his own question: . . .

Why Did He Call Her "Carfax"?

✂

QUENTIN DOWNES

✂

1895. A bad year for British prestige (nasty Notes from the United States, Venezuelan and Brazilian governments, all threatening war). A bad year, too, the Agent reflected, for British Toffs. He recalled 1895 well . . .

He was reading, in the autumn of 1911—sixteen years after 1895 —Watson's description of the case which has been recorded for all time as "The Disappearance of Lady Frances Carfax"; Watson's account appearing, for the first time, simultaneously in the *Strand Magazine* and the *American Magazine,* December 1911.

It was part of the Agent's job, in editing Watson's sometimes obscure and often indiscreet typescripts for world publication, to alter the real names. Charity—to avoid causing distress to the actual characters described; and prudence—to avoid those costly libel actions which were endemic in the overlitigious Victorian society, made this name-altering the Agent's first and principal consideration in marking up Watson's copy for press.

Because Watson has been permitted at times to claim responsibility for this prudent name-changing, it has been forgotten that, even where Watson did change the true names, the last word in the final selection of a "safe" name always rested with the Agent. It was his wide knowledge of the world—especially of the world of *Debrett, Burke, Jack, Dodd, Fairbairn,* and the rest of those reference books which record the pedigrees and honors of the aristocracy, which enabled the Agent to guide Watson, over a period of forty years (1887–1927), through the perilous ways of contemporary reporting.

The importance of the Agent in this connection cannot be overstressed, for it is by the Agent's choice that a real name has been replaced by a fictitious one. The clues, then, to the real names must be sought—and may be found only—in a constant awareness of the Agent's mentality: of his deep and even passionate interest in ancient and modern history, in genealogy and heraldry, in the romance of chivalry—which, for his romantic mind, had not altogether died with the Middle Ages. Borne constantly in view, also, should be the Agent's education, in which the normal Victorian classical foundation had carried the useful addition of a study of modern languages, in particular French and German. To this student of *Burke* and *Debrett,* the *Almanach de Gotha,* the *Genealogisches Handbuch des Adels, Ruvigny* and the many *Nobilaires* of titled Europe were as familiar as *Debrett.* It was his choice that the unhappy victim of Dr. Shlessinger's greed and brutality should appear in the Canon as "Lady Frances Carfax"—and it is a choice of pseudonym which has taken Sherlockian speculation far beyond the limits of a vulnerable single lady's persecution.

From this choice, the late Lord Donegall and others have argued that Holmes must have been up at Oxford, since the ancient center of that ancient city is the crossroads named Carfax. But there is an almost as well known Carfax in the center of the Sussex town of Horsham, and Horsham, by road, is somewhat less than twenty miles from Crowborough, in which pleasant Sussex town the Agent had his country house. Horsham would have been familiar to the Agent (it was certainly familiar to Holmes and Watson)—it was then the country town, and he could hardly have failed to become familiar with its central crossroads, its Carfax. I don't feel that the Agent had Oxford in mind when he selected the name Carfax—but whether or not he had, it was certainly in no Oxonian connection that he found and chose the name. Why he did so it is the purpose of this short article clearly to demonstrate.

A Bad Year for Toffs

As the Agent read Watson's account of what the infamous Dr. Shlessinger (*alias* Holy Peters) and his so-called wife, Annie Fraser, had done to a lady "traveling unaccompanied on the Continent with the remains of the valuable jewelry amongst her baggage," he recalled another titled lady, equally alone in the world, who had also got herself into considerable trouble in—yes, 1895.

The Agent remembered that terrible year well, a year in which, despite Great Britain's wealth and power, more humiliation had been heaped upon her than at any time since the darkest days of the first American war. To the Agent—a passionate believer in, and worker for, Anglo-American friendship—it was doubly terrible that the greatest humiliations had come from Washington, where Secretary of State Richard Olney was writing Notes ever more menacing; so that, to prevent what seemed certain war, the Prince of Wales took the unconstitutional (but eminently practical) step of writing privately to the owner of the *New York Times*. But not all this humiliation was caused by Britain's enemies or less-than-friends; the year ended with the greatest humiliation of all—the foolish and dangerous Jameson Raid, in which Dr. Starr Jameson, a friend of the Empire-building Cecil Rhodes, led a raid into independent Transvaal—an act which led directly to the disastrous Boer War of four years later.

And, as though the ill-fortune of a country is reflected in the ill-fortune of its governing class, strange tragedies noticeably involved what the Victorian common man called The Toffs.

Did the Agent remember that the train of tragedies had begun, on 5 March 1895, with the conviction of Edward *Holmes* for begging? Probably not. Such things are better forgotten. But he did remember these:

1.	15 March	Suicide of Baron de Nolde.
2.	13 May	Death of the Right Honourable Sir Robert Peel, PC, GCB, 3rd baronet, of hemorrhage of the brain.
3.	3 June	Suicide of William Leveson-Gower, collateral of the Duke of Sutherland (intimate friend of the Prince of Wales) and son-in-law of the 1st Baron Leigh (Chandos Leigh, the now-forgotten "poet").

4.	18 Sept.	Miles, Lord Beaumont, 10th Baron, lieut-colonel commanding the crack 20th Hussars. Accidentally killed by his own gun.
5.	28 Sept.	Viscount Parker, eldest son and heir of the 6th Earl of Macclesfield, found dead.
6.	15 Oct.	Richard Villiers-Stuart, a collateral of both the Earl of Clarendon and the Earl of Jersey. Accidentally drowned.
7.	26 Oct.	Suicide of John Henry de la Poer, 5th Marquess of Waterford, PC, KP, Master of the Buckhounds, 1885–86—who, with his brothers, was an intimate friend of the Prince of Wales.

And then, the Agent reflected, there was that distressing case of Frances, Lady Gunning . . .

The Lady Club-owner

Unlike Lady Frances Carfax, Frances Gunning—born Frances Spencer—was not the innocent victim of a designing and conscienceless rogue, but of her own panic-generated impulses. Yet, though she was convicted of deliberate forgery, for which she received Twelve Months at Hard Labour from the Common Serjeant, it is hard to withhold sympathy from "a widow since 1885, without any previous experience, [who] embarked on the gigantic enterprise [of founding and running] this Club."

Counsel for the Crown was the redoubtable Horace Avory (later a most famous High Court Judge), and the care with which he skated around the notable family background of Frances, Lady Gunning, "pleading Guilty to indictments ranging from 1892 to this present year, charging her with a series of forgeries," must instantly have excited the Agent's desire to know *whom* Crown Counsel was leaving discreetly out of the Court record. The Agent reached for his *Debrett* and looked up Frances Gunning.

Avory had quickly, rather too quickly, run through a brief, a very brief, account of the prisoner's background: "The Prisoner is the widow of a baronet, a clergyman of the Church of England, and daughter of another clergyman of the Church of England"—and then had gone on to detail the charges: of forging her father's signature to documents, so as to obtain money; of forging a Bill of

Exchange; of forging a renewal of a Bill; of forging a letter from her father; of forging a transfer of 500 shares, and so on. It all sounded very dishonest, especially when her Counsel, Mr. Holloway, had to admit that, of the subscriptions of £8,601, only some £868 were to be accounted for in the books of The Addison Club.

Yes, *Debrett* confirmed what Avory had said: the prisoner was the widow of the Reverend Sir Henry John Gunning, 4th baronet of Eltham, Kent, who died in 1885, and whom she had married in 1879, as his second wife. But—ah-ha!—what was this? Avory had merely mentioned that she was also the daughter of "another Church of England clergyman"—and so, indeed, she was. The entry under GUNNING in *Debrett* read:

> **Widow living of 4th Baronet**—FRANCES ROSE (*Lady Gunning*) da. of the Rev. the Hon. William Henry Spencer [*see* B. Churchill]: *m.* 1879, as his 2nd wife, the Rev. Sir Henry John Gunning, 4th baronet, who *d.* 1885.

So, the Agent marveled, *that's* who she is! Not simply the impecunious (and driven-to-crime) widow of a baronet-clergyman, but a relative of the Barons Churchill, and so a member of the powerful Ducal House of Marlborough, whose present head, the half-American 9th Duke, was the son of another of the Prince of Wales's pleasure-seeking (and -finding) cronies. The Agent turned up CHURCHILL in the Peerage, to find out exactly who Frances Spencer was in the long and complicated Spencer-Churchill genealogy.

Frances Rose Spencer, born 1840, was the daughter of the Reverend the Honourable William Henry Spencer (b.1819), son of the 1st Baron Churchill, who, before his elevation to the peerage of the United Kingdom in 1813, had been Lord Francis Almeric Spencer, DCL, 2nd son of the 4th Duke of Marlborough. Frances Rose was thus the great-granddaughter of the 4th Duke of Marlborough, while the present Baron's mother had been Lady Jane Conyngham, daughter of the 2nd Marquess Conyngham, a family raised to power through the first Lady Conyngham's improper association with King George IV. Here were powerful names indeed, especially when one considered that the present Lord Churchill was a Lord-in-Waiting to Her Majesty the Queen. No wonder that

the prisoner's unhappy connection with these Toffs was glossed
over by Crown Counsel, as "she is the daughter of another Church
of England clergyman." The wonder is, the Agent reflected, that
the Spencer-Churchills ever let the case come to Court.

The Carfax

If, as the Agent did, one turns up CHURCHILL in an end-of-the-
century *Debrett* and sees there the baronial arms, splendid with
griffin and wyvern supporters, and with the rather (so far as
Frances Rose was concerned) inappropriate motto, *Dieu defend le
Droit*—"God defend the Right!"—one will be struck by what struck
me, and what certainly struck the heraldry-conscious Agent: the
curious heraldic device in the second and third quarters of the
shield. It is called a *frette,* and at first glance it looks for all the
world like the map of a street intersection . . . a regularly patterned
crossroads . . . a *Carfax.*

Here, then, is the origin of the name, *Carfax.* The choice of
name does not imply any identification, in fact, of the real Frances,

Coat-of-arms of the Barons Churchill of Wychwood in the county of
Oxford; the title dates from 1779. Note (UPPER RIGHT AND LOWER LEFT)
the heraldic design called a *frette.* It was because of the *frette's* resemblance to a crossroads—or carfax—that the original of "Lady Frances
Carfax" got her fictitious name. *Contrad Research Library.*

Lady Gunning, with the real (but fictitiously named) Lady Frances Carfax. But that, to the tender heart of the Agent, there was a connection in sentiment, in pattern, the choice of the name Carfax makes clear. Both women got into avoidable trouble because, on their own, they were the prey either of rogues (this was equally true in Lady Gunning's case) or of their own unguided wrong-thinking—and in each case because those who could and should have looked after them failed criminally to do so.

That the rich and powerful Spencers—advisers and friends of the Reigning House—could have stood aside to let Lady Gunning, their relative, face the ignominy of a trial and serve a humiliating and degrading prison sentence with hard labor seemed to the crusading heart of the Agent a crime far worse than any with which Frances Gunning had been charged.

In his cryptic fashion, the Agent recorded his indignant contempt of all such titled Levites, who stood—and still stand—aside when they see another (even a relative) in trouble. To mark his sense of what the Spencers had done, he used, as an imaginary name, that of the most conspicuous element in the arms of the Spencers: the *frette,* or, as it looks at first glance, the "Carfax."

We all know the free and easy attitude that Holmes assumed toward crime in its relation to the law. Holmes had his own, often highly idiosyncratic, views of what constituted justice. After the particularly violent murder of—well, yes, he was a blackmailer: "the worst man in London"—Charles Augustus Milverton, Holmes not only permits the lady-murderer to escape, but remarks afterward: "I think there are certain crimes which the law cannot touch, and which therefore [emphasis added], to some extent, justify private revenge." There are many more such remarks, all demonstrating Holmes's self-confident ability to distinguish between the law and what he thinks of as justice. But, for all that many a Sherlockian commentator has called attention to this cavalier treatment of the law, no one yet has asked the pertinent question: Did Holmes actually know anything—anything at all—about the laws of England (and, perhaps, of some other countries) that he so contemptuously spurned? Did his disdain of legal forms come, not, as has been supposed, from a contempt for the law, but from an ignorance of the law? For the first time, this question is raised and answered here by an American lawyer who impartially presents . . .

The Case
Against Mr. Holmes

✳

ANDREW G. FUSCO

✳

Undoubtedly, Sherlock Holmes is one of the most written-about characters in literary history, but despite the great wealth of writings and research on the subject, many facets of his existence and character still remain obscured and disguised behind the heavy veil of inaccuracy and camouflage woven by Watson, the *sometimes* faithful chronicler.

Despite the fact that so many have written so much about the Master Detective, there are still far too many areas in which speculation alone remains. One of these areas is that of his education. No doubt there has been much commentary and speculation as to the university he attended, but the result has fallen far short of illumination. In fact, the only sure means we have of determining the nature of his education is to examine the Canon itself and try to use Holmes's own methods in the hope of shedding at least a little light on the subject.

Our detecting problem is compounded, however, by the fact that, throughout his recorded adventures, we are left with a record that shows Holmes to be well versed in almost all areas, after the form of the classical university education common during the

Renaissance. Apparently, he was well informed on a multitude of subjects; his mental abilities seem to approach those of his brother Mycroft, whose specialty was omniscience.

As Gavin Brend aptly put it, Holmes "was in fact a walking encyclopedia,"[1] although whether this was the result of his formal education or of many long hours in the reading room at the British Museum is another question. The problem, in essence, is one Holmes himself would have found challenging: we have too many facts, and to theorize on such a basis probably is a capital mistake, just as it is to postulate on insufficient data.

In order to maintain some degree of integrity from the standpoint of scholarship and analysis, it becomes necessary, then, to study the multifaceted detective from narrow viewpoints, individually, and, hopefully, to draw the total picture itself only after a separate analysis of each of its component parts.

To attempt to study all of these components goes far beyond the scope of this paper. Instead, it will be better to look at just one of the primary problem areas—Holmes's knowledge, or lack of knowledge, of the law. This is a question that has perplexed a few writers for many years, but unfortunately no consensus, and very little continuity, has ever been achieved on the subject.

We must start at the beginning: Watson the loyal, if not always faithful, narrator tells us early in *A Study in Scarlet* that Holmes possessed a "good, practical knowledge of British Law," and this bare statement has led numerous persons to believe and contend that Holmes had some sort of formal legal education, and that he perhaps was a trained solicitor or barrister (i.e., a lawyer). Another school of thought rejects this out of hand, usually with uncomplimentary reflection on the good doctor's standing (as a doctor not versed in the law) to judge anyone else's ability or knowledge in such a complex area. Since the latter school probably has the better basis upon which to form its conclusions, we must look elsewhere to find a definitive answer to the problem.

The second place to look for evidence of the nature of Holmes's education and knowledge would ordinarily be his university transcript, but, even at this late date in the annals of Sherlockian scholarship, no one seems to know quite where Holmes went to school, and all the likely institutional candidates disavow him. Was it Cambridge, Oxford, London, or some university on the

Continent? Or none of these? For the sake of argument, if we can accept the unpopular opinion of Dorothy Sayers and others that he attended Cambridge, we can probably rule out any formal legal training, albeit with a more than average degree of uncertainty, providing we further accept Miss Sayers's quite reasonable hypothesis that he pursued the Natural Sciences Tripos as opposed to the Law and History Tripos.[2]

So, if the Master Detective did not, in fact, receive any formal legal education while at Cambridge, the other alternatives are limited: (a) he studied British Law by tutor; (b) he studied British Law while on the Continent in the early 1870s; (c) he acquired the bulk of his legal knowledge by way of independent study; or (d) he had no real legal knowledge. The first of these possibilities we can probably reject out of hand, based on what little knowledge we have of Holmes's father and his attitudes.[3] That he could have received any valid education in British Law while traveling the Continent (if, in fact, he *did* travel the Continent during the early 1870s, during which time he must have acquired whatever semblance of legal knowledge Watson had observed) seems a doubtful prospect, at best—especially when one considers world sentiment concerning Great Britain at that time.

So, we are left with the latter two possibilities, and it is virtually impossible to answer the third possibility without first examining the fourth: Did Sherlock Holmes really possess any special legal knowledge, or was he no more informed than the average layman on the subject of the law?

Since the predominance of published argument seems to favor the theory either that Holmes was a lawyer or at least that he had a superior knowledge of British Law, let us first look at some of the principal tenets of that school:

1. The foundations of all such arguments rest on the previously quoted statement by Watson that would seem to support a contention that Holmes had at least *some* special legal knowledge.[4] But as noted above, we must consider the source of that evaluation. It was purely subjective, in that Watson could make his estimation based only on what *he* thought the law to be. To this date, careful research shows that no one has ever argued that Watson had any more knowledge of the law than the average layman, and he probably had less—surely his prescribing of strychnine

in large doses as a sedative for Thaddeus Sholto[5] was repugnant to the laws of medical practice, even in Watson's era. Further, though there is no question that Watson was loyal, steadfast, honorable, devoted and trustworthy, there is nothing to indicate that he ranked literary accuracy among the virtues. Need more be said?[6]

2. We also are asked to consider Holmes's use of legal terms—"deposes"[7] and "reversion"[8]—and urged to accept these as indicators of legal training or proficiency. What the espousers of this view have failed to do, however, is to look at the legal definitions of the words used and compare them with the context in which Holmes supposedly used them. Once done, there is no question that his usage was improper. For example, to "depose" is commonly defined as meaning to give written evidence under oath,[9] and there is nothing to indicate that this was the case when Holmes used the term in reference to Lady St. Simon's maid. Likewise, "reversion" most commonly indicates a future interest of a grantor or his heirs in property of which a present interest has been disposed of by, for example, the mechanism of life estate.[10] Can we really presume that Culverton Smith granted some kind of a property interest to his unfortunate nephew, reserving in himself certain residual or reversionary rights, and then murdered the nephew to recover what he had transferred? Most certainly not. What better evidence could we have that Holmes was not a lawyer? Even if we decide Holmes had some expertise in criminal law because of his frequent exposure to it, we cannot say he possessed the well-rounded background of the formally educated legal mind.

3. It has also been propounded that Holmes's possession of great legal knowledge is an inevitable conclusion if we consider the degree of proof he typically elicited in the solution of his cases.[11] As this writer has noted elsewhere, however, it is just as plausible that the proof and evidence Holmes sought (and usually gathered) were merely products of his mental compulsion toward absolute detail. Admittedly this proof generally would have been sufficient to satisfy a Victorian court, but can we honestly say that Holmes's mind would have been satisfied with anything less, irrespective of the desires or dictates of the Queen's Bench? This is especially true if we consider the fact that most of his solutions

were really nothing more than intricate factual puzzles to which he found the key. He sought all the facts and typically got them, no doubt much to the pleasure of the Queen's prosecutors, but without any particular regard for their legal implications.

4. Much has been made of the fact that Holmes required a signed receipt from Sandeford when he purchased the Sixth Napoleon (in which, unbeknownst to the seller, was concealed the Borgia pearl). Who but a lawyer would have thought of this?[12]

Where Sherlock Holmes could have acquired legal knowledge. The "Holbein" gateway (built in 1518) of Lincoln's Inn, one of the four remaining Inns of Court, or colleges of English Law. Bewigged counsel pass through the busy gateway in Chancery Lane, as this engraving of 1890 shows. *Contrad Research Library.*

Again, however, the argument fails.[13] In fact, it can be interpreted as being evidence that Holmes was remarkably ignorant of the law, if we consider the well-established legal principle that a thief cannot pass title to property.[14] Sandeford had no title to the pearl, because the chain through which his title was traced related back to a thief. For the same reason, Holmes got no title, and his receipt would not have protected his interest if title had been challenged. Further, under the prevailing law then and now, the contract itself probably was a nullity because of illegality: Holmes, in effect, was contracting to become a receiver of stolen goods. If doubts persist, it also can be argued that Holmes contributed to Sandeford's mistake as to the nature of the subject matter, and thereby Sandeford could later have rescinded the contract.

5. We are also reminded of Holmes's assisting in the defense of James McCarthy by providing counsel with helpful objections.[15] But were these related to the facts of the case, or to formal evidentiary matters? If to the former, the weight of the argument is minimized, for the reasons noted above.

6. Similarly,[16] Holmes's reference to lack of evidence for a search warrant[17] probably related more to his own vanity than it did to the laws of England regarding search warrants. As a private consulting detective with no official capacity, he had no standing to seek such a warrant, regardless of the evidence. And he no doubt would have been reticent to show his hand to Scotland Yard and allow its fellows to enjoy the fruits of his labor.

7. Finally, we are asked to consider Holmes's frequent assumption of the roles of judge and jury,[18] but such histrionics probably militate more against the conclusion that Holmes was a lawyer or had specific legal knowledge than in favor of it, for no lawyer (at least in those days) would show such disregard for the formalities and restraints of legal procedures and individual rights.[19]

Even if none of these rebuttals, individually, would seem sufficient to vitiate the conclusion that Holmes had good, practical legal knowledge, or that he was a trained lawyer, surely their cumulative effect is compelling. But, if there are still doubters in our midst, let us consider some other positive indications that Holmes was virtually ignorant of formal law as we know it.

As has been recounted by this writer at much greater length elsewhere,[20] Holmes's handling of the affair of Hall Pycroft smacks of complete ineptitude in legal matters. The Master Detective's conduct of the case demonstrates a complete lack of familiarity with the Statute of Frauds* (in force in England at the time) which by its very essence provided every business reason why "Arthur Pinner" should have sought a written memorandum of the sham employment agreement (had it not been a sham) with Pycroft. That Holmes could have ignored or overlooked such a monumental piece of British legislation (it was first adopted in the seventeenth century, and was the forerunner of identical or similar statutes in most of the capitalistic countries of the world) strongly bespeaks his lack of exposure to law as a discipline in and of itself.

Likewise, Holmes had little knowledge of the law of Domestic Relations because, in one adventure, he doesn't question the validity of a marriage without witnesses (at least not on that ground)[21] while in another he admits the absolute essentiality of the witness to the validity of the marriage ceremony.[22] Oddly enough, he does seem to be aware of some of the basics of the law of marriage, though, particularly regarding the need for a license and the void or voidable character of a marriage by force.[23] Probably most laymen also are aware of these rudiments, however.

It may be argued that Holmes's study of ancient English charters[24] bears some witness to possible legal skills, but the study of charters (which typically are grants of property rights by the Sovereign) does not require any particular legal ability, unless one is looking for possible defects. More likely than not, Holmes was more interested in the historical implications of the charters he studied, rather than any legal impairments that may have existed. Holmes probably was looking for some damaging evidence of abuse (if there is such a thing) of Sovereign authority.

Nor did he possess much knowledge concerning the law of wills, as others have pointed out.[25] For example, he said nothing to the

---

* The Statute of Frauds was originally enacted in *Statutes*, 29 Charles II, Chapter III, 1677, under the formal title, *An Act for the Prevention of Frauds and Perjuries*. Article 5, Section 4 of the Act requires any agreement, not to be performed within one year from the making thereof, to be in writing in order to be enforceable. Admittedly, there are technical exceptions to the rule, but the exceptions would still not justify Holmes's assertion that there was no earthly business reason for the purported agreement to be in writing. —*Ed.*

assertion that John McFarlane's clerk had witnessed the will of
Jonas Oldacre, when clearly two witnesses were essential to the
making of a valid will. Also, the fact that the signed will apparently had been only a draft copy "assumes a sinister significance."[26]

It is not doubted that Holmes possessed a number of legal books
in his library at 221B Baker Street,[27] but indications are that he
held such volumes for their worth as rare books, rather than as
reference items. Despite their inherent value, we can hardly believe
that he had much reason to refer to such works as Fitzher-
bert's *Great Abridgement of the Law* (London: 1516) or Little-
ton's *Tenures in English* (London: 1583) in his everyday work.
He most certainly did have many books on crime and criminals,
but our information would indicate that these were not of a technical legal nature such as one would require to study law itself.[28]

The "New Law Courts," opened to the
public in 1882 and still surviving, hardly
altered, in the Strand. This contemporary
drawing by Maclure retains old Temple
Bar (three-windowed building across
road on extreme right), but this was
removed permanently. Holmes could
have made a *practical* study of law in the
Courts' many Divisions and Benches.
Contrad Research Library.

Admittedly, most of the discussion so far has tended to disprove
the Master's possible legal knowledge in areas other than criminal
law, which is where one would ordinarily expect his greatest
proficiency to be. At this point, however, the evidence would seem
to clearly support a conclusion, without qualification, that Holmes
was no lawyer, and probably further that Holmes had no formal
legal training. This is true because no true legal education de-
votes itself to only one aspect of the law, except, perhaps, in graduate studies beyond an initial law degree. So even if we are later to
conclude that Holmes did have a good knowledge of the criminal
law, we may still state categorically at this point that Watson was
wrong and the Master Detective did not have a "good, practical
knowledge of British Law" in general.

We can presume, then, that if he had any specific legal skills,

they were the product of independent study, as was his custom in most areas. As to the more specialized area of criminal law, we have ample evidence of his knowledge, or lack thereof, and any evaluation of Holmes and the criminal law must necessarily commence and end with a discussion of his regard for it, and the manner in which he used and abused the criminal law to his own advantage.

As has been pointed out by numerous others,[29] Holmes was never above committing a felony or misdemeanor if it served his purposes. His chargeable offenses included blackmail,[30] burglary,[31] attempted larceny by trick,[32] concealing of material evidence,[33] accessory after the fact to homicide,[34] and accessory after the fact to various other crimes (by his condonation of same, or his allowing of the criminal to escape),[35] and many more.

The Master Detective never seemed to hold criminals in the same low regard as did the regular police force or the public in general. He points out that he would have made a "highly efficient" criminal,[36] and that burglary was always an alternate profession for him;[37] he almost praised John Clay, the thief, murderer and forger, by his reference to the criminal as being "at the head of his profession."[38] He also asserts that the "most winning woman I ever knew was hanged for poisoning her three little children for their insurance money."[39]

Nor did he feel any compunction about violating the civil rights of suspects. In fact, a great many of Holmes's successes were founded upon tactics and such illegally gained evidence as would have rendered a prosecution impossible if Scotland Yard had been in charge.[40]

Perhaps the most damning evidence, however, is his use of inconsistent terminology in relation to certain offenses in which a guilty person was allowed to escape prosecution, usually with Holmes's approval. Such references include his describing such an act as "commuting a felony,"[41] and stating that the Duke of Holdernesse "condoned a felony,"[42] and even admitting that he (Holmes) would have to "compound a felony."[43]

Much already has been written about his misuse of these terms, when what he probably meant was that he would have to be guilty of *misprision of a felony,*[44] the technical term for the un-

lawful failing of a person to report a felony, or perhaps the con-
cealment of a felony.[45] So again, Holmes's choice of words
reinforces the fact that he didn't really know much at all about the
law, even the criminal law. (If we can accept the assertion that
Holmes was an American,[46] or that he spent a great deal of time
in America,[47] a conceivable argument can be made that his
"terminological inexactitude" was not that at all, but rather a
typically Midwestern usage of American forms of the terms,[48] but
even this does not apply uniformly to his errors.)

Further, Holmes occasionally didn't even recognize crimes in
which he participated. In asserting,[49] for example, that no crimes
occurred in the Irene Adler[50] or Neville St. Clair[51] affair, the Master Detective exposes his ignorance of the "minor" offenses of dis-
orderly conduct and possibly larceny by trick (the heaving of the
smoke bomb as a diversion to get the picture) in the former case
and simple assault (forcible face-washing) in the latter.[52]

In the face of all the evidence, or the lack of evidence, that
Holmes knew the law, we can only apply his often quoted maxim
and decide, however improbable it may be, that Holmes was an
untrained dilettante when it came to matters of law. In answer
to questions (c) and (d) propounded much earlier in this already
too long diatribe, we must answer emphatically, and perhaps
regretfully, "No" and "Yes"—respectively.

None of this, however, should be construed as an assertion
that Holmes was as nearly completely ignorant of the criminal law
as he apparently was of the civil law. No one in such frequent contact with lawmen and lawbreakers as he was could have avoided
picking up some of the terminology and even a portion of the
theory of the criminal law. But the question before us relates to
his possession of especial or uncommon legal knowledge, not to his
possible absorption of bits and pieces as necessary incidents of his
work.

We have already noted that Holmes was never above taking
the law into his own hands, as judge and jury, and determining
guilt, innocence, and clemency. This, as already has been stated,
bespeaks a great disrespect for the regimens of formal law, but it
also may provide us with some insight into the character of
Holmes. Although he abhorred the emotions, and we cannot say

that sympathy or compassion usually motivated his actions, we can say that Sherlock Holmes did possess a great sense of moral right and wrong, even if his vanity did allow him to usurp the place of the Courts. As he once said, he would much rather "play tricks with the law of England than with my own conscience."[53]

On another occasion, Holmes stated, "It is every man's business to see justice done."[54] In theory, such an attitude is repugnant to all those things that are thought to comprise justice, primarily because there is felt to be an inherent danger in allowing any one person the power to determine and mete out justice. To allow such a magnificent burden to be placed within the purview and control of one man's caprices and idiosyncrasies is no doubt foolhardy. Foolhardy, that is, unless that one man is an emotionless, rational and always objective thinker like Sherlock Holmes, in which case the ends of justice may well be served better because of his existence and methods. For the purposes of conjecture, who would have been the better judge—the man on the street (say, for instance, John Hamish Watson) or Sherlock Holmes?

This is not in any way to say that we can condone his usurpation of the judicial function on so many occasions, but it is only meant to be an expression of gratitude that he used his powers wisely, to the lasting benefit of us all and not to our detriment.

Sherlock Holmes was not a lawyer, not even a bad lawyer. He was not a judge, not even a poor judge. He didn't know the law, not even in small quantity. But he was a manifestation of justice itself, whether the concept is repugnant to modern jurisprudence or not; and he continues to be, even for all his faults, one of the best and wisest men we have ever known. "And, unquestionably, he could have made a judge, sir, and a rare one."

Nonetheless, we should all whisper a prayer of thanks that the Master Detective apparently never sought to advise Sir Arthur Conan Doyle concerning the publishing contracts that he negotiated as Watson's literary agent. Had Holmes done so, the world might yet be waiting to learn of the life and times of Mr. Sherlock Holmes.

And further, we probably may speculate that Holmes *did* advise Watson concerning his agreement with Doyle—for what well-counseled author otherwise would have extracted so little credit and so few royalties from so prolific a writing career?

NOTES

1. Gavin Brend, *My Dear Holmes; A Study in Sherlock* (London: George Allen and Unwin, 1951).

2. Dorothy L. Sayers, "Holmes' College Career," in her *Unpopular Opinions* (London: Victor Gollancz, 1946).

3. *See*, e.g., William S. Baring-Gould, *Sherlock Holmes: A Biography* (London: Rupert Hart-Davis, 1962).

4. Albert P. Blaustein, "Sherlock Holmes as a Lawyer," *Baker Street Journal*, vol. 3, no. 3 (O.S.), 1948, pp. 306–08.

5. *The Sign of Four.*

6. *Accord,* Stephen G. Palmer III, "Sherlock Holmes and the Law," in *Sherlock Holmes: Master Detective*, Blegen and McDiarmid, ed. (LaCrosse, Wisconsin: The Sumac Press, 1952); *also*, S.T.L. Harbottle, "Sherlock Holmes and the Law," *Sherlock Holmes Journal*, vol. 1, no. 3, June 1953, pp. 7–10.

7. "The Adventure of the Noble Bachelor."

8. "The Adventure of the Dying Detective."

9. *Black's Law Dictionary* (St. Paul, Minn.: West Publishing Co., 1968), p. 526.

10. *Miller* v. *Dierken,* 153 Pa. Super. 389.

11. Fletcher Pratt, "Very Little Murder," *Baker Street Journal*, vol. 5, no. 2 (N.S.), 1955, pp. 69–76.

12. Blaustein, *supra* n. 4.

13. Harbottle, *supra* n. 6; *see also* Irving Fenton, "Holmes and the Law," manuscript copy, n.d. This item probably is identical to one of the same title in *Baker Street Journal*, vol. 7, no. 2 (N.S.), 1957, pp. 79–83.

14. The tenet is virtually universal in jurisprudence. E.g., the ancient maxim, *Nemo dat qui non habet* ("He who hath not cannot give"), 6 C.B., N.S., 478.

15. Blaustein, *supra* n. 4; *but see* Stuart C. Rand, "What Sherlock Didn't Know," in *The Second Cab* (Boston: Stoke Moran, 1947).

16. Blaustein, *supra* n. 4.

17. "The Adventure of the Bruce-Partington Plans."

18. Blaustein, *supra* n. 4.

19. Palmer, *supra* n. 6.

20. Andrew G. Fusco, "Or Some Written Memorandum Thereof . . . ," *Baker Street Journal*, vol. 22, no. 2 (N.S.), 1972, pp. 114–19.

21. "The Adventure of the Solitary Cyclist."

22. "A Scandal in Bohemia."

23. "The Adventure of the Solitary Cyclist."

24. "The Adventure of the Three Students."

25. Fenton, *supra* n. 13; Harbottle, *supra* n. 6.

26. Harbottle, *supra* n. 6.

27. Madeline B. Stern, *Sherlock Holmes: Rare Book Collector* (New York: Schulte, 1953).

28. *Id.*

29. Fenton, *supra* n. 13; Thomas L. Stix, "Sherlock Holmes Impeached (I),"

Baker Street Journal, vol. 15, no. 2 (N.S.), 1965, pp. 75–78; *and* Frederic A. Johnson, "Sherlock Holmes, the Criminal," *Baker Street Journal,* vol. 10, no. 3 (N.S.) 1960, pp. 172–74.

30. "The Adventure of the Mazarin Stone."

31. "The Adventure of Charles Augustus Milverton"; "The Adventure of the Retired Colourman"; "The Adventure of the Bruce-Partington Plans"; "The Adventure of the Illustrious Client"; "The Adventure of the Three Gables"; etc.

32. "A Scandal in Bohemia."

33. "The Adventure of Charles Augustus Milverton."

34. "The Adventure of the Abbey Grange"; "The Adventure of the Red Circle"; "The Adventure of the Devil's Foot"; "The Adventure of Charles Augustus Milverton"; "The Boscombe Valley Mystery"; etc.

35. "The Adventure of Charles Augustus Milverton."

36. *Id.*

37. "The Adventure of the Retired Colourman."

38. "The Red-headed League."

39. *The Sign of Four.*

40. Doyle W. Beckemeyer, "The Irregular Holmes," *Baker Street Journal,* vol. 2, no. 1 (N.S.), 1952, pp. 18–20.

41. "The Adventure of the Blue Carbuncle."

42. "The Adventure of the Priory School." In the same case Holmes asserts that a person who embarks on one criminal venture is *morally* guilty of all the crimes that result. At best, this is an oversimplification, though it does have some valid basis.

43. "The Adventure of the Three Gables."

44. S. Tupper Bigelow, "Sherlock Holmes and Misprision of Felony," *Baker Street Journal,* vol. 8, no. 3 (N.S.), 1958, pp. 139–46; "E.J.C.," "An Opinion from British Counsel," *Baker Street Journal,* vol. 3, no. 3 (O.S.), 1948, pp. 309–13; Allen Robertson, "An Opinion from American Counsel," *Baker Street Journal,* vol. 3, no. 3 (O.S.), 1948, pp. 313–16.

45. 23 Emory Law Rev. 1095 (1974).

46. Christopher Morley, "Was Sherlock Holmes an American?" in *221B: Studies in Sherlock Holmes,* Vincent Starrett, ed. (New York: Biblo & Tannen, 1969).

47. Willis B. Wood, "Sherlock in Kansas," in *The Second Cab* (Boston: Stoke Moran, 1947).

48. "E.J.C.," *supra* n. 44.

49. "The Adventure of the Blue Carbuncle."

50. "A Scandal in Bohemia."

51. "The Man with the Twisted Lip."

52. Irvin M. Fenton, "An Analysis of the Crimes and Near-Crimes at Milverton's," manuscript copy, n.d. This item probably is identical to one of similar title in *Baker Street Journal,* vol. 6, no. 2 (N.S.), 1956, pp. 69–74.

53. "The Adventure of the Abbey Grange."

54. "The Adventure of the Crooked Man."

Professor James Moriarty, of binomial theorem and asteroidal dynamics fame, was, as Holmes said, "the Napoleon of Crime . . . organizer of half that is evil and nearly all that is undetected in this great city." Clearly, Holmes was impressed with the intellectual qualities of this criminal Napoleon. "He is a genius, a philosopher, an abstract thinker"—but obviously no academic dreamer, no philosophical slouch, when it came to organizing crime. If Holmes called Moriarty a "Napoleon," then that Napoleon ruled an empire—and it is the nature and quality of that dark empire that the English biographer of Moriarty describes for us here. Dark, indeed, was that empire, yet like that other contemporary empire, the British Empire of Queen Victoria, it was lively (if never enlightened) with that inexhaustible energy, that insatiable urge to acquire, that almost frenetic individualistic go-getting which characterized every aspect of Victorian life, even—indeed, not least—

Moriarty and
the Real Underworld

✄

JOHN GARDNER

✄

Mention the name of Professor James Moriarty to anyone who has even a nodding acquaintance with Sir Arthur Conan Doyle's Sherlock Holmes, and a picture is immediately conjured—the tall, gaunt, scholarly figure threatening Holmes in his Baker Street rooms; the fight on the ledge at the Reichenbach Falls; a vast army of criminals ready to do his bidding; the clop of horses' hooves in the streets, and the rumble of hansoms; gaslight casting eerie shadows; the thick yellow fogs, "London particulars," creeping up from the river; sinister figures lurking in alleys and passageways; robbery, murder, extortion, violence; the sly tongue of the confidence man, the quick fingers of the pickpocket, the wheedling of the beggar, the wiles of the whore: the whole wretched, dingy, yet compulsive aura of the nineteenth-century underworld.

Holmes himself is reported to have said of the Professor (in "The Final Problem"), ". . . his agents are numerous and splendidly organized. Is there a crime to be done, a paper to be abstracted, we will say, a house to be rifled, a man to be removed— the word is passed on to the Professor, the matter is organized and carried out. The agent may be caught. In that case money is found for his bail or his defense. But the central power which uses the agent is never caught—never so much as suspected."

This description has a strangely modern ring to it. It certainly indicates that Moriarty undoubtedly would have spent the bulk of his time within the underworld of his era, rubbing shoulders

One of the most notorious of the London slums, in which Dr. Moriarty recruited his "villains"—and which, to a large extent, resisted "respectability" until very recent times: St. Giles's. *Contrad Research Library.*

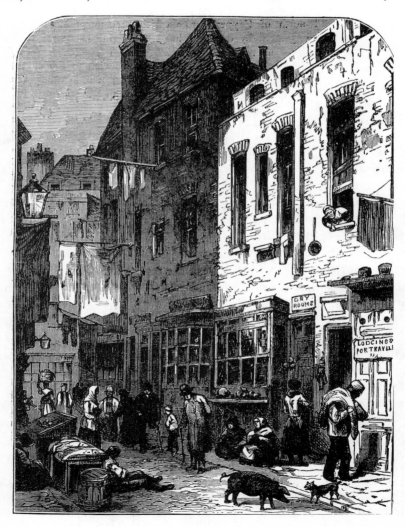

and passing the word of command throughout that society of villains which proliferated during the century.

Here we have a definite link which joins that shadowy world to the organized crime of our own time, for the sprawling regiment of criminals in Moriarty's day referred to themselves, collectively, as The Family.

"*Antigarotting Collar*"—a spoof advertisement from *Punch*, issue of 27 September 1856. Though a rather labored Victorian "joke," this advertisement perfectly reflected, in a factually sinister manner, the principal danger and preoccupation of contemporary Londoners. *Contrad Research Library.*

In 1841 an article in *Tait's Magazine* speaks of " 'The Family' . . . the generic name for thieves, pickpockets, gamblers, house-breakers *et hoc genus omne*." The term was certainly still in use at the end of the century, and villains spoke of each other as family men and family women.

We all know that today The Family, in criminal terms, takes on sinister connotations. So Doyle's Moriarty could well have been the Victorian equivalent of the twentieth-century Godfather. His influence would certainly have its starting point in the whirling vortex of the nineteenth-century underworld.

Briefly, then, one sees Moriarty as a ruthless criminal leader of high intellect and advanced organizational talents—the scientific criminal—a man determined to rule his chosen universe.

What sort of empire would he have ruled? Over what kind of subjects would he have held sway?

The picture we have of the London underworld during the first half of the nineteenth century is one of a perpetual war waged between the respectable middle and upper classes, and the great horde of criminals, many of them specialist technicians, who lived in the Rookeries—those swamped, fetid, and congested areas on the outer perimeter of the metropolis. These parasites would emerge from the Rookeries to perpetrate their villainy, only to disappear again into the warrens of courts, alleys, and cellars of the tightly packed, rogue-infested hives such as the great St. Giles's Rookery around Holborn—known as the Holy Land—or the Devil's Acre around Pye Street, Westminster; and a dozen more, including the terrain of Whitechapel and Spitalfields, which contained such unlovely byways as Flower and Dean streets, and Dorset Street—at one time known as the most evil thoroughfare in London.

It appears to us now, looking from the distance of a hundred years or so, that there was a marked contrast, a frontier almost, between the glittering West End of London and the impoverished areas. Yet the whole period was one of gradual and massive prog-

Another Victorian slum: Field Lane, Clerkenwell. The actual names of "Scrooge" and "Fagan" (*sic*) indicate that Charles Dickens must have known this haunt of criminality well. *Contrad Research Library*.

ress. Great changes made themselves felt at all levels. Legal, penal and social reform, a more effective police force, the cutting of roads through the Rookeries—all played a part in bringing the crime rate down by the end of the century. But the criminal, while adept at altering his techniques, is basically conservative in outlook: so the underworld of the eighties and nineties still clung to past ways. Thus, while London's criminal society became more diffuse toward the end of the century, its business methods altered little.

Playing a major part in the life force of the underworld were the fences—the receivers of stolen property. Almost anything could be disposed of through the small back-street pawn brokers, the market traders, the hordes of middlemen and the few really big fences who often set up or instigated large robberies.

The most colorful of these to emerge during the first half of the century was the great and legendary Ikey Solomons, who lived, in a house full of secret trapdoors and hidden rooms, at the heart of Spitalfields.

Solomons was almost certainly Dickens's model for Fagin in *Oliver Twist,* and when he was finally arrested, two coachloads of stolen goods were removed from his home on the first visit, while the officers had to return at least twice before the place was cleared of loot.

Working hand in glove with the fences were, of course, the cracksmen, screwsmen, and sneak thieves. They still operate today with as much verve as they did in Victorian London, and in Moriarty's time they stood high in the criminal hierarchy. The sneak thief was a particularly cunning operator, an expert in picking his moment to nip through an open window, or indulging in the occupation of "area diving"—slipping down the area steps of terraced houses and into the basements, taking what came to hand before making a fast exit.

Into this same category one can place the snoozer, who would plan his jobs with considerable care, posing as a respectable businessman, staying at good hotels, mixing with his fellow guests in order to pick the best victims before stealing from them as they slept—snoozed.

Cracksmen and screwsmen were possibly the most sophisticated of thieves, developing a whole armory of tools and cutting devices ranging from skeleton keys to the Jack-in-a-box—or screw jack—

for prizing off the doors of safes. Before the end of the century, these gentlemen were expert in the use of explosives and oxy-acetylene cutting devices.

Thieves of this kind certainly took their profession very seriously, using ingenious methods and careful preparation. Nowhere is this more clearly illustrated than in the great train robbery of 1855. This was probably the most sensational theft of the century, having an obvious parallel in the Great Train Robbery of 1963. In all, over £12,000 in gold and coin—a most considerable sum at the time—was stolen from a shipment en route from London to Paris.

The conspirators, Pierce and Agar, both professional cracksmen, and Tester, a railway clerk, spent over a year preparing the crime, going to great lengths in order to get information, to bribe the guard of the London-Folkestone passenger train on which the bullion was carried, and to provide themselves with duplicate keys to the three Chubb safes used for transporting it.

The crime was carried out with great flair. Pierce and Agar boarded the train with bags containing lead shot sewn into special pockets. Through the corrupted guard, they gained access to the guard's van, unlocked the safes, removed the gold, and substituted the lead.

The culprits were eventually caught in a classic manner. Agar's mistress, suspecting that she was being done out of her fair share, informed on them.

If the Victorian was not safe from burglary in his own home, the streets were also full of hazards. By far the largest number of criminals worked in the streets. Many were pickpockets, a problem still with us today, as warning signs in public places tell us. It is doubtful if the Victorian Londoner needed any warning, for the artful mobsmen, toolers, whizzers and dippers, together with their stickman accomplices, were everywhere in the crowds, in the underground, on railway trains and omnibuses. It is, perhaps, indicative of their proliferation that Havelock Ellis in his book *The Criminal*, published in 1890, illustrates his chapter on criminal slang with a passage describing events in a pickpocket's life, in the dipper's own words:

"I was jogging down a blooming slum in the Chapel," he says, "when I butted a reeler, who was sporting a red slang. I broke off his jerry, and boned the clock, which was a red one, but I was spotted by a copper, who claimed me. I was lugged before the beak, who gave me a six doss in the Steel. The week after I was chucked up I did a snatch near St. Paul's, was collared, lagged and got this bit of seven stretch."

The translation follows:

"As I was walking down a narrow alley in Whitechapel, I ran up against a drunk who had a gold watch guard. I stole his watch, which was gold, but was seen by a policeman, who caught me and took me before the magistrate, who gave me six months in the Bastille [the House of Correction, Coldbath Fields]. When I was released I attempted to steal a watch near St. Paul's, but was caught again, convicted, and sentenced to seven years' penal servitude."

The streets also had their fair share of confidence tricksters, often layabouts who practiced simple dodges like pretending to find a gold ring which they would sell for a mere five shillings (fawney dropping,* as it was called), or even children crying over a smashed milk jug, to whom the tender-hearted were fine prey. Begging also became a complex and truly histrionic art.

Demanding with menaces, mug-hunting and general foot-padding were common enough crimes in the badly lit streets, and in mid-century, law-abiding Londoners went in real terror from garotters who would choke their victims insensible before fleecing them. Only strong penalties, including the barbarous cat, together with better policing and street lighting, brought this epidemic to an end.

Yet even in daylight one was not safe from the macers, magsmen and sharps—tricksters, frauds, swindlers and cheats, the fore-runners of every cheapjack and con man on our own streets and doorsteps and in the police files.

There were other villains who practiced their arts behind closed doors: the forgers, the shofulmen (the coiners), and the screevers, the writers of false character references and testimonials. Their heyday was in Moriarty's time, when anything which could be faked, from documents to bank notes to coins and jewelry settings, was duplicated in small crude dens or elaborate work-shops equipped with molds, presses, engraving tools and electro-plating devices.

Whatever its cause, vice has always been a magnet to criminals,

---

* The modern U.S. "phoney," which is thus revealed as a re-importation.—*Ed.*

Then, as now, the vagrant unemployed were ripe for mischief—and employment by the "Napoleon of Crime." *Contrad Research Library.*

The Victorian "peeler" preferred to combat the "crime" of "unlawful entertainment" rather than risk the dangers of pursuing the real criminals. *Contrad Research Library.*

and Victoria's London reeked of it. In mid-century it was estimated that there were over 80,000 prostitutes working in the city—
good money for the cash-carriers (nineteenth-century ponces), the
minders and madams—words which, like racket, mob and pig,
have not altered with time. Many of these women doubtless doubled as pickpockets' accomplices and skinners—who literally
stripped the clothes from the backs of terrified children; certainly
women predominated among the "palmers"—adroit shoplifters,
often working in pairs—while the "canary," who carried a cracks-
man's tools and loot from a robbery, was usually a woman.

These, then, were the rank and file with whom, and through
whom, a man like James Moriarty would have worked.

With this raw material at his disposal, it is easy to imagine how
a man with the intelligence and standing of a James Moriarty
could skillfully mold a criminal community.

One can clearly see him, as Holmes suggested in "The Final
Problem," sitting "motionless, like a spider in the center of its
web, but that web has a thousand radiations, and he knows well
every quiver of each of them."

In his article in this anthology, Colin Wilson writes the startling sentence: "Holmes is magnificent because he seems to be, in a sense, larger than his creator." And a little further along in the same article occurs this even more striking conclusion on the author's part: "In short, Doyle failed to think his creation through to its logical conclusion, thereby demonstrating that he was not the intellectual equal of Sherlock Holmes." This is very daring—even shocking—stuff: but how much are such be-damned-to-you statements justified by the facts? It has long puzzled people that Conan Doyle permitted himself to investigate (at the cost, his son afterward complained, of more than £250,000) the Occult, while giving Holmes a character to which such matters were abhorrent. Holmes did develop, for all the arguments to the contrary; indeed, the title "From Aesthete to Hearty" would be no bad one for a sketch of Holmes's psychological progress; but he did not, nor was ever permitted to, develop to the stage of an investigator of the Occult. We clearly recall the shock with which the "spirit photographs," accepted as genuine by Conan Doyle, were received—it will now be more than fifty years ago; but the shock lay, not in the obviously (to us, at any rate) faked look of the photographs, but in their unquestioning acceptance by the respected, even revered, Arthur Conan Doyle. The matter of Conan Doyle's involvement with "the Fairies" is here examined in detail, not only from the point of view of a nonpsychic investigator, but from the point of view of one as interested in Conan Doyle as in the Holmes that he created.

The Irrelevance of Conan Doyle

MARTIN GARDNER

"What has that eminent Spiritualist . . . to do with Sherlock Holmes?"

—T. S. Eliot

Questions similar to Eliot's can be asked about many another famous scrivener whose name has been associated with allegedly fictional characters. What has that sixteenth-century Spanish drifter and one-armed soldier to do with Don Quixote and Sancho Panza? What has that kinky-haired, pie-faced French mulatto, lecher, spendthrift, and literary hack to do with Athos, Porthos, Aramis and d'Artagnan?

The answer, of course, is, Nothing. The case of Cervantes is particularly instructive, because it has so much in common with that of Conan Doyle. The two books about the adventures of the Knight of La Mancha tell the story of a long friendship between a dreamer—yet man of action—and his faithful down-to-earth companion. We now know, thanks to the recent efforts of Spanish scholars, that these adventures were written, not by Cervantes, but by Sancho Panza. After the death of his master, Sancho sold his memoirs to Cervantes, who, scoundrel that he was, kept them hidden until Sancho, too, had died.

One should have suspected this long before the truth came out. Cervantes had little interest in Don Quixote. It was his poetry and plays, all written in a careful, classical style, of which he was proud. Only because he was seriously in debt did he allow his name to appear on Sancho's sprawling, carelessly written work.

Sancho was, of course, a much greater writer than Cervantes. He was far from the slow-witted person he made himself out to be, but like James Boswell and John Watson he modestly under-played himself to pay greater homage to his friend. Unfortunately, his stories about the Don were written in his old age, when his memory was starting to fade, and they are filled with lapses that Cervantes would never have allowed to remain in the manuscript had he troubled to go over it carefully. Cervantes had so little interest in the first half of Sancho's memoirs that it was not until ten years later, when he desperately needed money again, that he issued the sequel. This time he edited more carefully, adding passages in which he tried to explain the contradictions he had failed to catch in the earlier volume.

There are many reasons for believing that Doyle had as little to do with Watson's manuscripts as Cervantes with Sancho Panza's. Like Cervantes, Doyle had no interest in—indeed, he had contempt for—the stories he pretended were his own. But as soon as they became great popular successes, bringing him an income needed for other projects, he let them continue to appear under his own name, touching them up here and there, but editing them so hastily that many of Watson's contradictions, like those of Sancho's, were allowed to remain.

The strongest internal evidence that neither Cervantes nor Doyle wrote the stories for which they became famous is simply the enormous contrast between the mentality and philosophical outlook of supposed author and hero. Don Quixote was a man of firm Roman Catholic faith and high moral principles, with a passion for chivalry. Cervantes hated chivalry. He allowed his name to appear on Sancho's books because he mistakenly supposed them to be attacks on faith and chivalry. His infidelities to his wife, the episodes involving his mistresses, the affairs of his daughter—all were so sordid that early biographers of Cervantes fell back on Latin when they supplied details.

The equally great contrast between the minds of Holmes and Doyle has often been noted. Was Gilbert Chesterton the first to point out how much more Doyle had in common with Dr. Watson? It is true that Doyle and Watson were both medical men, slow thinkers, good writers, and sensitive to the poetry of London; yet there was one overwhelming difference between the two men that has not, I believe, been sufficiently recognized. I refer to Watson's abiding respect for rationality, science, and common sense.

It has many times been pointed out that Holmes's so-called deductions were actually inductions. Like the scientist trying to solve a mystery of nature, Holmes first gathered all the evidence he could that was relevant to his problem. At times he performed experiments to obtain fresh data. He then surveyed the total evidence in the light of his vast knowledge of crime, and of sciences relevant to crime, to arrive at the most probable hypothesis. Deductions were made from the hypothesis; then the theory was further tested against new evidence, revised if need be, until finally the truth emerged with a probability close to certainty.

Although Watson seldom played a role in this complex process, with enormous respect he watched it unfold. Frequently mystified by the speed and efficiency of Holmes's method, he never failed to admire it, to accept its final results, and on one occasion, after the procedure had been explained to him, to exclaim, "How absurdly simple!"

Nothing could be more remote from the mind-set of Watson's alleged creator. Doyle spent the last twelve years of his life in a tireless crusade against science and rationality. It is a period usually glossed over quickly in biographies of Doyle, but, in view of today's explosion of interest in spiritualism and all things occult, it is good to review it as an object lesson. Above all, it provides overwhelming evidence that Doyle had almost nothing to do with either Holmes or Watson.

It has been said that Doyle's conversion to spiritualism, like the recent case of Bishop James Pike, was an emotional reaction to the death of his son. Not so. Even when he was a young ex-Irish-Catholic, Doyle had a strong interest in psychic phenomena. His crusade for spiritualism began in 1916, two years before his son died. Although several British scientists were caught up in the craze, notably Oliver Lodge and William Crookes, Doyle rapidly became the movement's most influential fugleman. He lectured and debated everywhere. His literary labors for the cause were prodigious. In addition to innumerable pamphlets, magazine articles, introductions to books by others, letters, and book reviews, the following volumes of spiritualist apologetics flowed from his pen: *The New Revelation, The Vital Message, The Wanderings of a Spiritualist, Our American Adventure, Our Second American Adventure, The Case for Spirit Photography, Psychic Experiences, The Mystery of Spiritualism, The Land of Mist,*[1] *The Edge of the Unknown,* and, not least, a monumental two-volume *History of Spiritualism.*

It is no good to say that Doyle had become senile. Clearly he had not. His final years were remarkably vigorous and productive. His last book, *The Edge of the Unknown,* published in 1930, the year that he died at age seventy-one, is a model of lucid, beautifully structured prose. Thousands of people were deeply influenced by his books and lectures. Dr. Joseph B. Rhine, the eminent parapsychologist, is on record as saying that it was a speech by Doyle that first inspired him to turn from botany, in which he had been trained, to the study of psychic phenomena.

In *Memories and Adventures* (pp. 392–94), Doyle gives a dramatic summary of why he believes in spiritualism. He had seen his dead mother and nephew so plainly that he could have counted the wrinkles on one, the freckles on the other. He had conversed at length with spirit voices. He had smelled the "peculiar ozone-like smell of ectoplasm." Prophecies he heard were swiftly fulfilled. He had "seen the dead glimmer up upon a photographic plate" untouched by any hand but his own. His wife, a medium whose writing fingers would be seized by a spirit control, had produced "notebooks full of information . . . utterly beyond her ken." He had seen heavy objects "swimming in the air, untouched by human hand." He had seen "spirits walk around the room in fair light and join in the talk of the company." On his wall was a painting done by a woman with no artistic training, but who had been possessed by an artistic spirit.

He had read books written by unlettered mediums who transmitted the work of dead writers, and he had recognized the writer's style, "which no parodist could have copied, and which was written in his own handwriting." He had heard "singing beyond earthly power, and whistling done with no pause for the intake of breath." He had seen objects "from a distance projected into a room with closed doors and windows." Why, Doyle concludes, should a man who has experienced all this "heed the chatter of irresponsible journalists, or the head-shaking of inexperienced men of science? They are babies in this matter, and should be sitting at his feet."

Those are the strong words of a profoundly sincere man. They are also the words of a man with a temperament utterly alien to that of both Holmes and Watson. The bitter truth is that Doyle was an incompetent observer of supposed psychic events. He was ignorant of even the rudiments of magic and deception, hopelessly naïve, capable of believing anything, no matter how flimsy the evidence. Over and over again the great mediums of the day who produced psychical phenomena were caught in fraud by the Holmeses and Watsons of science. Over and over again Doyle refused to recognize even the possibility of fraud except in a few cases where it was so patently obvious that everyone in the spiritualist movement recognized it. Even in such rare cases Doyle was quick to explain deception away as a temporary aberration on the part of genuine psychics. Were they not pressured into cheating by the incessant demands of skeptics for phenomena that could not always be produced at will?

In many cases Doyle flatly refused to believe fraudulent mediums even when they made full confessions and explained in detail exactly how they cheated. The most sensational of such confessions was by Margaret Fox, one of the Fox sisters of upper New York State whose ability to produce spirit raps by cracking the first joint of a big toe had started the modern spiritualist craze. Margaret Fox's remarkable confession, made in 1888 when she was eighty-one, appeared in the New York *World,* October 21, and you can read it in Harry Houdini's *A Magician Among the Spirits.* That night, on the stage of New York's Academy of Music, under the close scrutiny of three physicians, Margaret took off a shoe, put one foot on a stool and demonstrated her toe-cracking technique to a hushed audience.

How did Doyle react to her confession? Like other prominent spiritualists, he refused to believe it. Nor did he believe Houdini when the magician tried to persuade him that prominent conjurors of the day who were capitalizing on the spiritualist movement by claiming supernormal powers were not genuine psychics. The Davenport brothers, for example, were friends of Houdini. He knew their methods well but was unable to convince Doyle that they were tricksters. Julius Zancig, another magician and friend of Houdini, had perfected a secret code by which he could transmit information quickly to his wife. Just as some magicians today pretend to be genuine mind readers because it enhances their reputation and increases their earnings, so the Zancigs found they could make more money posing as psychics than by doing straight magic. Doyle never doubted the authenticity of their telepathic abilities. Magicians found this as hilarious then as they do today whenever a famous writer or scientist goes on record as believing that some magician-turned-psychic has supernormal powers.

Indeed, Doyle even refused to believe Houdini's repeated denials that he, Houdini, was not psychic. Doyle's essay, "The Riddle of Houdini,"[2] is one of the most absurd documents in the history of parapsychology. Here is Doyle, the supposed creator of Sherlock Holmes, arguing soberly that his friend Houdini was in reality a medium who performed his escapes by dematerializing his body!

Houdini's protests fell on uncomprehending ears. Doyle readily admitted that Houdini was a skilled conjuror, but he argued that the magician's escapes were on such an "utterly different plane" from that of other magicians that it was an "outrage of common sense to think otherwise." Why, if Houdini was a genuine psychic, did he deny his singular powers? "Is it not perfectly evident," Doyle answered himself, "that if he did not deny them his occupation would have been gone forever? What would his brother-magicians have to say to a man who admitted that half his tricks were done by what they would regard as illicit powers? It would have been 'exit Houdini.' "[3]

There is scarcely a page in any of Doyle's books on the occult that does not reveal him to be the antithesis of Holmes. His gullibility was boundless. His comprehension of what constitutes scientific evidence was on a level with that of members of London's flat-earth society. Consider, for example, the story he tells in *The Coming of the Fairies*.[4]

In 1917, in the Yorkshire village of Cottingley, a sixteen-year-old girl, Elsie Wright, was being visited by her ten-year-old cousin,

Frances Griffiths. Elsie was a dreamy little girl who for years had loved to draw pictures of fairies. She had a fair amount of artistic talent, had done some designing for a jeweler, and once worked a few months for a photographer. The two girls loved to spend hours in a glen back of the cottage where, they told Mr. and Mrs. Wright, they often played with fairies.

One day the girls borrowed Mr. Wright's camera, and Elsie snapped a picture of Frances in the woods. When Mr. Wright developed the plate he was astonished to see four scantily clad Tinkerbells, with large butterfly wings, prancing merrily in the air under Frances's chin. Two months later Frances took a picture of Elsie that showed her beckoning a tiny gnome wearing black tights and pointed hat (a bright red hat, the girls recalled) to step into her lap.

The two photos reached Doyle by way of Edward L. Gardner, a theosophist and occult journalist. Doyle wrote to Houdini in great excitement: "I have something . . . precious, two photos, one of a goblin, the other of four fairies in a Yorkshire wood. A fake! you will say. No, sir, I think not. However, all inquiry will be made. These I am not allowed to send. The fairies are about eight inches high. In one there is a single goblin dancing. In the other, four beautiful, luminous creatures. Yes, it is a revelation."

In the December 1920 issue of the *Strand Magazine,* the monthly that had printed so many of Watson's marvelous tales, Doyle and Gardner collaborated on "An Epoch-Making Event— Fairies Photographed." The article blew up a storm. Several newspapers attacked the pictures as fakes, but hundreds of readers wrote to Doyle about the fairies that they, too, had seen in their gardens. Three years after the first two fairy pictures had been taken, Gardner brought the two cousins together again at the same cottage (the girls insisted the fairies would not "come out" unless both were there) and let them borrow his camera. Eventually the girls succeeded in obtaining three more fairy photos. Gardner was not present during any of this picture-taking. Why? Because the girls convinced him the fairies were extremely shy, and would not come out for a stranger!

The three new pictures appeared in the *Strand* in 1921, and the following year Doyle reproduced all five in his book, *The Coming of the Fairies.* Of the three new photos, one shows a fairy with

"Fairy" photographs warmly endorsed
by Sir Arthur Conan Doyle.
From The Coming of the Fairies
by Edward L. Gardner.

yellow wings (the girls always supplied details about the colors) offering a posy of "etheric harebells" to Elsie. A second shows an almost nude young lady, with lavender wings, leaping toward Elsie's nose.

Neither girl is in the third photograph. A winged fairy is on the left, another on the right. Both are either partly hidden behind twigs, or the twigs are showing through their transparent bodies. The girls recalled seeing the two creatures, but said they had noticed only a misty glow between them. On the photograph this glow proved to be something that looks like nothing more than a piece of silk hanging on some branches. According to Doyle's caption in the book's first British edition, it is "a magnetic bath, woven very quickly by the fairies, and used after dull weather and in the autumn especially. The sun's rays through the sheath appear to magnetize the interior and thus provide a 'bath' that restores vitality and vigour."

Doyle was now firmly persuaded that the fairies were not "thought forms" projected into the camera by the girls, like the photographs which Jule Eisenbud argues, in his *World of Ted Serios* (William Morrow, 1967), were projected onto Polaroid film by a Chicago bellhop. Doyle believed that the fairies belonged to "a population which may be as numerous as the human race . . . and which is only separated from ourselves by some difference of vibrations."

Moreover, Doyle was convinced that a revelation of the existence of these little people would go far toward combatting the materialism that dominated modern science, and so pave the way for an acceptance of the greater revelation of spiritualism. In 1920 he wrote to Gardner:

I am proud to have been associated with you in this epoch-making incident. We have had continued messages at séances for some time that a visible sign was coming through—and perhaps this was what is meant. The human race does not deserve fresh evidence. . . . However, our friends beyond are very long-suffering and more charitable than I, for I will confess that my soul is filled with a cold contempt for the muddle-headed indifference and the moral cowardice which I see around me.

Doyle noticed that one of the four fairies, in the first picture taken by the girls, is playing a double pipe. A similar pipe is held by the gnome in the second picture. Is not this the traditional pipe of Pan? According to the girls, it made a "tiny little tinkle" that could barely be heard when all was still. And if the fairies have pipes, why not other belongings? "Does it not suggest a complete range of utensils and instruments . . . ?" Doyle asks. "It seems to me that with fuller knowledge and with fresh means of vision, these people are destined to become just as solid and real as the Eskimos."

One of the funniest (and saddest) aspects of Doyle's preposterous book is that the five pictures he so proudly displays are not even clever fakes. The lack of modeling on the fairy figures, and their sharp outlines, indicate that Elsie had simply drawn them on stiff paper, then the girls had cut them out and stuck them in the grass or supported them in the air with invisible wires or threads. (The pictures could have been faked in other ways, but this seems the most likely.) The little ladies have hairdos that were fashionable at the time. There is not the slightest blurring of their fluttering wings. In every picture the fairies look as flat as paper dolls. The London *Star,* 20 December 1921, reported that the ladies in one picture, except for their wings, were line-for-line copies of figures on a poster that for years had advertised the wares of Price and Sons, a firm of candle makers.

Unlike Dr. Watson, Doyle could never bring himself to exclaim, "How absurdly simple!" Not once did he doubt the genuineness of the fairy photos, although he did own that proof of their authenticity was less "overwhelming" than for the authenticity of photographs of discarnates on the "other side." The two girls never obtained another fairy picture. Doyle reports on a visit in 1921 to the Cottingley glen by a clairvoyant named Geoffrey Hodson. He was accompanied by the two girls. The place swarmed with elves, gnomes, fairies, brownies, goblins, water nymphs and other elusive creatures, all seen and vividly described by Hodson and the girls, but the little people refused to appear on any camera plates.[5]

In 1971 both Elsie and Frances were interviewed by the BBC. The two elderly ladies insisted that their father had not faked the pictures. When Elsie was asked point blank if she or Frances had faked them, she was unwilling to deny it. "I've told you they're photographs of figments of our imagination," she said, "and that's what I'm sticking to." The same question was put to Frances, who was interviewed separately. Frances asked how Elsie had answered it. When told, she said she had nothing to add.[6]

Well, what is one to make of an eminent writer who believed that Houdini dematerialized his body to perform his escapes, and that the glens of England teem with wee folk who now and then allow themselves to be seen and photographed by us mortals? However you answer, one thing is certain. Such a man could never have constructed, as figments of *his* imagination, the coldly rational Holmes or his admiring Dr. Watson.

It was not, I think, Doyle who made this pair immortal. It was the other way around. Holmes and Watson, intent on guarding their privacy, permitted Sir Arthur to take credit for inventing them. In doing so, they conferred upon him that earthly immortality which his authentic but undistinguished writings could never have provided.

NOTES

1. *The Land of Mist* is actually a novel, but one that rattles with spiritualist drum-beating. Doyle's fictional scientist, George Edward Challenger (of *Lost World* fame), now a widower, is converted to spiritualism when he gets a message from his discarnate wife. Before the *Strand* serialized the novel, Doyle called it *The Psychic Adventures of Edward Malone*.

One of the strongest indications that Holmes was not Doyle's creation is that Holmes, unlike Professor Challenger, never became a spiritualist. True, he once remarked (in "The Adventure of the Veiled Lodger"), echoing one of Doyle's favorite themes: "The ways of fate are indeed hard to understand. If there is not some compensation hereafter, then the world is a cruel jest." But had Doyle actually written this story at the time he claimed, when his interest in spiritualism was at its zenith, Holmes surely would have said more than that.

2. This essay was first published as a pamphlet and serialized in the *Strand Magazine* as "Houdini the Enigma," vol. 74, August and September 1927. It is reprinted in Doyle's *The Edge of the Unknown* (1930), currently in print as a Berkley paperback.

3. On Doyle's relationship with Houdini, see *Houdini and Conan Doyle: The Story of a Strange Friendship,* by Bernard M. L. Ernst and Hereward Carrington (New York: Albert and Charles Boni, 1932). Consult also the chapter on Doyle in Houdini's *A Magician Among the Spirits* (New York: Harper and Brothers, 1924), and the many references to Doyle in *Houdini, the Untold Story,* by Milbourne Christopher (New York: Thomas Y. Crowell, 1969).

4. *The Coming of the Fairies* was first published in 1922: in London by Hodder and Stoughton, in New York by George H. Doran. An enlarged edition, to which Doyle added more fairy photographs from England and other lands, was issued in London in 1928 by Psychic Press. Samuel Weiser, New York, reprinted the Doran edition in paper covers in 1972.

5. Hodson gives a full account of this in his book, *Fairies at Work and Play*, published in London by The Theosophical Society Publishing House, 1921. The same house, in 1945, published Edwin L. Gardner's *Fairies: The Cottingley Photographs and Their Sequel*, a book containing the best reproductions of the five photos. The fourth revised edition appeared in 1966. Both books are still in print.

The latest retelling of the story of Doyle and the fairy pictures is "Exploring Fairy Folklore," a two-part article by Jerome Clark, *Fate* magazine, September and October 1974.

6. Tapes of the BBC interviews with Elsie and Frances are owned by Leslie Gardner (son of Edward L. Gardner), who also owns much unpublished material on his father's investigation of the fairy pictures. For comments on the BBC interviews, see Robert H. Ashby's letter in *Fate*, January 1975, pages 129–30, and "The Cottingley Fairy Photographs: A Re-Appraisal of the Evidence," by Stewart F. Sanderson, in *Folklore*, vol. 84, Summer, 1973, pages 89–103. The latter article is a presidential address given by Sanderson at the Folklore Society's annual meeting in London, March 1973. It is an excellent summary, by a skeptic, of the history of the fairy photos.

Who was the richly uniformed, masked nobleman who entered the Baker Street consulting rooms on that dark night in March 1888—an arrogant foreigner trying to escape the consequences of his indiscretions? His identity has remained hidden from even the most diligent Sherlockian scholars, until now. Who the masked visitor was is at last revealed in . . .

Sherlock Holmes
and the King of Bohemia
The Solution of a Royal Mystery

✄

MICHAEL HARRISON

✄

1. Dr. Watson as Censor

In presenting to the public what I claim to be the correct
identification of Count von Kramm, principal male character of
"A Scandal in Bohemia," I feel that an explanatory word should
be said here on Watson's conception of his duties as editor and
censor in his telling of Mr. Sherlock Holmes's triumphs of
detection.

While recognizing that the identities of all his friend's clients—
illustrious and otherwise—have been concealed by Watson under
more or less interpretable pseudonyms, critics of the Doctor have
not hesitated to accuse him of the most slapdash approach to the
matter of dating his reminiscences. The critics complain of gross
inconsistencies in giving dates; and much, perhaps most, of that
part of the higher criticism involved with Watson has been concerned with adjusting his hopelessly confused dating with what
the critics think should have been the correct timetable and correct sequence of detective adventure.

From *A Sherlock Holmes Commentary,* by D. Martin Dakin,
I select what all readers of Sherlockian criticism will instantly
recognize as a typical attitude toward Watson's chronicling:

A SCANDAL IN BOHEMIA
The date
Watson says it was in March 1888; but for reasons
already explained in the last story, *this must be
changed to 1889.* [Emphasis added.]

This peremptory attitude toward the revision of Watson's dating is, it must be observed, rather the rule than the exception with the critics; and far more eminent Sherlockians than Dakin have not hesitated to be more arbitrarily corrective.

Much of this "putting Watson right" is due to the unfortunate conviction on the part of many critics that they know best, or—only slightly less dictatorial—they know what Watson intended to say.

Thus the greatly respected Sherlockian scholar and critic, the late William Baring-Gould, after having supplied his own date for the case of "A Scandal in Bohemia" (Friday, 20 May 1887: "Watson's account of the case dates it as beginning 'on the 20th of March, 1888.' *This is clearly an error*"*), goes on to cast doubt either on what Holmes's noble visitor said of himself, or on what Watson recorded.

The reader will recall that the self-styled Count von Kramm, in replying to Holmes's "Oh, dear! That is bad. You have compromised yourself seriously," says, "I was only Crown Prince then. I was young. I am but thirty now." To which remark, Baring-Gould appended a footnote: "Crown Prince he was still. But thirty he was not. He was forty-six at the time."

The reason for this footnote is that Baring-Gould, despite the many correct statements that Watson makes and records in this case, has already convinced himself that Count von Kramm is none other than His Royal Highness Albert Edward, Prince of Wales (1841–1910), the future King Edward VII. Much as I respect Baring-Gould's Sherlockian scholarship, I must say here that there is nothing but prejudice to support such an identification; but in order to support it, Baring-Gould arbitrarily rejects the positive statement of his age given by the Count, a statement carefully recorded by Watson. As we shall see, the Count *was* thirty—he

---

* Emphasis added.

was born on 5 April 1857, at Verona, not Windsor—and was thus not quite thirty-one when he asked Holmes to recover the compromising letters and photographs in the possession of Irene Adler, adventuress and international opera star.

As I shall show, all the clues for the correct identification of Holmes's noble visitor are given by Watson, both in the Count's age and in the sonorous titles by which, realizing that Holmes knows his identity (has known it all the time), the foreign nobleman proclaims his rightful rank. The names deserve careful study: each of them is significant in providing a clue to the nobleman's identity. Taken all together, these clues make the identification certain beyond all doubt.

Too little attention has been paid, not so much to who Watson was, as to what he was, and to how such people as he had been trained to act in the highly deportment-conscious society of late-Victorian times.

Watson was a doctor of medicine in a period when the professional manner and professional reticence were esteemed more highly than any purely medical skill. Watson had been trained to observe and say nothing; to respect confidences; to guard those painful details of private indiscretion and private suffering from the public gaze. He had to alter names, and—this is what the critics should have realized—often he had to alter dates. There is no harm in the pleasant task of redating the Watsonian chronicles; there is every reason why Watson should not be blamed for wrong or confused dating. Watson decidedly knew very well what he was about in making his necessary changes.

But in his record of the singular case of "A Scandal in Bohemia," there was even more need for care in preserving the secret of the Count's identity from the ordinary reader. Though the Count was *not* the Prince of Wales, Baring-Gould was right in sensing a connection between Holmes's noble client and the British Royal House. In the indiscreet Count, Holmes and Watson were meeting one of the royal family's most petted favorites; one for whom both Queen Victoria and her eldest son, the Prince of Wales, had incurred the bitter and unrelenting enmity of Prince Wilhelm of Prussia, the future Kaiser Wilhelm II. Wars are not fought any more for dynastic reasons: they are fought for food, for markets. So that it would not be correct to attribute to Wilhelm's hatred for his grandmother ("That old hag!") and for his uncle ("That old peacock!") the war of 1914; but it is correct to say that that hatred made it impossible for the British government even to come to a peaceful discussion with the vain, arrogant, military-minded Kaiser.

But, as well as being one of the British Royal Family's principal favorites, the Count was a member of one of the most successful noble houses to have arisen during the nineteenth century: a house whose brilliant capacity for success has not diminished in this present century, and which, over the past century, has allied itself with the most ancient houses of Europe.

Now let us briefly recapitulate what "A Scandal in Bohemia" might have been had matters gone differently; always bearing in mind that the tale, as Watson tells, and we read, is something of an allegory rather than a sober record of fact.

But the Count did call on Holmes, and Watson has left us all the clues for establishing the Count's identity.

2. The Plot Recalled

In all the Sherlockian Canon of sixty cases—not all of them recorded by Watson—"A Scandal in Bohemia" is surely the most memorable of all. It has, as they say, everything to commend it to the attention and to the memory. True, it has no murder, either of an exotic or ordinary kind; it has not even any of that horror, as in the cases of "The Illustrious Client" and "The Veiled Lodger," which seems so often to inform the cases noted in the Doctor's records.

It has, I suggest, something more important to explain its popularity with a world-wide readership over the past eighty years: it has romantic overtones that "The Speckled Band" and "The Reigate Squires" could not possess.

Folly in high places; indiscretion which might have been even vice, save that, in the latter case, Holmes would not have consented to help; the presence of an adventuress—the harlot purified and made socially acceptable by both intelligence and financial success, who so fascinated the Victorians of all classes and of all standards of morality;* the unequivocal display of wealth hinting at illimitable riches on call:

A man entered who could hardly have been less than six feet six inches in height, with the chest and limbs of a Hercules. His dress was rich with a richness that would, in England, be looked upon as akin to bad taste. . . .

Holmes laughed. "It is quite a pretty little problem. . . ."
"But a very serious one to me. . . ."
"Very. . . . Then, as to money?"
"You have carte blanche."
"And for present expenses?"

No one who has ever read Watson's account of the case will forget how the richly clad visitor drew a heavy chamois leather bag from under his cloak and laid the bag on the table: "There are three hundred pounds in gold, and seven hundred more in notes." And for a receipt, Holmes scribbled on a sheet from his notebook! (Though one feels that the noble visitor would still have left the money and large white Bank of England notes had Holmes, in his usual manner, scribbled the receipt on his own starched cuff.)

The arrival of the visitor was preceded by the arrival of an un-dated, unsigned note, written on thick pink-tinted paper which was not then quite the solecism that it would be today.

There will call upon you tonight, at a quarter to eight o'clock, a gentle-man who desires to consult you upon a matter of the very deepest mo-ment. Your recent services to one of the royal houses of Europe have shown that you are one who may safely be trusted with matters which are of an importance which can hardly be exaggerated. This account of you we have from all quarters received. Be in your chamber then at that hour, and do not take it amiss if your visitor wears a mask.

We are thus instantly made aware that the case about to be described by Dr. Watson involves affairs at the very highest level. By 1888, Holmes had rendered services to several of the royal

---

* For a detailed examination of the rise of the adventuress in the Victorian world see my *Fanfare of Strumpets* (London: W. H. Allen, 1970).

houses of Europe; but Holmes guessed that the phrase in the anonymous note, "your recent services," could hardly refer to any other than his services, of the previous year, to the reigning family of Holland. And as those services involved the indiscretions of the late Crown Prince,* it is apparent—though not, it would seem, to Watson—that Holmes had already guessed, even before his masked visitor's arrival, the nature of the services that the great private consulting detective would be asked to render: the recovery of some compromising letters; the (almost certainly extra-legal) suppression of a blackmailer.

And though Holmes does not call Watson's attention to the use of the word "we" in a sentence that he selects for comment: "And the man who wrote the note is a German. Do you note the peculiar construction of the sentence—'This account of you we have from all quarters received' "—any more than the various Sherlockian commentators have done, I shall do so here. To me, Holmes's refraining from comment on this unusual word is proof that the letter told him, not only that he was being asked to deal with royal troubles, but that his caller was himself a King. Only in Latin is the use of the first person plural a sign of affected humility, and this letter was in English. Holmes realized, even if Watson didn't, that the writer was a man used to expressing his commands with the "royal we."

In consequence, Holmes's examination of the writing paper itself may be seen, not as a piece of Holmesian detective bravura, but as something introduced into the text of the account to be an added clue to the future identification of the visitor.

Holmes, you may remember, asks Watson to tell him what the watermark might suggest as to the origin of the paper. Watson fails in the attempt, and Holmes then tells him that the paper was made by a firm in "Eg." Holmes turns to their Continental Gazetteer to find a town beginning with Eg., and comes across Egria. "It is a German-speaking country—in Bohemia, not far from Carlsbad." Then he reads from the gazetteer: " 'Remarkable as being the scene of the death of Wallenstein, and for its numerous glass factories and paper mills.' "

---

* See my *The World of Sherlock Holmes* (London: Muller, 1973).

The conversation now takes on a mysterious quality, if all that it concerns is the not very difficult task of tracing the origin of a piece of writing paper. Holmes snaps the volume of the Continental Gazetteer shut and says, " 'Ha, ha, my boy, what do you make of that?' His eyes sparkled and he sent up a great blue triumphant cloud from his cigarette."

Watson is obviously puzzled to relate the air of triumph with the apparently insignificant feat of discovering that the paper was made in Egria.

"The paper was made in Bohemia," Watson ventures, seeing that some comment is expected of him.

"Precisely. And the man who wrote the note is a German. Do note the peculiar construction of the sentence . . ."

Now, though he does not record this, Holmes's answer must have puzzled Watson even more. If, from the construction of the letter's sentences, it was obvious that the writer was a German, of what significance could it be that the paper, too, was German? Had the note been written on Claridge's writing paper, would that have made the writer any less of a German?

At that moment, the noise of hooves and a sharp tug at the bell announced the arrival of their visitor. Holmes glanced out of the window, whistling as he saw the smart turn-out: "Yes. . . . A nice little brougham and a pair of beauties. . . . There's money in this case, Watson, if there's nothing else."

So that Watson never had a chance to ask why the identification of the writing paper as German (or Bohemian) was so important. Perhaps we may detect a trace of his nearly century-old sulks in his offer to leave: "I think I had better go, Holmes."

And, seeing that he has ruffled the feelings of the affectionate but often obtuse Watson, Holmes goes out of his way to pay his friend one of those compliments that Watson so rarely got: "Not a bit, Doctor. . . . I am lost without my Boswell."

And a few minutes later, after their masked visitor has arrived— "You may address me as the Count von Kramm, a Bohemian nobleman"—Holmes insists that Watson stay. Watson rises to go, but Holmes pushes him back into his chair, telling the Count: "It is both, or none." At which the visitor shrugs his shoulders and says, "Then I must begin."

He does begin—by telling Holmes that he represents an august personage; but Holmes will have none of this charade. He tells the Count that he is already in possession of much of what he is about to be told:

"The circumstances are of great delicacy, and every precaution must be taken to quench what might grow to be an immense scandal and seriously compromise one of the reigning families of Europe."

"I was also aware of that. . . . If Your Highness would condescend to state your case, I should be better able to advise you."

The Count then springs from his chair, showing great agitation; but after pacing up and down the sitting room for some seconds, he comes to a resolve to be more open with Holmes: "You are right. I am the King. . . ." Holmes replies he is aware of addressing Wilhelm Gottsreich Sigismond von Ormstein, Grand Duke of Cassel-Falstein, and hereditary King of Bohemia.

I now call the reader's attention to what has, so far, been noted by no Sherlockian scholar, erudite or shallow: Holmes's addressing a man whom he knows to be King as "Your Highness." I have had reason to call attention to Watson's seeming unfamiliarity with common English usage in regard to titles of nobility—I mean, quite apart from his legitimate devices to conceal identity; but this impressive, almost violent, apparition of royalty in the person of a six-foot-three Hercules, dressed "with a richness which would, in England, be looked upon as akin to bad taste," could hardly have failed to impress itself unforgettably on the prim Doctor's mind. The King of Bohemia would not have been the first monarch to whom Watson had been presented: as a regular officer of the Army Medical Service, he would have been eligible for presentation at one of the Queen's drawing rooms and for attendance at any of the Prince of Wales's levees. Indeed, as the anonymous author of *The Glass of Fashion* wrote in 1881:

Formerly, only persons of undisputed rank and breeding claimed access to the royal presence; but this privilege is now extended to the clergy, military and naval officers, physicians and barristers, and their wives and daughters, as well as to the families of merchants, bankers, members of the Stock Exchange, and manufacturers of the higher class. Artists and littérateurs of repute are also admitted, but not necessarily or usually any member of their families.

As he was both a physician and a military officer (retired), Watson's application for a presentation would not have been refused. He would have seen, not only the Queen of Great Britain, Empress of India, but also many of those foreign monarchs who visited one another as today presidents pay all-expenses-paid visits to their opposite numbers abroad. On the other hand, royalty in the person of a King of Bohemia would not be lightly forgotten; so that Watson would hardly have been likely to record that Holmes called his royal visitor "Highness," unless Holmes had not only done so, but had explained afterward to Watson why he had not used the customary "Your Majesty."

This, again, is one of the most important clues in establishing the identity of the visitor.

The Grand Duke of Cassel-Falstein then explains what Holmes had already guessed: that there has been an exchange of letters; that there is a compromising photograph. The lady involved is a certain Madame Irene Adler.

Holmes tells Watson to look her up in the Baker Street files.

"Let me see," said Holmes, reading the entry. "Hum! born in New Jersey in the year 1858. Contralto, La Scala. Prima donna, Imperial Opera of Warsaw. Retired from the operatic stage, living in London— quite so. Your Highness, as I understand, became entangled with this young person, wrote her some compromising letters, and is now desirous of getting those letters back?"

—which sums up the situation. Except, as the King of Bohemia explains, that the lady refuses to give them back, or even to sell them, but proposes to send them to his fiancée, Princess Clotilde Lothmann von Saxe-Meningen (sic).

Holmes, as is well known, does obtain the return of the letters and photograph, but not through any detective or persuasive skill of his own; merely through the generosity of the King's ex-mistress who, having married a young English barrister named Godfrey Norton, is too happy in her new life to harbor thoughts of revenge upon her royal ex-lover.

Baring-Gould, noting Holmes's use of the phrase, "this young person," has this somewhat sarcastic comment to make: "When one considers that, at the time of the adventure, Irene was 29 years

Lillie Langtry, the real "Irene Adler"—in the advertisement which cost her £30,000. She charged Pears' Soap £137 (the number of pounds that she weighed!) for the use of her "endorsement"—but Adam Worth, the "Master Criminal," copied her signature from the ad and stole her jewels from the Bank. *Contrad Research Library.*

of age, and that Holmes himself was a mere 33,* this superior attitude begins to look a little absurd."

Superior, perhaps—but only in a moral sense. The eminent Sherlockian had not studied sufficiently the euphemisms of the Victorian age by which the harlot was able to be referred to in polite hearing. I list many of these euphemisms in my *Fanfare of Strumpets;* it will suffice here to say that among them was "young person."

Kept women belonging to the stage were invariably referred to as "young persons of the theater" (or footlights), and no one in Victorian times, reading Watson's account of the case, could believe that any but a high-class tart was the subject of the King's call on Holmes. I have been taken to task—by Pamela Hansford Johnson, among others—for having bluntly stated that Irene Adler was a *Grande Horizontale:* but what other deduction can one make from the conversation between the King and Holmes?

Since we are now approaching the point at which the visitor will be identified from the generously provided clues, I call attention to the significance not only of the name, "Irene Adler," but also of the date of her birth: 1858. It will be seen also that the mention of the Imperial Opera, Warsaw, is not at all unintentional.

And now, as they say in the entertaining preambles to the stories in *Ellery Queen's Mystery Magazine,* the reader is in possession of all the clues needed to solve the mystery. Who, then, was Wilhelm Gottsreich von Ormstein, Grand Duke of Cassel-Falstein, and hereditary King of Bohemia?

3. The Puzzle of "Bohemia"

No deliberate Watsonian deception has caused more brow-furrowing, more useless hunts among unprofitable genealogical and historical byways, than Watson's reference to the hereditary kingship of Bohemia.

In the before-mentioned *A Sherlock Holmes Commentary,*

---

* That is, according to Baring-Gould's revised chronology—but the two ages remain, of course, in the same relation to each other: Holmes only four years the elder.

Dakin gives what is more the usual approach than the usual opinion when he writes:

THE KING OF BOHEMIA

But was he? The trouble is that from 1620 to 1918 Bohemia was a province of the Austro-Hungarian Empire, and if it had a king at all, the title was one of the subordinate appellations of the emperor, though he never seems to have used it. . . .

Dakin then runs through a list of persons who have been, at various times, proposed as candidates for identification with the King of Bohemia, from the unhappy Crown Prince Rudolph to the Prince of Wales; but, as he rightly remarks, these two were men of such openly immoral life, and of such capacity for getting into scandalous situations, that they would hardly have been embarrassed by the presence of compromising letters or photographs.

Yet, though there was no King of Bohemia in 1888—the title, as I shall show, hides that of another sovereignty—the mention of a claim to a Kingdom of Bohemia is not unintentional on Watson's part.

The ancient house of which Wilhelm Gottsreich was a member —it was founded in the eighth century—developed, at the beginning, several branches, of which the counts of Louvain became extremely prominent in late-medieval European affairs. This branch, founded by Gerberg of Lotharingia, eventually became dukes of Lower Lotharingia, margraves of Antwerp and dukes of Limburg, and, after 1191, dukes of Brabant. The male line of this branch was ended in 1355 with the death of Duke Jean III the Triumphant, of Lotharingia, Brabant and Limburg, and in the female line by the death in 1406 of his daughter, Jeanne of BOHEMIA and Luxemburg. On her death, her possessions passed to the House of Burgundy.

Now, if it seems unlikely that any claim to a throne of Bohemia could subsist on such frail genealogical foundations, consider for a moment one established historical fact: that Oliver Williams, better known as Oliver Cromwell,* intended, had he lived, to

---

* But it was in his real name of Williams, and not that of Cromwell, that he married Elizabeth Bourchier at St. Giles's, Cripplegate, built on the former temple of the ancient Roman fertility god, Semo Sancus Dius Fidius.

claim the Holy Roman Empire on the grounds that he had usurped the crown of the king whose sister had been Queen of Bohemia. The historical fact is that the House of Hesse—of which the senior surviving branch is that of Hesse-Cassel (now spelled Kassel)—does not make, nor did it make in 1888, any claim to the defunct Bohemia kingship; but the name was introduced into the account by Watson as the first of those clues by which the identity of the King of Bohemia with a member of the House of Hesse might be established.

4. Identifying Holmes's Noble Client

Let us now assemble the clues as they have been presented in Watson's narrative, remembering that certain non-Watsonian refinements may well be credited to the Agent who handled Watson's MSS for publication, since this Agent, a distinguished man of letters in his own right, was also profoundly interested in both European history and European genealogy.

As concerned as was Watson in preserving the incognito of Holmes's clients, the Agent yet added those subtle touches which will now enable us to make a positive identification of the masked visitor.

Which are the first facts about the visitor given in Watson's narrative? Let us list them.

1. He is a German.
   "The man who wrote the note is a German."
2. He has some connection with Austria.
   The writing paper was made in "a German-speaking country—Bohemia, not far from Carlsbad."
3. He declares himself to be a king.
   The interpretation of his titles will come later.
4. Though a king, something has happened to his kingdom.
   This explains why Holmes calls him "Highness," rather than "Majesty," and why he himself refers to his sovereignty as "hereditary," rather than as "actual" or "reigning."
5. He is at the center of some grave political situation, with which the affair of the compromising letters and photograph is connected intimately, but is not the matter of the threatened scandal itself.

"The circumstances are of great delicacy, and every precaution must be taken to quench what might grow to be an immense scandal *and seriously compromise one of the reigning families of Europe.*" [Emphasis added.]

"I was also aware of that. . . . If Your Highness would condescend to state your case . . ."

6. He is connected in some way with Poland, and in particular with Warsaw.

"Some five years ago, during a lengthy visit to Warsaw, I made the acquaintance of the well-known adventuress, Irene Adler."

7. Irene Adler's year of birth is given in Holmes's records as 1858.

8. He states that he himself was born in 1857 or 1858: i.e., thirty to thirty-one years before his meeting with Holmes. (In fact, it was in 1857.)

9. He became acquainted with Irene Adler at some time before he ascended the throne.

"I was only Crown Prince then. I was young. I am but thirty now."

Inferred or deduced facts

1a. He is rich.

It is true that he may have raised the £1,000 in order to impress and retain Holmes; but this is unlikely. Said Holmes: "There is money in this case, Watson, if there is nothing else." Holmes was rarely at fault in these material matters.

2a. He seems to be well connected in London.

What Watson's obviously prejudiced pen describes as richness of dress bordering on bad taste sounds very much like uniform or elaborate (foreign style) dress clothes or court dress. The reference to the visitor's cloak—ample enough to conceal a heavy chamois leather bag of money beneath its folds—makes it sound as though he had come from some grand, possibly court, function; a theory to which the transport—"a nice little brougham and a pair of beauties"—lends support, since this was the type of carriage favored by the Prince of Wales for his less public outings.

3a. He is above the usual height.

Watson, who must have been a man of average stature, is impressed, obviously against his will, with the physical characteristics of the visitor.

4a. He is probably a soldier.

All Germans of his class would have had at least nominal membership of the army; but there is something in the visitor's peremptory manner which speaks of the military, rather than the royal, habit of command.

5a. He may be the subject of a learned pun in the name "Egria."
6a. He may have a connection—by blood or by similarity of name—with the great Wallenstein, properly Albrecht von Waldstein, Duke of Friedland Sagan and Mecklenburg, the Bohemian general.

Summing-up of the first set of facts

Our visitor is a tall man of thirty, probably a professional soldier, who has sat on a throne and has been either temporarily or permanently deposed; but who is still rich, still well connected; and who, in himself, is the epicenter of a gathering political storm. He is unmarried; a playboy of obviously great physical attractions (the fact that neither Holmes nor Watson thinks so has caused this part of the description to be somewhat played down); and—judging by the apparent use of a Marlborough House brougham—he is on good terms with the British Royal Family; at least with its heir.

Before I name this then most important person, I should like to present this evidence of the Watson-or-Agent-devised word-play in the fictitious names and titles of the visitor.

It will be apparent that one of these word-plays is really comprehensible and significant only after the identity of the visitor has been at least guessed; but I should prefer to give the clinching evidence of the names and titles so as to make it quite clear that the identification has been correctly made.

The evidence of the names and titles

Wilhelm Gottsreich Sigismond von Ormstein, Grand Duke of Cassel-Falstein, and hereditary King of Bohemia. What are the real names behind this orotund mouthing of the sonorous?

The first name to be examined is obviously Cassel-Falstein, for Cassel (Kassel) is a real name, and this real name might yield a real clue.

Cassel can suggest *only* senior Hesse; and the mention of a Grand Duchy instantly calls to mind Grand Ducal Hesse, or any *Grossherzog von Hessen und bei Rhein*. Our man, then, is either the Grand Duke or a member of the Grand Ducal Hesse family. But what of the curious name, "Falstein"?

The name suggests the well known and genuine *Falkenstein*, a family which has intermarried with all the famous families of Europe, including the various branches of the Hesse.

But the clue to the meaning of the manufactured "Falstein" lies in the pronunciation, which may be represented phonetically as "falsch-stein," which again suggests *falsch Stein,* to be translated not so much "false stone" as (perhaps, in this ingenious but malicious context), rather, "dubious foundation."

Is the suggestion of this coinage then that we are dealing with one who is a member of the Grand Ducal Hesse family in an irregular fashion?—a by-blow or the scion of some morganatic union? But we shall return to genuine Falkenstein later.

"Wilhelm," I think, is a false clue, designed to turn the attention of the ordinary reader to the (erroneous) conclusion that the visitor might have been Prince Wilhelm of Prussia, later Kaiser Wilhelm II. On the other hand, our word-players here may well have had in mind that the name "Wilhelm" could be held to be compounded of German, *wild,* "wild," and *Helm,* "rudder": "wild rudder"—no bad description of a playboy hell-bent on pleasure.

Sigismund, German Emperor, was King of *Bohemia* from 1419 to 1437; but three better-known Sigismunds were Kings of *Poland.* So that the name Sigismund recalls the fact that the punsters wish to emphasize the connection of the visitor both with *Bohemia* and with *Poland.*

The manufactured "Von Ormstein" has, I confess, caused me much pondering; but it may represent—bearing in mind the proposed meaning of the equally made-up "Falstein"—*von Norm Stein,* "deriving from the standard (family) foundation." Not at all good German, but something which might have been thought up for English-speaking readers by Watson or the Agent.

But the most convincing clue of all is in the name *Gottsreich,* which certainly sounds like "God's Empire"—the sort of name for the New Germany that the future Kaiser Wilhelm would be likely to give it. (Ein Reich, Ein Volk, Ein Gott only slightly improved by the next-in-line German megalomaniac dictator into *Ein Volk, Ein Reich, Ein Fuehrer.*)

But the manufactured name here is not, in reality, Gottsreich,

God's Empire, but (same pronunciation, of course) *Goths-reich,*
"the Kingdom of the Goth"—for it was in the old lands of the
Goths, in Southeastern Europe, in that part of Roman Dacia
which lies south of the Danube, and which was once protected by
the great Danubian fortresses of Singidunum, Viminacium, Rati-
aria, Novae, Durostorum and Troesmus, besides the immense
earth-wall of Dobrudja, that the visitor—His Serene Highness
Prince Alexander Joseph of Battenberg—once had ruled as sovereign.

5. *"Sandro" of Battenberg*

Queen Victoria, in a memorable letter, talks of what *she* thinks
would be the best way of maintaining the family and of conserving
its power in what is evidently to be a very different future world.
She advises, first and foremost, the democratization of the family
—let it, she advises, look for its wives and husbands outside the
tradition-stifled ranks of the old royalty; let it find its mates—and
so, the Queen claims, its survival—in alliances with persons of
nonroyal, even of nonaristocratic, blood who may bring fresh talents, fresh strength, to the royal stock.

In that, as I write, the eleven-hundred-year-old monarchy, of
which Queen Victoria was so exalted an ornament, still survives
in apparent health and general public acceptance, the wisdom of
the old Queen's advice—which is now seen to have influenced the
policy of her descendants—has been amply justified in events.

In the pursuit of her wish to "de-royalize" her family, to detach
it from the dynastic glory but, at the same time, the dynastic nar-
rowness of the old alliance patterns, Queen Victoria gave her most
powerful patronage to those new families which had sprung, by
morganatic marriages, from the old stems. Of these new houses,
the Tecks and the Battenbergs were the most favored; but in
terms of success the Battenbergs far outshone the Tecks, the
former marrying into most of the royal families of Europe, while
becoming exceptional protégées and protégés of the Queen.

In 1851, at Breslau, Prince Alexander Ludwig Georg Friedrich
Emil von Hessen und bei Rhein (1823–1888), Imperial, Royal
and Hessian Grand-ducal General of Cavalry, Major General of
the Imperial Russian Army, etc., married Julie, Countess Hauke

"Bertie," Prince of Wales, in "Balkan" uniform. Was it the circulation of this photograph which originated the myth that Bertie was that "Count von Kramm" who was being menaced by "Irene Adler"? *Contrad Research Library.*

"His dress was rich with a richness that would, in England, be looked upon as akin to bad taste." "Sandro"—His Serene Highness Prince Alexander of Battenberg, first sovereign ruler of Bulgaria—and the real "Count von Kramm." A contemporary (1879) engraving by A. Weger, from a photograph especially taken for his coronation. *Contrad Research Library.*

*Alexandre Ier
Prince de Bulgarie*

Queen Victoria, the warm admirer and faithful friend not only of "Sandro" von Battenberg but also of the man who saved the Prince from disaster: Sherlock Holmes. A photograph taken at the time of the "King of Bohemia" case—1888—by W. & D. Downey, of London. *Contrad Research Library.*

—note how the name sounds when pronounced in the English fashion—who was the daughter of Moritz, Count Hauke, General of Artillery in the Imperial Russian Army, Senator and War Minister in the Kingdom of *Poland,* then a fief of the Russian Empire, as, indeed, it is today.

The marriage was a morganatic one, and by no means the first in the grand-ducal family of Hesse. The Prince's elder brother, Prince Heinrich Ludwig, had morganatically married twice, while their uncle, the Grand Duke Ludwig III, had also contracted a morganatic second marriage.

It was the progeny of the morganatic marriage between Prince Alexander and Countess Julie Hauke who were to show to what heights of social success and worldly power the sons and daughter of an irregular marriage could come.

Julie Hauke, immediately on her marriage to Prince Alexander, was created Countess of Battenberg, with the rank of Highness, and, seven years later, Princess of Battenberg, with the rank of *Durchlaucht* (Serene Highness)—all her children to bear the title of Prince or Princess of Battenberg, with the rank of Serene Highness.

And how well those children did!

1. Prince Ludwig (Louis), born at Graz, 1854; died in London, 1921; Admiral of the Fleet and First Sea Lord of the British Navy. At Darmstadt he married, 1884, Princess Victoria of Hesse and the Rhine, the daughter of Grand Duke Ludwig IV of Hesse and Princess Alice, *the daughter of Queen Victoria.* To this Battenberg grandson-in-law the Queen always showed exceptional favor. In 1917, when the English Battenbergs renounced their German family name of Battenberg for that of Mountbatten, Prince Louis became Marquess of Milford Haven, Earl of Medina and Viscount Alderney. His younger son, Albert Victor Nicholas Louis Francis, has gained notable distinction, first as Lord Louis Mountbatten, and later as Admiral of the Fleet Lord Mountbatten of Burma.

2. Prince Alexander Joseph, born at Verona, 5 April 1857, died at Graz, 17 November 1893. This is the glittering "Sandro" of our story—the details of his life and career will be told separately.

3. Prince Heinrich Moritz, born at Milan, 5 October 1858, died at sea off Sierra Leone, 20 January 1896. Married at Osborne, 23 July 1885, Princess Beatrice, *daughter of Queen Victoria.*

4. Prince Franz Joseph, born at Padua, 24 September 1861, died at Schaffhausen, 31 July 1924. Married at Cetinje, 6/18* May 1897, Anna, Princess Petrovitch Njegosch, daughter of King Nicholas I of Montenegro.

Their children married quite as successfully: one became Queen of Sweden, another Queen of Spain. Only one of the Battenbergs has so far become a ruling monarch: that was the second son of Julie Hauke, Prince Alexander (Sandro). On 17/29 April 1879— when he was just twenty-two years of age—he became the first monarch of independent Bulgaria; and it is with the troubles which arose out of that singular elevation that Holmes and Watson, in 1888, and we today, are chiefly concerned in this study.

6. The Plot Against Sandro

"The Golden Boy" was a phrase invented at the very end of the nineteenth century, after Sandro's glittering career—"though more in the nature of a Roman candle than of a long-range rocket," as a contemporary statesman acidly observed—had fizzled and spluttered out to its singularly quiet end.

But of all the romantic figures which captured the popular fancy in every European country save Germany, none achieved so heroic a fame as Sandro of Battenberg, Sovereign Prince of Bulgaria, a monarch at twenty-two.

His handsome face, his ancient lineage, his *irregular* membership of Europe's oldest royalty, his defiance of irresistible power, his frustrated love—all these made him the ideal fantasy-hero for every romantic novelist, from the hack writers of *The Boy's Own Paper* to the rather more polished author of *The Prisoner of Zenda*.

The all-conquering impulses which had led the Osmanli Turks from farther Asia to the gates of Vienna, and which had overthrown the Roman Empire of the East and had absorbed all the former provinces of Byzantium, had almost exhausted themselves by the end of the seventeenth century. Though even at the out-

---

* The first date is New Style; Bulgaria had not then abandoned the Julian calendar.

break of World War I, Turkey still ruled an immense continental empire, the *drive* had long passed; and already, before 1700, the emergent Russian state had begun to prey upon its "legitimate victim," Turkey. With the exceptions of Polish, Finnish, and Baltic territory, almost every gain that Russia has made since Ivan IV changed his title from King to Caesar (Csar) has been at the expense of Turkey or of Turk-protected states. By the end of the nineteenth century, Russian political thinking had come to accept as inevitability that what remained of Turkey's possessions must become Russian.

There is no need here to rehearse the tried propagandist tricks —we have seen them all in our generation—by which the various Russian governments sought to throw a mantle of legality over the bare face of plunder. But Russian intentions in Turk-ruled Europe had to be speeded up because a doomed but still vigorous empire—that of Austria-Hungary—was capable of beating Russia to the punch. So that Russia had to work quickly to detach the predominantly Christian vilayets of Wallachia, Moldavia, and the rest from Turkish suzerainty, so as to incorporate them into Russian Europe.

Much of what Russia wished she got with her victory in the Russo-Turkish War of 1878, but not all. Other powers were fearful of Russian ambitions, and so there had to be an intermediate step between the freeing of certain districts from Turkish rule and their being incorporated into Holy Russia. The intermediate step was in their being granted independence, under a ruler appointed by the powers—which term included Turkey.

Greece had already been freed, and had two Royal Houses supplied: a German—which the Greeks soon threw out—and a Danish, which is still more or less on the throne as I write.

Now, after the Berlin Congress which ended the Russo-Turkish War, it was the turn of Bulgaria to follow into freedom from Turkey both Greece and Rumania. By the Treaty of Berlin, 13 July 1878, an independent Principality of Bulgaria was erected, its first monarch being the German Prince Alexander of Battenberg, even though it had been Russian arms that had liberated Bulgaria. The other newly independent Balkan state of Rumania, formed from the old principalities of Moldavia and Wallachia, had a German monarch too—Prince Charles of Hohenzollern-Sigmaringen, who was not only *not* born of a morganatic marriage, but was also allied to the ruling house of the newly formed German Empire.

The Russians were prepared to accept even a German prince as ruler of their Bulgaria, provided that he showed his willingness to act in all things as a puppet-ruler directed by Russian orders. This, however, Sandro was not prepared to do: it is possible that he relied on the fact that he was, through the marriage of one of his aunts, a first cousin of the Russian Emperor, who would go easy with him. In this belief he was mistaken: with the Emperor, as with all previous and later Russian rulers, Russian expansion came first, all other considerations very poor seconds and thirds. Blood relationships could not be permitted to stand in the way of expansionist aims.

In 1884, Sandro's brother, Prince Ludwig (Louis), married the daughter of the Prince of Wales's sister, a marriage which gave great offense to the blood-conscious and relatively *arrivé* Hohenzollerns, already shocked by the liberal sentiments of the German Crown Princess, Queen Victoria's daughter. So that when it was suggested that Princess Victoria, daughter of the Crown Prince and Crown Princess of Germany, should marry Prince Sandro, Prince Wilhelm, their eldest son—afterward Kaiser Wilhelm II—protested furiously, and, in his protests, carried most of German aristocratic opinion with him.

At the wedding at Darmstadt of Prince Ludwig of Battenberg with the Prince of Wales's niece, Sandro, in Sir Philip Magnus's words,* had "bewitched" Queen Victoria, who wrote to her daughter, the Crown Princess (15 December 1886): "I think he may stand next to beloved Papa, and he is a person in whose judgment I would have great confidence. I think him very fascinating, and (as in beloved Papa's case) so wonderfully handsome."

In the year following his brother's brilliant marriage, Sandro added the former Turkish territory of Eastern Roumelia to his kingdom (it was not until 1908 that Bulgaria was formally pro-

---

* *King Edward the Seventh* (London: John Murray, 1964).

nounced so; but Sandro was a king in all but name); so that, as an independent monarch, he was doing well by his new subjects, though not (in their opinion) by the Russians.

However, even though German, he was morganatic, and Prince Wilhelm of Prussia, who already hated his English mother and thoroughly despised his liberal father, wanted none of him.

The British Royal Family, on the other hand, could not do enough to show their affection and partiality for the Battenberg monarch. After the wedding at Darmstadt, the Prince of Wales canceled some important London meetings in order to accompany Sandro to Berlin, where "Bertie" persuaded his sister, the Crown Princess of Germany, to bring her husband around to a favorable view of a wedding between Sandro and Princess Victoria, who was deeply in love with the handsome playboy.

In his diary, under the date 12 May 1884, Frederick von Holstein noted that: "At the banquet at the New Palace two days ago, the Crown Prince, who was sitting between the Prince of Wales and the Prince of Bulgaria, treated the latter with quite unusual cordiality. A few days earlier, he had spoken with the loftiest disdain of all Battenbergs. So the Crown Princess has got round him again."[*]

Now, though Bismarck had warned the Prince of Wales that "the affections of princesses counted for nothing in the balance against German interests," and the aged Kaiser Wilhelm I—on Bismarck's representations—had forbidden any further meetings between Sandro and Princess Victoria, the Prince of Wales arranged, with his sister's connivance, clandestine meetings between the lovers.

Nothing but trouble followed this matchmaking on Bertie's part; on 15 March, the Kaiser had ordered Sandro to make formal renunciation of Princess Victoria's hand; Bismarck insulted the Prince of Wales by neglecting to return a call; and the Russians, who had no wish to see Sandro strengthen his position by a marriage into the German Imperial House, prepared, in the traditional Russian way, to "get" their bad investment. Queen Victoria asked that Prince Wilhelm of Prussia refrain from calling on her at Windsor. All around, Bertie's matchmaking had stirred up trou-

---

[*] *King Edward the Seventh, op. cit.*

ble; but the lovers, encouraged by both Queen Victoria and her son, had not given up hope that, with the death of the Kaiser—he was nearly ninety—the next Kaiser would permit them to marry.

It was in the hope of this marriage that Sandro came to see the great detective at Baker Street; and it was because of the possibility of this marriage that the recovery of the compromising letters and photograph from "Irene Adler" became so imperative.

The independent attitude that, encouraged by the British government, no less than by the British Royal Family, Sandro had adopted in a state then regarded as within the Russian sphere of influence, had maddened the Russians, and now the Austrian government regarded him with dislike. He had fought and beaten the Austrian client-prince, Milan of Serbia; and now the Russians knew that if they attacked Sandro, neither Germany nor Austria would lift a finger to help the Battenberg monarch. Accordingly, on the night of 21 August 1886, the csarist secret police had surrounded the royal palace at Sofia, kidnaped Sandro, and forced him, literally at pistol point, to sign an instrument of abdication.

As Magnus writes, "Queen Victoria and the German Crown Princess were almost prostrate with grief and rage; the Prince of Wales was exceedingly angry; and the young Prince William [of Prussia] rejoiced."

The throne of Bulgaria was now offered around once more; Prince Waldemar of Denmark, a younger brother of the Princess of Wales, indignantly refused it (though he could hardly have done otherwise and still spared his sister humiliation); and the crown eventually went to another German prince, related to but not overfriendly with the British Royal Family: Ferdinand of Coburg—"Ferdy the Fox." He did what the Russians told him to do, so it seemed, and for a while got on well with his masters.

The brutal expulsion of Sandro from his Balkan (Gothsreich) kingdom had not rendered him any less eligible a *parti* in the eyes of the British Royal Family and, now, of the Crown Prince and Crown Princess of Germany.

Watson is right in dating the Count's call as in March 1888, and the revisers of this dating are wrong, no matter what ingenious arguments they present to justify their "correcting" the Watsonian record.

For March 1888 was the decisive month in Sandro's later career —that is to say, in his career as the prospective husband of Princess Victoria of Prussia—seeing that his career as a monarch was ended. For a development was now apparent which made a speeding-up of all the plans essential: the old Kaiser, now ninety-one, could not hope to live much longer; and his heir, the Crown Prince Frederick, was dying almost as certainly and a great deal more quickly of cancer of the throat. The unhappy man had already undergone a tracheotomy to avert suffocation when the Prince of Wales went (10 February 1888) to San Remo to see his dying brother-in-law. Bertie wrote to his son George (later King George V), "Poor Aunt Vicky is worried to death. There are 7 doctors and some 50 reporters of various newspapers! The former do not, alas!, agree among themselves. It is all very sad . . ."

It *was* all very sad; and it fully accounts for the urgency apparent in the Count's approach to Holmes. For, on 16 March 1888—that is, hardly more than a month after the Prince of Wales had gone to San Remo to see the doomed Crown Prince, and to report the facts to Queen Victoria and to Prince George—the Prince of Wales again left London, this time to represent his mother at the funeral of Kaiser Wilhelm I. The dying Crown Prince was now the Kaiser Frederick I.

The urgency, then, arose from the fact that Frederick was now Emperor, but was dying; and that, if the marriage of Sandro with Princess Victoria of Prussia was to be consummated, it must be accomplished at once, while the Emperor was still alive to authorize it. For, with the Emperor dead, and his son Wilhelm on the Imperial throne, Sandro might whistle for his Princess!

No *open* scandal, then, must come to strengthen Prince Wilhelm of Prussia's already strong protests against the marriage, and we know, from Watson's record, how rapidly—and successfully, of course—Holmes got to work on the recovery of letters and photograph.

But there were developments that, even had Holmes foreseen or expected them, could not have been prevented by him. After a reign of only fourteen weeks, the Emperor Frederick died.

His son, Kaiser Wilhelm II, acted immediately to show his hatred of his mother and his intention to rule strongly—he locked up his mother and seized her papers. Only by confiding some of those papers to the English physician Sir Morell Mackenzie did the Empress Frederick manage to save some of her more private papers from the unfilial rapacity of her twisted son.

This, then, was the end of Sandro's romance with Princess Victoria. He accepted that, with Wilhelm on the throne, there could be no more hope of Victoria's becoming Princess Alexander of Battenberg. He returned to the family home in Darmstadt, and now something very curious indeed happened to this, on the whole, very curious young man: he fell in love with an operatic singer!

It was not, of course, odd that he should have done so; he had already fallen in love with a lady of the stage, "Irene Adler." It was merely odd that he should, so soon after he had been rejected by the new Kaiser, have shown what must have been his real preferences. Only this time he proposed to marry the lady.

Her name was Johanna Loisinger, and she had been born at Pressburg, BOHEMIA (now Bratislava, Czechoslovakia), on 18 April 1865. Preparatory to his marrying Fraülein Loisinger, Sandro made arrangements to abandon his princely rank, and by a grand-ducal decree of 11 January 1889—ten months after he had stamped regally into the sitting room at Baker Street—Prince Alexander of Battenberg became the Count von Hartenau. He retained his rank of major general in the Royal and Imperial German Army.

On 6 February 1889, the newly named Major General Count von Hartenau married, at Mentone, Fraülein Loisinger.

The marriage, which was a happy one, was soon over. Sandro died at Graz on 17 November 1893, a little less than five years later. His widow, who died at Vienna on 20 July 1951, and so survived Sandro by nearly sixty years, did not let the memory of his origins vanish in a more republican Europe: in her widowhood, she preferred to call herself Countess von Hartenau-Battenberg.

Where, I think, we might not so much amend as clarify Watson's chronology is in the matter of dating the promise that Holmes gave to Prince Sandro not to publish a record of "A Scandal in Bohemia" until after two full years had passed.

In my opinion, the undertaking was given later—after Holmes had recovered the letters and photographs, and after the accession of Prince Wilhelm to the Imperial throne had made all hope of Sandro's marrying Princess Victoria out of the question. The Emperor Frederick died, after his brief reign of ninety-nine days, on 15 June 1888; his son became Emperor on the same day. Parted forever from Princess Victoria, Sandro must soon after have reconciled himself to the prospect of life in a humbler condition; decided upon a marriage to Fraülein Loisinger as a count, and, as a consequence, requested the grand duke to relieve Sandro of his princely rank. I feel that it was not until after his marriage to the operatic singer that Sandro made the condition—to which Holmes instantly agreed—that no account of the case would be given (by Watson, for general publication) until after the lapse of two years. Watson's account, under the title of "A Scandal in Bohemia," appeared in the *Strand Magazine* for July 1891. Allowing for the facts that the account had to be written, checked—almost certainly heavily subedited by the Agent—and finally submitted to the editor of the *Strand,* before being set in type and illustrated with halftone engravings from the original line-and-wash drawings of Sidney Paget, the account must have been written by Watson in the early part of 1891. Two years back from, say, March 1891 gives us a date at around the first quarter of 1889—and this agrees well with my theory, since it was on 6 February 1889 that Sandro married Johanna Loisinger at Mentone. It is, I think, the fact that the space of a year elapsed between Holmes's recovery of the compromising documents from Irene Adler and Sandro's extracting the promise of two years' secrecy from Holmes which has so confused our meticulously creative Sherlockian chronologists, and has set them to work adjusting the Watsonian calendar.

It should be noted, in passing, that Sidney Paget's well-known drawing of the King of Bohemia provides much confirmation for my theory, as being consistent with the fact that Watson minutely described the King to Paget, without, of course, revealing to the artist the identity of the King. The small points at which Paget's drawing differs from any photograph (without his beard) of Prince Alexander of Battenberg is explained by the fact that, not having been told of the King's identity, Paget could not copy a photograph.

And now . . . who was "Irene Adler"?

7. The Identity of "Irene Adler"

Adler, in German, means "eagle," and the name must have seemed a little too splendid a pseudonym to Watson, who disapprovingly thought of the lady more as the most rapacious of hawks —of vultures, even—than as an eagle.

Still, for all its heraldic nobility, the eagle is no less a bird of prey than the vulture; and there were good reasons why Watson could not give the lady names that meant either "harpy" or "hawk." In the latter case, the mother of Sandro von Battenberg had been born Julie *Hauke*—a name which, in English pronunciation, would sound identical with hawk. Though of bourgeois origin, Countess (later Princess) Julie was of irreproachable reputation, so that a chance identification (through the word "hawk") of the notorious strumpet, Irene Adler, with the spotless and most powerfully connected Countess Julie Hauke, Princess of Battenberg, was a danger to be avoided by Holmes, Watson, and the Agent at all costs.

In the former case, Irene Adler herself was no inviting target for criticism, however well merited. She, too, was most powerfully protected, as a Mr. Adolphus Rosenberg found to his cost.

He was the owner-editor of a scandal sheet, *Town Talk,* and in this scurrilous journal had criticized the lady and her noble and exalted friends.* Roundly abused by Justice (Hanging Judge) Hawkins for having smirched the reputation of a lady "honoured," as her counsel pointed out, "with the acquaintance and, I might say, the friendship of Their Royal Highnesses the Prince and Princess of Wales," Rosenberg was fined £100 and all the costs and sent to prison, with hard labor, for eighteen months. ("I wish that it had been in my power to make it more," the Judge charitably remarked.)

Irene Adler, then, was no person to be lightly provoked.

---

* See my *Painful Details: Twelve Victorian Court-cases* (London: 1962), for a full account of this grotesque action-at-law.

Besides, there was Holmes's infatuation with the lady to insure that she be presented in the best possible light.

There may be no possible doubt that, in Irene Adler, we must recognize the character of Lillie Langtry, born Emilie Le Breton; one of the most impudent, courageous* and financially successful harlots of the later nineteenth century—the century of the Grand Harlot.†

She was the red-headed, violet-eyed daughter of the Very Reverend Dr. Le Breton, Dean of *Jersey* ("You daren't trust Father within a yard of any woman," Lillie recalled)—"Let me see," Holmes said. "Hum! born in New *Jersey* in the year 1858 . . ."— and though Lillie was born a little before 1858, she never specified her age, and 1858 was generally mentioned as the year of her birth.

Lillie married a gentleman named Edward Langtry ("I married him for his yacht"), on whose rapidly diminishing capital she set up house at 17 Norfolk Street, Park Lane, as that *point d'appui* from which to embark on the oldest profession in the world . . . but at the very top.

She didn't begin at the topmost levels of the top, of course, but she managed to find the men who could help her do so: artists such as the Royal Academicians, Millais, Leighton and Watts, who put glorified pictures of her (especially the famous one in which she is wearing a bonnet) into the Royal Academy, which thus became as it were her first shop window.

Oscar Wilde not only publicized her—as he had done that other great strumpet, Sarah Bernhardt: the notorious Oscar's help, as regarded Lillie, was of a strictly practical kind—he lent her his arty little apartment in Cecil Street, Strand, so that she might meet there her Royal "friend," the Prince of Wales.

Lillie's first important, nonroyal, capture was Moreton (note the name) Frewen, rich American brother-in-law of Lord Randolph Churchill, father of Sir Winston Churchill.

Frewen not only bought her a horse, Redskin, but—much better

---

* Courageous . . . ? Indeed! One of her least inhibited lovers, the alcoholic maniac George Baird, "Squire of Abington," once broke into her hotel in Paris, and, in a paroxysm of jealous anger, smashed up the room, tore all Lillie's clothes off, and put her into hospital. It took three days in a French prison to cool Baird off.

† For a description of these women—and a full account of Lillie's own career as a *Grande Horizontale*—see my *Fanfare of Strumpets* (London: 1970).

—passed her on to the impressionable and dying Leopold, Duke of Albany, younger brother of Bertie, Prince of Wales. Leopold was severely rebuked by his mother, Queen Victoria, for hanging a picture of The Lily over his bed. From Leopold, Lillie passed on to the Prince of Wales (though neither was to be regarded as faithful), Bertie getting himself mixed up in the unsavory business of Lady Mordaunt,* Lillie to capture another member of that Royal Family to which Bertie belonged: Leopold II, King of the Belgians.

But the romance, if one may use such a word in this connection, which brought her into touch with Holmes was Lillie's affair (all strictly commercial, of course) with His Serene Highness Prince Ludwig von Battenberg, always known in England as Prince Louis of Battenberg.

Prince Louis, destined to wind up as Admiral of the Fleet and First Sea Lord in 1914, was—at the time of Lillie's hooking him—a mere lieutenant in the Royal Navy, but a favorite and relative of the British Royal Family. (He called the Prince of Wales "Uncle Bertie.") He was the elder brother, by three years, of Prince Sandro—and this fact must be kept carefully in mind.

For Lillie's favors ran, as it were, in families: Lord Randolph Churchill and his brother-in-law, Moreton Frewen; Prince Leopold, Duke of Albany, and his elder brother, the Prince of Wales; the Prince of Wales and his cousin, King Leopold of the Belgians; and now Prince Louis of Battenberg and his younger brother, Prince Sandro . . . about to marry Princess Victoria of Prussia— if nothing went wrong.

And, as Holmes must have reflected, plenty could go wrong. Lillie had now been around and about for more than a decade; she had forced the Prince to display her in public; she had insisted on being invited, not only to the Prince's private house, and there entertained by his wife; she had insisted on, and had won, being presented at Court to the Queen herself. Holmes must have reflected that, in dealing with Lillie, he was dealing with a formidable woman indeed.

What was worse, by 1888 she was no longer *maîtresse en titre* of the Prince of Wales, who had succumbed to the more pressing rapacity of Daisy Maynard, Lady Brooke (later Countess of War-

---

* See *Painful Details, op. cit.*

wick). A little weary of Lillie's charms, Bertie had economized on a redundancy payment or severance payment by starting her on a self-supporting stage career. She was not, as Watson made her out to be, an operatic star, but an actress who was also, in the slang phrase of the 1880s, a "singer"—that is, a prostitute; and that Watson had no other meaning in mind is shown by his giving her an address in St. John's Wood, then the locale of high-class brotheldom and prostitution. Respectable women did not live in St. John's Wood.

In leaving the Prince of Wales, Lillie had not lost her grip on men. In America she had hooked Freddie Gebhard, heir to a $5,000,000 dry-goods fortune, who, though no alcoholic, spent $200,000 (£40,000) on drink alone in the eight years that he was Lillie's escort. And when, on her completely successful theatrical tour, she crossed the United States, it was in a magnificent railway coach supplied by Colonel William D'Alton Mann, "a legitimate Civil War colonel; a newspaperman with a skin-peeling style and a penchant for blackmail"—exactly what Prince Sandro had come to see Holmes about.

The mention of forgery in Holmes's interview with Sandro certainly links "Irene Adler" with Lillie Langtry:

> "There is the writing."
> "Pooh. A forgery."
> "My private note-paper."
> "Stolen."
> "My own seal."
> "Imitated."

Holmes's cynical attitude here has puzzled, and even distressed, some Sherlockian commentators; but his (and Watson's) attitude becomes understandable if one remembers that it is of Lillie Langtry that the men are talking, and that few at that time could think of Lillie without remembering the impudent forgery of which she had been the victim.

Adam Worth, master criminal of the nineteenth century, had coolly copied Lillie's signature from an advertisement in which she had, for a fee, endorsed the purity of a certain soap. Over this forged signature Worth wrote an order, purporting to come from

Lillie, instructing the Union Bank to deliver to the bearer jewels worth £40,000 ($200,000). Later, the bank was very fortunate to be able to settle with Lillie for a mere £10,000.

Holmes, as Watson has recorded, found Lillie far less easy to hoodwink.

What Watson did not tell us, though he correctly named the year in which the King came to seek Holmes's help, was that Lillie was now a free woman—free legally as well as by the conventions of her ancient trade. She had, despite her many lovers, managed to obtain a divorce from Langtry; and this must have made her

seem, to the terrified Sandro, doubly dangerous. Three years earlier, even closer links between the morganatic Battenbergs and the British Crown had been forged by the marriage of Sandro's younger brother. Heinrich Moritz (known conventionally as Prince Henry of Battenberg) had married Queen Victoria's daughter, Princess Beatrice. A freed-by-divorce Lillie could certainly threaten the brilliant prospect of Sandro's marriage to Princess Victoria of Prussia, and, as we have seen, that had to be effected while her father, the dying Emperor Frederick, still lived.

Why did Watson choose to call Lillie "Irene"? If we accept—and I think we must—that the prim Watson thoroughly disapproved, not only of Prince Sandro's blackmailer, but of Holmes's having fallen for her (that phrase is anachronistic, but expressive: so I use it here), then we must look for some cynicism in the choice of pseudonyms, whether or not it was Watson or the Agent who chose them.

The name Lillie and the object, a lily, were both very common in the Britain of the 1870s to 1900s. The flower adorned four Christmas cards out of ten, and almost every religious picture or improving text. The lily was an emblem of peace.

Now the antonym of the rapacious hawk is the peaceful dove —so that the dove, as well as the lily, was an emblem of peace.

Eirene, in Greek, means "peace, a time of peace, the Goddess of Peace." So that Lillie got her pseudonym of Irene from Watson's having equated the sarcastic "dove" with "peace"—and turning that word into Greek.*

So that, though for prudential reasons, Watson or the Agent has made the recognition of the original hidden behind the name "Irene Adler" more difficult than the recognition of the original behind "the King of Bohemia," the clues are all there:

"Irene Adler"	*Lillie Langtry*
Born New Jersey	Born Jersey
Born 1858	Stated to have been born 1858

---

* This familiarity with Latin and Greek should not astonish. Both Watson and the Agent were doctors of medicine, and, in order to become medical students, they would have had to pass a stiff examination in both the classical tongues.

A top level tart	A top level tart
"Friend" of Royalty	"Friend" of Royalty
Connection with religion: Holmes, looking up her name in his records, finds her name next to that of a priest (a rabbi)	Connection with religion: Lillie's father was a priest (Church of England Dean)
An "operatic star" (with secret pun on the word "singer"—i.e., prostitute)	Went on the stage to act and *sing*
Marries Godfrey Norton in 1888	Divorced—i.e., changes her state—in 1888
Wife of Godfrey *Norton*	Mistress of *Moreton* Frewen
Norton is a *barrister*	Brother is a barrister
Holmes suggests to the "King of Bohemia" that "Irene Adler's" blackmail might be countered by a claim that the letters are *forged*	Lillie is robbed of jewels worth £40,000 by means of an order which is *forged*
"The King" calls her "the well-known adventuress" (i.e., an upper-grade harlot)	Lillie Langtry was certainly the best-known *Grande Horizontale* of her day
Holmes called her "the daintiest thing under a *bonnet* on this planet"	The picture which first advertised her charms was the ludicrously demure portrait painted by Watts, which shows her in a *bonnet*

There are many other points of identification. Perhaps the reader would like to find them?

Holmes, Watson tells us, was fascinated by this outrageous strumpet; to Holmes, Watson adds, she was always *"the* woman"—a character and personality unique in an all too identically patterned world. But what Watson never saw—or, perhaps, never tells us that he saw—was this: the case of "A Scandal in Bohemia" demonstrates that it is not beyond belief that, to Lillie Langtry, Holmes was always *"the* man."

For, at least in his relations with Lillie Langtry, "the well-known adventuress," he too showed himself to be unique. Con-

sider the facts: to Holmes, in panic, comes His Serene Highness
Prince Alexander of Battenberg, sent to Baker Street by the
Prince of Wales, and in one of the Prince of Wales's discreet
broughams. And whatever it is that the royal visitor is about to
demand, there will be no obstacle of cost ("There's money in this
case, Watson, if there's nothing else . . ."); and, in the matter of
getting back the indiscreet letters that Lillie Langtry is holding,
Prince Sandro confirms Holmes's view of the money involved
when he tells the Master Sleuth, "You have *carte blanche* . . . ,"
and makes his point by handing over £1,000 as starters.

Holmes, as we know, recovered the letters. I do not believe in
the factuality of those events with which Watson ends the account; I believe that this contradictory and quite incredible explanation of how Lillie handed back the royal letters is a badly
imagined substitute for some more truthful but politically un-
publishable account. Out of it we may, I think, accept one statement as the truth: that Holmes did recover the letters, and that he
did not *buy* them back.

And that alone would entitle him to be thought unique. Of all
the men whom Lillie had met and fascinated, only Holmes escaped
with a whole skin and an intact pocketbook.

The case of "the Red-headed League" has excited more interest, and probably presented more problems, than any other in the Canon: the objects of deepest Sherlockian study being the characters of the several dramatis personae—chief among them the well-bred (though basely born) gentleman-crook, John Clay—and the physical difficulties involved in the actual excavation work undertaken by Clay in his felonious attempt to nick a bank's wealth. But for all this close attention to Clay and his ignoble (but arduous) labors, no Sherlockian commentator yet has attempted to look at the story's apparent inconsistencies from a mathematician's point of view. So here, for the first time, a mathematician (and a renowned one) looks carefully at the mathematics of Clay's proposed removal of London clay. This classic Sherlockian case gets an entirely fresh look in . . .

Red Faces and "The Red-headed League"

※

BANESH HOFFMANN

※

In the adventure of "The Red-headed League," John Clay and his partner in crime wish to dig a tunnel from the cellar of Jabez Wilson's pawnshop in Saxe-Coburg Square to the nearby cellar of the Coburg branch of the City and Suburban Bank, with a view to stealing some of the bank's gold.

To this end, Clay, under an alias, takes a job as assistant in the pawnshop. Because Wilson's presence hampers the tunneling, the criminals concoct the extraordinary scheme of the Red-headed League, exploiting the remarkable coincidence that both Wilson and Clay's partner have red hair of a most distinctive fiery hue. Seeking to persuade the reluctant Wilson to go to the League's office in response to its advertisement, Clay reassures him with these words: "The work is slight; it need not interfere very much with one's other occupations."

But for most people the work would very much interfere with their other occupations, since, as Wilson later learned, it required his continuous presence at the office of the League from 10:00 A.M. till 2:00 P.M. without fail every weekday, Saturday included. Thus Clay's remark was a lie.

Yet there is mitigation. As Wilson later remarked to Holmes, "a pawnbroker's business is mostly done of an evening." So one could say that Clay had spoken the truth, at least so far as Wilson was concerned, even though his phraseology was more general than the truth demanded.

We can find further mitigation. Recall that Watson dropped in on Holmes on a Saturday morning, heard Wilson tell his tale of the Red-headed League, and patiently waited some fifty minutes in silence while Holmes pondered what he referred to as "quite a three pipe problem"; and that when Holmes then suggested that the two of them go to St. James's Hall after lunch—and, as it turned out, after visiting Saxe-Coburg Square—Watson acquiesced, saying, "I have nothing to do to-day. My practice is never very absorbing." Clearly, Clay's remark would apply not only to Wilson but to Watson as well. It was thus somewhat less of an untruth than even Clay may have imagined. Yet it was still a lie.

Before the visit to Saxe-Coburg Square, Holmes had already deduced the existence of a tunnel. On beating the pavement in front of the pawnshop with his stick he silently concludes that the tunnel does not extend in that direction. He therefore leads Watson around the corner and then to the bustling main street, and while standing there says brazenly, "I should like just to remember the order of the houses here. It is a hobby of mine to have an exact knowledge of London."

The first of these two sentences is a deliberate deception of the long-suffering Watson, since Holmes is specifically interested in noting the presence of the bank, which he then recognizes as the obvious destination of the tunnel. As for the second sentence, it may well be defended as true, yet precisely because it immediately follows the first, it too becomes, to all intents and purposes, a deliberate lie.

We were probably not overly distressed to catch Clay in an untruth. After all, we expect a criminal to lie. But we can hardly avoid a feeling of regret that Holmes should have been untrustworthy merely for the sake of mystifying his good friend Watson—especially when we realize, as Holmes undoubtedly did, that the good Watson would probably have been just as mystified even if Holmes had been candid.

What were Watson's feelings when he began to sort his notes

and write up the details of the case of the Red-headed League? Surely he realized by then that Holmes had deliberately misled him. Did he feel hurt? The answer is undoubtedly yes. For, as will be seen, he had his revenge, even if it was a subtle one. Telling of the incident in Saxe-Coburg Square in front of the pawnshop, he writes: "Finally [Holmes] returned to the pawnbroker's and, having thumped vigorously upon the pavement with his stick two or three times, he went up to the door and knocked." Much later in the narrative, when Holmes is explaining how he solved the case, Watson quotes him as saying: "I surprised you by beating upon the pavement with my stick. . . . Then I rang the bell, and, as I hoped, the assistant answered."

What Watson is gently telling us is that although Holmes actually knocked on the door, he later said he had rung the bell. Admittedly, this is a small discrepancy, and Watson could easily have eliminated it. Why did he retain it? Recall here the annoyance with Holmes that Watson openly admitted at the start of *The Valley of Fear,* and the manner of his quick revenge, which led Holmes to express the need to guard himself against Watson's "pawky humour."*

> "I am inclined to think—" said I.
> "I should do so," Sherlock Holmes remarked impatiently.
> I believe that I am one of the most long-suffering of mortals; but I'll admit that I was annoyed at the sardonic interruption. "Really, Holmes," said I severely, "you are a little trying at times."

A few minutes later Watson has his revenge, as is seen in the following dialogue:

> "You have heard me speak of Professor Moriarty," [said Holmes].
> "The famous scientific criminal, as famous among crooks as—"
> "My blushes, Watson!" Holmes murmured in a deprecating voice.
> "I was about to say, as he is unknown to the public."
> "A touch! A distinct touch!" said Holmes. "You are developing a certain unexpected vein of pawky humour, Watson, against which I must learn to guard myself."

Here, in the case of the Red-Headed League, by retaining the above discrepancy, Watson is expecting us to link it with the earlier occasion when Holmes indulged in a purposeless lie. And if, even despite the earlier instance, we still cannot bring ourselves to look on Holmes as a petty prevaricator, Watson is giving

---

* The opening of *The Valley of Fear* is as follows:

us the option of believing Holmes honest, in which case he expects us to draw the natural conclusion that Holmes's much-vaunted memory for detail was less reliable than we had thought. A pawky fellow, this Watson, when his feelings are hurt!

For most of his readers, Watson's plan unfortunately misfires —and through no fault but his own. For, so splendidly has he presented Holmes to us as a superman that we are loath to think of him as either a habitual prevaricator or a man with a less than perfect memory. Nevertheless, once the data have been properly presented to us we begin to wonder about the image we have hitherto formed of Holmes. And this leads us to further insights.

There is something particularly strange about Holmes's knocking on the door of the pawnshop and actually hoping that the assistant would be the one to answer. Consider the situation. Though Holmes had never set eyes on Clay before, he had at once recognized him from Wilson's description of the man who had come to work for him as assistant in the pawnshop: "Small, stout-built, very quick in his ways, no hair on his face, though he's not short of thirty. Has a white splash of acid upon his forehead." On hearing this, Holmes sits up in his chair in considerable excitement and says, "I thought as much. Have you ever observed that his ears are pierced for earrings?" the answer from Wilson being, of course, that he had.

Later Holmes tells Watson that he considers Clay "the fourth smartest man in London." Considering that the first three, in Holmes's view, were presumably Holmes, brother Mycroft, and Moriarty, this is high praise indeed. Let us keep it in mind.

Why, when he knocked on the door of the pawnshop, did Holmes hope that the assistant would be the one to open it? Not so that Holmes could catch his first glimpse of Clay: he already knew that the pawnbroker's assistant was none other than Clay. Holmes himself tells us the real reason: to observe the knees of Clay's trousers.

The whole confrontation can hardly have lasted as much as ten seconds. If you doubt this, try timing the entire dialogue, which was brisk and went like this—although I have added the first four words: "Won't you step in?" "Thank you. I only wished to ask you how you would go from here to the Strand." "Third right, fourth left." Upon this the door was promptly closed, and my own timing is five seconds, even when I recite Holmes's part relatively slowly.

This brief confrontation sufficed for Holmes to note that the knees of Clay's trousers were worn, wrinkled, and stained, thus confirming the hypothesis that Clay had been engaged in digging.

But now recall the high rating Holmes gave to Clay's intellectual powers. What went through Clay's mind during those few seconds? Surely he needed but an instant to recognize Holmes in the figure standing before him on the pavement; not only was Holmes famous, but in addition Clay, as a criminal, had a professional as well as a layman's interest in him. And the presence of Watson can only have hastened the identification. Imagine Clay's shock on recognizing the redoubtable Holmes right there, literally within yards of the telltale tunnel; and Clay's inner consternation on noting, as he could not fail to note, that though Holmes was ostensibly asking the way to the Strand, his attention, during the short time available, was clearly preoccupied with the telltale knees of Clay's trousers. Right away, Clay must have realized that the game was up. To continue with the plan would now be utter folly. Only flight was left. Holmes would never have become lost in the heart of London so close to the Strand. Even a fool would realize that.

But now we find ourselves face to face with a baffling problem: What was Holmes's reason for confronting Clay? We can at once dismiss the possibility that it simply never occurred to Holmes that he might be recognized; such modesty was not numbered among his virtues.

Did Holmes deliberately present himself to Clay in order to scare him, knowing full well that Clay would recognize him? Was Holmes trying to cause Clay and his partner to flee without using the tunnel to steal the gold? Certainly it was not essential for Holmes to see either Clay or the knees of his trousers. He could have learned all he needed by obtaining permission to thump the floor of the bank cellar with his stick and noting that it rang hollow —as it was to do later when the bank director Merryweather struck it that same Saturday. This would certainly have revealed to Holmes the presence of the suspected tunnel. If we conclude, then, that there was some ulterior motive in Holmes's presenting himself to Clay, we come back to the basic problem of what that motive may have been. It is an extraordinarily difficult question. The only motive with a chance of making sense would apparently be to put such fear into the criminals' hearts that they would flee forthwith. Yet this could not possibly have been what Holmes had in mind; if he believed they would not go through with their attempt to rob the bank, what point was there in setting up the police trap and organizing the vigil in the cellar of the bank? Surely Holmes's strategy ought to have been to leave the criminals in total ignorance of impending doom, so that they would fall into the trap and be captured without the need for a widespread manhunt.

We have to conclude that although Holmes deliberately presented himself to Clay, for some obscure reason he confidently expected that the criminals would suspect nothing and thus that the confrontation would not affect their course of action. And the strange thing is that evidently the criminals did attempt to go through with their plan without change.

As Holmes was wont to say, after one has eliminated the impossible, whatever remains, however improbable, must be the truth. We have found a situation in which no explanation seems to make sense. We must therefore go back over our reasoning to find a possible loophole. The only one that seems promising is that Clay was, in fact, not at all as intelligent as Holmes had made out. This would explain Clay's failure to recognize in the sudden appearance of Holmes an unequivocal sign that his plan was doomed. But all along we have had an indication supporting unflattering conclusions concerning Clay's mental acuity. For, looked at dispassionately, his whole plan was incredibly ill-conceived. It violated that cardinal precept of criminal conduct: do not leave a back trail.

Clay's plan, far from concealing his identity, actually drew attention to it; and to his partner's identity too. Assume, for the sake of argument, that Holmes had not become involved in the matter till afterward, that the gold had been stolen according to plan, and that the thieves had made a complete getaway. They could not possibly have remained anonymous. Sooner or later, the bank would have discovered the loss of the gold. And then even the police unaided by Holmes would have realized the presence of the tunnel and followed it back to the cellar of Wilson's pawnshop. Wilson would have been closely questioned—at first as a prime suspect—and the whole fantastic story of The Red-headed League would have come pouring out. Wilson would have described his erstwhile assistant with the hairless face, the white splash of acid, and the pierced ears, and Holmes, and surely others, would immediately have realized that one of the wanted men was Clay. As for the other—who was also describable by Wilson—his most distinctive feature was undoubtedly his fiery red hair. But instead of hiding it, the partners made it the most conspicuous feature of their scheme. This laying of so brazen a back trail may well have been sheer bravado. But was it intelligent?

We know from the vivid testimony of Peter Jones of Scotland Yard that Clay was elusive. On being told in the bank cellar that Clay was involved, Jones exclaimed:

"John Clay, the murderer, thief, smasher, and forger . . . he is at the head of his profession [an estimate echoed verbatim by Holmes] and I would rather have my bracelets on him than on any criminal in London. . . . His brain is as cunning as his fingers, and though we meet signs of him at every turn, we never know where to find the man himself. He'll crack a crib in Scotland one week, and be raising money to build an orphanage in Cornwall the next. I've been on his track for years and have never set eyes on him yet."

Let us give Clay his due. Perhaps, having found how easily he could elude the obviously none-too-resourceful Scotland Yard, he felt he could afford to take chances with the police. But after the

startling and ominous confrontation in Saxe-Coburg Square, would an intelligent man have compounded the already compounded risk by continuing with his plan, thus taking chances with Sherlock Holmes?

Having found reason to doubt Clay's intelligence, let us consider these two mutually exclusive alternatives concerning Holmes's estimate of Clay: (1) that Holmes showed poor judgment of intellectual capacity; and (2) that he was literally accurate in his estimate.

If the first, the picture of Holmes as a superman is once again tarnished.

What if the second? What if Clay was in fact the fourth smartest man in London, and at the head of his profession? Then once more Holmes would seem to come off badly. For if even the most intelligent criminals were as mediocre as Clay, if even the best of them exhibited as little intelligence as Clay did, what merit could there be for Holmes in outwitting them?

One might offer a Machiavellian theory more favorable to Holmes: the confrontation in Saxe-Coburg Square was deliberately designed to simulate a blunder so that, believing Sherlock Holmes to have lost his grip, Clay would fall into the trap exactly as Holmes had planned.

It will not do—and this quite apart from its internal inconsistencies. The facts are against it. For, suppose it were true, then in explaining to Watson how the case was solved, Holmes would certainly have told of the subtle trick he had played. But he made no mention of any such trick. There seems no escape from this sad conclusion: In seeking the confrontation, Holmes blundered; but luckily for him Clay then bungled too. Or, as one might venture to put it: Defeat of Clay came despite the feet of clay of Holmes.

Shall we, then, sum up with the dubious salutation: "Hail to Sherlock Holmes, who was a match for bunglers"?

Considering the enormous pleasure that Holmes has given—and continues to give—to all of us, let us try to end on a happier note, even if the attempt turns out to be not wholly convincing. What if most of the criminals Holmes hunted were not overly intelligent? Is that necessarily devastating? One could argue that it is harder to solve a mystery created by a criminal of mediocre intelligence who acts irrationally than it is to solve one in which the criminal's acts form a rational, comprehensible pattern: mere logic is nonplussed by irrationality.

So hail, indeed, to Sherlock Holmes, who was a match for bunglers.

Addendum

Since I have been discussing the case of "The Red-headed League," let me add a sort of postscript dealing mathematically with one of the outstanding problems connected with the case.

First the mathematics: Let us write out the integers in order, like this:

$$1, 2, 3, 4, 5, 6, 7, 8, \ldots$$

Now let us delete the odd integers, leaving only the even ones:

$$2, \quad 4, \quad 6, \quad 8, \ldots$$

It is obvious that the number of even integers is only about half the number of all the integers. Until more than three-quarters of the way through the nineteenth century, everyone would have agreed that this is so. But then it occurred to the mathematician Georg Cantor to count the even integers, which he did by listing all the integers as before and putting beneath each one of them the integer with twice its value, like this:

$$1, \quad 2, \quad 3, \quad 4, \quad 5, \quad 6, \quad 7, \quad 8, \ldots$$
$$2, \quad 4, \quad 6, \quad 8, \quad 10, \quad 12, \quad 14, \quad 16, \ldots$$

Cantor then argued that since to each integer there corresponds a unique even integer, with all the even integers uniquely accounted for, the number of even integers must be the same as the number of all the integers. This sounds not merely naïve but utterly ridiculous. And in fact Cantor's ideas along these lines were greeted with widespread scorn among professional mathematicians—who were about the only people who heard of them in those days. Nevertheless, they constituted a mathematical revolution of the first magnitude, and they form a basic part of the very fabric of modern mathematics.

It behooves us, then, to take them seriously. Why do we have difficulty doing so? Because as we look at the integers lined up with those having double their values, we realize that the further we go, the greater the debt we are piling up that will have to be paid when we stop. For example, by the time we have got as far as

$$1, \quad 2, \quad 3, \quad 4$$
$$2, \quad 4, \quad 6, \quad 8$$

we have counted the even integers up to 8, but all the integers only up to 4. And by the time we reach number 100 of the regular integers, we will have had to reach as far as the even integer 200 to fill our quota. The further we go before we stop, the greater the debt we must repay. The matching is thus illusory. It is a fraud, a little like kiting checks.

Admitted. But that is because we are considering what the situation is at the stage at which we stop. What if we never stop? What if we keep going forever? Then we shall never be called on to repay our ever-mounting debt, and shall therefore never be confronted by a discrepancy: the even integers will match the integers one by one without exception, forever. And because, since we are dealing with the integers, there is indeed no end, no stopping place, we conclude that the number of even integers is indeed equal to the number of all the integers. The key point is that we never stop; that we are dealing with infinity; and that, as Cantor showed, if we want to take the concept of infinity seriously, we must be prepared for strange results that deal harsh blows to our preconceived notions.

Take another case, more immediately relevant to "The Red-headed League." Though it is somewhat simpler than the above, it involves essentially the same concepts: the number of integers 2, 3, 4, 5, . . . is equal to the number of integers 1, 2, 3, 4, . . . Using the Cantorian method of counting, we can easily see that the statement is valid. We merely line up the two sets of integers like this:

$$1, \quad 2, \quad 3, \quad 4, \quad 5, \quad 6, \quad 7, \quad 8, \quad . . .$$
$$2, \quad 3, \quad 4, \quad 5, \quad 6, \quad 7, \quad 8, \quad 9, \quad . . .$$

Only if we stop will there be a discrepancy. If we go on forever, there will be perfect matching one for one.

What has this to do with "The Red-headed League"? When Clay, and presumably also his partner in crime, were digging their tunnel, they dug enormous quantities of earth out of the ground. Where did they put it? No satisfactory answer has been proposed.

If we wish to be facetious, we can suggest that they dug a second tunnel into which they dumped the earth excavated from the first. If we are asked what they did with the earth excavated from the second tunnel, we reply that they dug a third tunnel and put the earth excavated from the second tunnel into that. What of the earth excavated from the third tunnel? Obviously, they dug a fourth tunnel in which to stow it. And so on.

It is a pleasant joke while it lasts. But suppose it goes on forever? Suppose there is no limit to the number of tunnels they dig? Then we are dealing with infinity, and what began as a pleasantry becomes a deadly serious exercise in Cantorian mathematics. For if we label the tunnels 1, 2, 3, etc., the number of the excavated tunnels labeled

$$1, 2, 3, 4, 5, \ldots$$

is the same as the number of receptacle tunnels, labeled

$$2, 3, 4, 5, 6, \ldots$$

and if each tunnel held the same amount of earth, the total amount of earth in the receptacle tunnels would be equal to the total amount of earth excavated.

Mathematically this is unexceptionable, and it constitutes a valid theoretical solution of the problem of the disposal of the excavated earth. Do you ask whether I regard it as a practicable solution? Please do not do so. Being neither a professional criminal nor a consulting detective, I cannot tell a lie.

It has been remarked elsewhere in this anthology that the parodies of the Master were already numerous and established within a few years of his first appearance at the Christmas of 1887: this is a fact generally well known to Sherlockians. What is certainly not so well known—what, indeed, is hardly known at all, even to hardcore Sherlockian scholarship—is that the dramatizing of Sherlock Holmes may even antedate the publication of the first parody. We have read, in the Lord Chamberlain's archives at the Public Record Office, the curtain raiser by Charles Brookfield and Seymour (later Sir Seymour) Hicks titled Under the Clock: An Extravaganza. *As literature it is beneath contempt; as theater, it is the most appalling nonsense to which our insatiable archivistic curiosity has even accidentally brought us. But as Sherlock Holmes appeared in it as early as 1893, only six years after the first publication of* A Study in Scarlet, *it has historic importance quite out of proportion to any intrinsic quality that it might possess. The many stage and screen Sherlocks—the good and the bad; the mediocre and forgettable; the brilliant and memorable—are all remembered here, as the author presents them in . . .*

The Impersonators
Sherlock Holmes on Stage and Screen

❦

ANTHONY HOWLETT

❦

Mr. Sherlock Holmes, who "loathed every form of society with his whole Bohemian soul," turned away with disdain from popular notoriety. It is not surprising, therefore, that he refused any part in the numerous dramatizations of his adventures on the stage and in films.

That he would have made an excellent actor is undeniable. Dr. Watson has related many examples of his friend's amazing powers in the use of disguises and how "his expression, his manner, his very soul seemed to vary with every fresh part he assumed. The stage lost a fine actor, even as science lost an acute reasoner, when he became a specialist in crime." This was no mere Watsonian adulation; even Inspector Athelney Jones was forced to admit: "You would have made an actor, and a rare one." Mr. Holmes himself admitted that he could never resist a touch of the dramatic, and at the dénouement of "The Six Napoleons," when Watson and Inspector Lestrade "with a spontaneous impulse . . . broke out clapping as at the well-wrought crisis of a play," we are told that "a flush of color sprang to Holmes's pale cheeks, and he bowed to us like the master dramatist who receives the homage of his audience." Unfortunately Mr. Holmes's powers as an actor were not displayed to the general public, so we can only consider how he has been portrayed by professional actors.

Sherlock Holmes in the Theater

The first portrayal of Sherlock Holmes in the theater was in a satirical sketch in 1893, an extravaganza titled *Under the Clock*. It was written by Charles Brookfield and Sir Seymour Hicks, who portrayed Holmes and Watson respectively. But the first serious play appeared six months later. This was a lurid melodrama much inspired by the sensational Jack the Ripper murders. The author was Charles Rogers, and the play was called simply *Sherlock Holmes*. It had its first production in Glasgow in May 1894, with John Webb in the title role. In an age when barnstorming melodramas were very popular, it enjoyed extensive tours for many years.

The next play was, however, the most famous and enduring of them all. It had its genesis very appropriately with Sir Arthur Conan Doyle. He entered the theatrical field in 1897 with a five-act Holmesian drama, although, as he remarked in a letter, "I have grave doubts about putting Holmes on the stage at all." The play, having been earlier sent to Sir Herbert Beerbohm Tree, was sent to the impresario Charles Frohman in New York. Frohman turned it over to the American actor-playwright William Gillette, who undertook to rewrite it, having been given carte blanche by Conan Doyle, whose attitude to Holmes at the time is illustrated by his much-quoted, "You may marry or murder or do what you like with him."

Gillette steeped himself in the Holmes stories, and, relying primarily on "A Scandal in Bohemia" and "The Final Problem," he produced his own drama in four weeks. No copy of Conan Doyle's original play has survived, but it is known that Gillette extensively rewrote it and tailored the part of Holmes to suit his own personality. The only copy of Gillette's first draft was destroyed in a hotel fire, but shortly afterward he had rewritten the play yet again. *Sherlock Holmes*, this "absurd, preposterous, and thoroughly delightful melodrama," as it has been called, was an immediate success. It opened in 1899 and ran for 236 performances in New York, with Gillette as Holmes. After tours in America, it was brought in 1901 to London, where it ran at the Lyceum for another 216 performances.

Even then the play's triumphant career had barely started. It was translated into Danish, Dutch, French, German, Russian, and Swedish. It toured across Europe, again and again in America, and it repeatedly toured throughout England; at one period, five companies, including Gillette himself, were on tour simultaneously with the play. In 1903 a young actor made his professional debut in the role of Billy the pageboy: the program gave his name as Master Charles Chaplin.

No small measure of the play's initial success was due to the performance of William Gillette in the title role. His physical appearance, temperament and personality have caused him to be remembered by many as one of the greatest Holmeses of the footlights. Although many other actors have appeared in the part, such was the attraction of Gillette that over thirty years after the original production, when he was in his seventies, he could still achieve an outstanding success with a farewell tour.

At last in the 1930s, by which time one has completely lost count of the number of performances, Gillette's *Sherlock Holmes* was apparently at an end. Thereafter there was still the occasional repertory theater production, such as one at Birmingham in 1952 with Alfred Burke and Paul Daneman, but it seemed that the play had really run its allotted span.

However, in 1974, seventy-five years after the first production, came a renaissance from a very surprising quarter. The Royal Shakespeare Company presented *Sherlock Holmes* for the Christmas season at the Aldwich in London. Here was Gillette's play back again in a splendid period production, with superb sets and a top professional cast. John Wood was an effective Holmes in the Gillette tradition, and such was the unexpected success that the run had to be extended until the following autumn. After 106 performances, the play went to the United States, to meet with similar acclaim there.

But, back to the turn of the century. Only a month after *Sherlock Holmes* had opened at the Lyceum, a popular burlesque appeared at Terry's Theatre in the Strand titled *Sheerluck Jones* (or *Why D'Gillette Him Off?*), with Clarence Blakiston in the lead. Indeed, in the early years of the century there were truly prolific theatrical portrayals of Sherlock Holmes.

Before Gillette's play had reached England, in 1900 Max Goldberg had written *The Bank of England: An Adventure in the Life of Sherlock Holmes,* which toured England for several years and subsequently went to the States. In the early 1900s many such unauthorized plays were produced in America and in Europe. In Spain, too, the popularity of the detective was considerable, and he was pitted against such celebrated criminals as Raffles and Arsène Lupin in incredible adventures.

The fame of Sherlock Holmes made him an inevitable subject for the music halls and vaudeville, and at this period numerous sketches, dramatic or otherwise, were produced. Gillette himself wrote and appeared in a frivolous "curtain raiser," *The Painful Predicament of Sherlock Holmes,* in 1905, originally at the Metropolitan Opera House in New York and later at the Duke of York's in London. The American cast included Ethel Barrymore, and the English, Dame Irene Vanbrugh, with Charlie Chaplin again as Billy.

Then in 1910 came a Sherlock Holmes play by Conan Doyle himself, which he wrote in a week. It was a stage version of "The Speckled Band" and was produced at the Adelphi Theatre with H. A. Saintsbury as Holmes—a part which he had played nearly a thousand times on tour in Gillette's play—and Lyn Harding made an outstanding success as the formidable Dr. Grimesby Rylott [*sic*]. This "snake-on-the-bellrope" drama rapidly became almost as popular as Gillette's, and the familiar pattern repeated itself: long runs, extensive tours in England and America, translations into several languages, and numerous revivals. It was professionally produced again as recently as 1970 in Manchester.

Conan Doyle was delighted at his own first real stage success, and recorded in his memoirs:

We had a fine rock boa to play the title-rôle, a snake which was the pride of my heart. . . . We had several snakes at different times, but they were none of them born actors and they were all inclined either to hang down from the hole in the wall like inanimate bell-pulls, or else to turn back through the hole and get even with the stage carpenter who pinched their tails to make them more lively. Finally we used artificial snakes, and everyone, including the stage carpenter, agreed that it was more satisfactory.

The next production on the London stage was another play written by Conan Doyle in 1921 titled *The Crown Diamond: An Evening with Sherlock Holmes,* with Dennis Neilson-Terry as Holmes. It must frankly be admitted that it was a poorly written play, and it failed after only a week's run. Doyle adapted it into a short story under the title of "The Mazarin Stone," which appeared in the *Strand Magazine* in October 1921, and even in this form it is probably the least successful of the Holmes stories.

Two years later Harold Terry and Arthur Rose collaborated in writing the play *The Return of Sherlock Holmes.* It was based mainly upon the stories, "The Empty House" and "Lady Frances Carfax." It had a long run at the Princes' Theatre, with Eille Norwood (who had just completed an excellent series of Holmes films) in the title role. Although an undoubted success both in London and on tour, and in Amsterdam and Copenhagen, the days of the outstanding theatrical success like Gillette's *Sherlock Holmes* and Conan Doyle's *The Speckled Band* were over. Audiences were not the same after World War I; times were changing with great rapidity, and the rival claims of the cinema were being felt. This was really the last of the major Holmes plays. Extensively revised by Arthur Rose and Ernest Dudley in 1953, it was successfully revived at the New Theatre, Bromley, in a production which set it back into the period of the 1890s and for the first time paid close attention to the finer points of Holmesian detail. A notable portrayal of Sherlock Holmes was given by Geoffrey Edwards, whose physical appearance was probably closer to the Holmes of the Paget illustrations in the *Strand* than any of his predecessors.

When another new play appeared in 1933, however, the picture had changed drastically, and it was the last Holmes play, apart from revivals, to be seen for the next twenty years—well after World War II. After brief trial runs outside London, *The Holmeses of Baker Street* appeared at the Lyric Theatre, with Sir Felix Aylmer as Holmes and Sir Nigel Playfair as Watson. Many years previously, Gillette had dared to show Holmes in love, but this amazing play by Basil Mitchell revealed him as a widower with a grown-up daughter! "When I have written to this man and told him that I hold him . . . responsible . . . we will have no more trouble," said Sherlock Holmes in "The Creeping Man"—he must have taken similar action here, for the play was quickly withdrawn.

It was not until the 1950s that some revival of interest in theatrical portrayals of Holmes began, so thoroughly had the cinema ousted the theater—especially during the intervening war years. The first theatrical revival took the form of a ballet, *The Great Detective,* performed by the Sadler's Wells Ballet Company in 1953, with Kenneth Macmillan providing psychological overtones by dancing the roles of both Sherlock Holmes and Professor Moriarty.

The greatest disappointment of this era was a play which started with such high hopes in view of the reputation of the leading actor. Basil Rathbone was one of the finest impersonators of Sherlock Holmes. He was certainly the last of the few—those three or four actors out of so many who have been truly satisfying in the immortal role. A celebrated stage and film actor, he had made fourteen very well known Holmes films and had played the role 218 times on American radio and also on television. In 1953 he made his stage debut as Holmes in a play, *Sherlock Holmes,* written by his wife, Ouida Rathbone. It was given an expensive production with a strong supporting cast and, after the usual trial runs, finally came to New York. It was, alas, not a well-constructed play, and even Basil Rathbone's portrayal could not save it: a disastrous failure, it ran for only three days.

The times were not propitious for a theatrical Holmes. In 1961 James Goldman wrote a curious play about a judge who, after a nervous breakdown, imagined himself to be Sherlock Holmes. Under the title *They Might Be Giants,* it was produced at the Theatre Workshop, Stratford, London, with Harry H. Corbett (later of "Steptoe" fame) in the lead. Like the film version eleven years later, this humorous, evocative, and at times poignant play was acclaimed by some critics but was "caviare to the general."

The first two decades after World War II saw the universal popularity of the American musical. The musical adaptation of Bernard Shaw's *Pygmalion* into *My Fair Lady* was probably the most outstanding example. It was inevitable that, sooner or later, someone would attempt the same treatment with Sherlock Holmes. In 1965 Jerome Coopersmith wrote *Baker Street,* with music and lyrics by Marion Grudoff and Raymond Jessell. It ran for several hundred performances in New York, with Fritz Weaver as Holmes and Peter Sallis as Watson, but never came to England. Its musical content was not outstanding, but it was nevertheless reasonably successful.

As we have seen, after the initial and prolific triumphs of Holmes plays in the early years of this century, a decline set in following World War I, rapidly increasing during the twenties and thirties. After World War II, there was a sporadic resurgence of interest but in quite different patterns, none wholly successful. Once again it looked as if Holmes's theatrical career were over. But the Master Detective, in spite of competition from the cinema, radio and, more recently, television, was not yet finished. The pendulum is now beginning to swing back, and in recent years there has been a marked renaissance—mainly in the sphere of the repertory and London's non–West-End theaters.

The first signs were seen in *Sherlock Holmes and the Speckled Band* in 1968. This drama by David Buxton did not follow Conan Doyle's play of 1910, but went back to the original story of "The Speckled Band." It was produced by the Colchester Repertory Theatre, with Roger Heathcott as Holmes. Two years later, in Perth, Joan Knight attempted with considerable success the ambitious undertaking of adapting *The Hound of the Baskervilles* for the stage, with Tim Preece as Sherlock Holmes. In 1974 the Open Space Theatre in London produced *Sherlock's Last Case* by Matthew Lang—an original play not based on the Conan Doyle stories, but allegedly inspired by Basil Rathbone's films, with Julian Glover in the lead. Fortunately, it was not Holmes's last case, and the encouraging return to adaptations of the original stories was restored. Also in 1974 John Southworth made a strange adaptation of three adventures, "A Case of Identity," "The Mazarin Stone" and "The Dying Detective," which were presented separately in the same program under the title of *Sherlock Holmes of Baker Street*. The play was performed by the Ipswich Drama Centre with Richard Franklin as Holmes, and it was played elsewhere in other repertory theaters in 1975.

The production of four wholly new Sherlock Holmes plays in the last seven years, as well as the recent outstanding revival of

Gillette's *Sherlock Holmes* by the Royal Shakespeare Company,
is indeed a significant augury for the continuance of the splendid
game.

Sherlock Holmes in the Cinema

The views of Sherlock Holmes upon his impersonators and
their adventures in the cinema are, it is feared, like the case associated with the Giant Rat of Sumatra, "a story for which the world
is not yet prepared." The earliest films may perhaps be excused
to some extent, for the cinema was in its infancy, but it is difficult to resist applying Dr. Watson's graphic description of
"ineffable twaddle" to many of the later films—although the exceptions were sometimes memorable and outstanding.

The earliest Holmes film was made in 1900 in America. Titled
Sherlock Holmes Baffled, it was made for a peep-show machine of
the what-the-butler-saw variety. Nevertheless, although only forty-
nine feet in length, it was a true film and not a series of still
photographs mechanically flicked over to give an appearance of ani-
mation. It also used simple trick photography to enable a burglar
to appear and disappear with astonishing rapidity and ultimately
baffle a figure in a dressing gown, who was presumably Sherlock
Holmes. By a fortunate chance of fate, a copy of this film has
survived the years, has been expertly restored, and can still be seen.

The earliest known actor to portray the Master on the screen
was Maurice Costello in *Sherlock Holmes* (or *Held to Ransom*), an
American film of 1903. Although the titles of one or two Holmes
films of European origin in the next five years have been traced,
the first significant stage came between 1908 and 1911, when the
Nordisk Film Company of Denmark embarked on a series of
eleven Holmes films, six of which were written and directed by
Viggo Larsen, who also played Holmes. Another actor who played
Holmes in the Nordisk series was Alwin Neuss, who went on to
play the same role in several later German films. Larsen himself
repeated the role in another series of five films by Vitascope in
Germany and in sundry other films. Such was the success of the
Nordisk series that American, French, German, Hungarian, and
Italian film companies quickly followed suit, and right up to the
early 1920s, numerous Holmes films were seen regularly in the

cinemas. Holmes was pitted against Raffles, Arsène Lupin, and various master criminals, often in incredibly lurid adventures. One such masterpiece, *Sherlock Holmes in The Great Murder Mystery* in 1908, explained that "Holmes goes into a trance to pin a murder on an escaped gorilla—not based on Conan Doyle."

In 1912 came the first authorized series, when Sir Arthur Conan Doyle sold the film rights to the Eclair Company of France. "When these rights were finally discussed and a small sum offered for them . . . it seemed a treasure trove and I was very glad to accept. Afterwards I had to buy them back again at exactly ten times what I had received, so the deal was a disastrous one." Eclair made eight films between 1912 and 1914, all fairly closely based on the original stories; they were made in England with a substantially British cast, although a Frenchman, Georges Treville, portrayed Holmes.

Even though between 1914 and 1918 England and Germany were at war, Germany still continued to make some twenty-one Sherlock Holmes films in this period, including the first version in 1914 of the most filmed of all the stories, *The Hound of the Baskervilles*. Not content with the original ending, one company made five sequels!

The first British Sherlock Holmes film was *A Study in Scarlet*, made by G. B. Samuelson in 1914, and the press was lavish in its praise. Such was the universal popularity of Sherlock Holmes on the screen at this time that an American company hastily made another version of *A Study in Scarlet* in the same year. Encouraged by his success, Samuelson made another Holmes film in 1916. This time it was *The Valley of Fear,* and he cast in the lead H. A. Saintsbury, who had already played Holmes over a thousand times on the stage.

The same year, 1916, saw the now historic film version of the famous play *Sherlock Holmes,* made by Essanay in America, with William Gillette in his original role.

But the real turning point in the history of Sherlock Holmes in the cinema was in 1921 when the Stoll Film Company of Great Britain released *The Adventures of Sherlock Holmes,* first of several series of extremely good films featuring Eille Norwood; forty-seven films were made in all. They were of a very high standard, sincere and, except for modernization, faithful to the

James Bragington, the first British actor to play Sherlock Holmes in the cinema. Here he is in the now standard "Sherlock get-up" as he appeared in the Samuelson production of *A Study in Scarlet,* 1914. *Private collection of Mr. Anthony Howlett.*

Eille Norwood, the British actor, whose filmic Holmes ranked second only to Basil Rathbone's masterly delineation. This still from the Stoll (British) production of *The Adventures of Sherlock Holmes,* 1921, shows the typical Norwood "Holmes" as it became famous throughout the 1920s in no fewer than forty-seven films and numerous stage productions. *Private collection of Mr. Anthony Howlett.*

original stories. Norwood's fine portrayal earned widespread praise, and Conan Doyle himself wrote: "He has that rare quality which can only be described as glamour, which compels you to watch an actor eagerly even when he is doing nothing. He has the brooding eye which excites expectation and he has also a quite unrivalled power of disguise."

One of the last silent films was *Sherlock Holmes* (British title: *Moriarty*) in 1922, starring John Barrymore and Roland Young. The character of Holmes was altered to suit Barrymore's more romantic personality; the plot was substantially that of Gillette's play; and a prologue to the film dealt with Holmes's youth and college career.

The advent of the talking film was an occasion for prompt revival of interest in Sherlock Holmes, and between 1929 and 1939 very many Holmes films were produced in England and America and on the Continent. The first sound film was *The Return of Sherlock Holmes* in 1929 and featured Clive Brook. It illustrates the faults all too familiar in many films of this decade—negligible resemblance to the original stories, glaring anachronisms, and distortions of style and character, even though it must be conceded many were quite good ordinary detective-adventure films of the period. A major fault was that, although the impersonator of Holmes was often a well known and accomplished actor, he all too frequently lacked any physical resemblance to the accepted portrait of Sherlock Holmes, established by the old *Strand Magazine* illustrations and sentimental tradition.

Notwithstanding that the features and figure of Clive Brook were not really Holmesian, he was again cast in *Sherlock Holmes* in 1932. When Raymond Massey (*The Speckled Band,* 1931) and Robert Rendel (*The Hound of the Baskervilles,* 1932) played the role, enthusiasts sighed woefully.

An example of misconceived casting gave Reginald Owen a curious claim to distinction. In 1932 he was Watson to Clive Brook's Holmes, and less than a year later he was cast as Holmes in an unrecognizable version of *A Study in Scarlet.*

The year 1931 was, however, a significant one. It marked the debut of Arthur Wontner as Sherlock Holmes. In the prime of his distinguished career, Wontner gave a portrayal which is widely held to be authoritative. In the words of the late Vincent

Starrett, "No better Sherlock Holmes than Arthur Wontner is likely to be seen and heard in pictures, in our time . . . his detective is the veritable fathomer of Baker Street, in person. The keen, worn, kindly face and quiet, prescient smile are out of the very pages of the book." Lady (Jean) Conan Doyle in a letter to Wontner also expressed her delight in "your really splendid acting . . . and masterly personation of Sherlock Holmes." Arthur Wontner was seen in five films, *The Sleeping Cardinal* in 1931 (based on "The Empty House" and "The Final Problem"), *The Missing Rembrandt* in 1932 (based on "Charles Augustus Milverton"), *The Sign of Four* later the same year, *The Triumph of Sherlock Holmes* in 1935 (a close adaptation of *The Valley of Fear*), and *Silver Blaze* in 1937. These five films are now classics of the Holmesian cinema.

Wontner's successor was nevertheless a formidable challenger, and it is a moot point which was the more satisfactory Holmes. The answer is, of course, neither: each made his own unique contribution. But it is probably true to say that the best-known Sherlock Holmes of the last forty-odd years is Basil Rathbone. In 1939 he made his Holmesian debut in *The Hound of the Baskervilles*. This film has, by almost universal acceptance, come to be regarded by Holmesians as probably the finest Holmes film ever made. For the first time in film history the story was kept correctly in period and, allowing for adaptations necessary in changing to a film medium, followed the original narrative fairly closely. Although Rathbone was to repeat his characterization many times over the following years, he never quite equaled the heights reached here; it was an immensely satisfying portrayal. Later the same year Rathbone appeared in *The Adventures of Sherlock Holmes,* another careful and expensive production by the same studio, Twentieth Century–Fox Film Corp., and one which ranks second only to *The Hound.*

Then came a marked change of style when Basil Rathbone and Nigel Bruce (who had played Watson) moved to the Universal Film studio, where they made a series of twelve more films between 1942 and 1946. This series has been much criticized, mainly because of the poor quality of many of the plots, which were only very remotely based on the original Conan Doyle stories, and also because of the obtrusive modernization. The first three films

Another famous British Holmes: Arthur
Wontner, in a scene from *Silver Blaze*,
1937. Ian Fleming played Dr. Watson,
and John Turnbull made a convincing
Inspector Lestrade. Wontner's portrayal
is widely held to be authoritative, and,
appearing in five Holmes films, Wontner
was the unchallenged Holmes of his day.
*Private collection of Mr. Anthony
Howlett.*

The most famous and enduring Holmes-Watson partnership of them all: two magnificent British film actors in an ideal American setting. Basil Rathbone and Nigel Bruce in a scene from *The Adventures of Sherlock Holmes,* made in the United States, 1939. *Photograph copyright Twentieth Century–Fox, Inc.*

showed Holmes in a wartime setting (one even had Professor
Moriarty as a Nazi agent), but the remaining nine were better
and set in an indeterminate modern period. The best was probably
an adaptation of "The Musgrave Ritual" in 1943 under the title
of *Sherlock Holmes Faces Death*. Today this Universal series has
acquired almost a period charm of its own and, owing to innumerable repeat showings on television, is perhaps the most
widely known.

By the end of the 1940s, television was beginning to oust the
cinema in popular appeal, and film companies were turning over
to films specially made for the new medium. There were odd
abortive attempts which are best forgotten, and it is only necessary to mention a series of thirty-nine films titled *Sherlock Holmes*
made in 1954, with Ronald Howard in the lead. They were incredibly poor and were never accepted for showing in the United
Kingdom.

The next major production was by Hammer Films in 1959 and,
inevitably, *The Hound of the Baskervilles*. It was the first Holmes
film in color, but was a feeble and disappointing production.
Although Peter Cushing, who played Holmes, had meticulously
studied the part, he presented a rather lightweight and prissy
Holmes.

There followed the occasional Holmes film in various parts of
the world, including Germany: *Sherlock Holmes and the Deadly
Necklace* (1962) has a good claim to being the worst Holmes film
ever made since the days of the early silents.

Luckily this depression of the fifties and early sixties did not last,
and 1965 saw an immense improvement with the appearance of
A Study in Terror. It was made in association with the Sir Arthur
Conan Doyle Estate and had John Neville and Donald Houston
as a fine Holmes and Watson. The film related how Sherlock
Holmes solved the Jack the Ripper murders of the 1890s, and although an apocryphal story, the screen play was convincing, and
the gruesome theme was tastefully handled. It was a splendid production, and not since Rathbone's *Hound* of twenty-six years
previously had so fine a Holmes film been seen.

Although there were other Holmes films in 1970–1975, the last
major film was *The Private Life of Sherlock Holmes* in 1970. Directed by the famous Billy Wilder, it was the most expensive and
lavish Holmes film of them all. Originally intended as a revival

of the Holmes tradition, as the London *Times* critic said, "If Wilder came to scoff, he remains to pray at the shrine." The film had of course very considerable merit, but the overall result was disappointing. Robert Stephens's Holmes left much to be desired.

Five years before, *A Study in Terror* had shown the way for Holmesian films in the cinema of today, but it is nevertheless uncertain how the pattern will go in the future. One thing is clear: the indestructible Sherlock Holmes goes on. He will need his indestructibility, for, at the time of writing, another new film is making its rounds. It features Gene Wilder as *Sherlock Holmes's Smarter Brother*.

Some statistics

It is somewhat astounding to recall the number of impersonations of Mr. Sherlock Holmes there have been. The statistics, albeit only approximate, are impressive. There have been some thirty-two legitimate stage plays in the professional theater (it is impossible to estimate the countless revivals or the innumerable translated versions) and at least fifteen music hall or vaudeville sketches and burlesques, probably more. There have been some 196 films, and if one includes comedy films, the total number increases to around 264. In England and America alone there have been over 630 radio plays, and if one includes other countries and also the numerous television plays throughout the world, the number probably approaches a thousand. Sherlock Holmes has also been featured in a ballet, in a musical, in cartoon films, in commercials, in documentary films, in newsreels, and on records. Whatever the medium, the Master is there.

These figures alone demonstrate the affection and esteem with which the world regards this great man who truly became a legend in his own lifetime. It is therefore fitting that the tributes of the theater and the cinema (albeit some are of dubious and questionable memory) should be recalled.

NOTE: This article is an extensively revised and expanded version of one which I wrote in 1954. That article made use of some factual research which had been undertaken with my friend Michael Pointer, and it was published under joint authorship. Pointer has recently written a book which is the definitive work on the subject, *The Public Life of Sherlock Holmes* (Devon: David & Charles, Ltd., 1975).

To refer to the brilliant young author of the most successful Sher-lockian book of recent years, The Seven Percent Solution, *as up-and-coming may seem both patronizing and unjustified. But Mr. Meyer is, for all his success, a newcomer to the Sherlockian scene, and it is precisely this quality which enables him to see certain trends in Sherlockian scholarship with a fresh and discerning eye. Though written independently, and in ignorance of the other contributions to this anthology, Meyer's article reads, not only like percipient general criticism of modern Sherlockian exegesis, but as the shrewdest criticism of some other articles here. His percep-tion of critical trends would appear to be unequaled, as is ap-parent from what he has to say on . . .*

Psychological Directions in Holmesian Criticism
Some Thoughts on the Phenomenon

NICHOLAS MEYER

While Sherlockian criticism may claim to be in a class by itself, when contrasted with more conventional literary commentary it must also be acknowledged that despite this distinction, it does conform to criticism generally in that it has evolved, and will continue to evolve, over a period of years.

Just as one can follow chronologically the patterns of Shakespearean study, it is also possible to view from the present the development of Sherlockian studies over the past eighty or so years. One can see the initial witty experiments of Father Knox grow into complex arguments of chronology and consistency, and from there lead to startling and oftentimes ingenious theories to account for discrepancies and errors in the good Watson's reportage. Besides Father Knox, certain people—illustrious, not to say immortal—gaze down upon us today from their secure place in the pantheon of Sherlockian study: Smith, Starrett, Baring-Gould, Brend, Bell, Holroyd, and Harrison. Together with literally hundreds of others, they have constructed a dynasty of criticism which is unique in literature.

Yet even among themselves, over the years, one can glimpse

changes and permutations in *Weltanschauung*. Oddly enough, the current interest in the Master and his amanuensis appears to be from the psychological point of view, and it is here, for the first time (though the psychologists and their brethren are probably used to it by now), that the first ugly mutterings and imprecations against critical evolution are heard.

Why?

There are reasons; and perhaps, in examining them, we may better come to understand what the psychological viewpoint is about, or rather, what it is supposed to be about. Discovering that, we may find ourselves less threatened by the presence of these "new boy" Holmesians.

In the first place, we must acknowledge that psychological criticism has been with us from the very beginning, though not always dignified with its name. Holmes himself was every inch a psychologist (once he had exhausted the physical clues), when the game was afoot. His search for motivation would have done credit to a Stanislavski ("You would have made a fine actor, Mr. Holmes!") or a Sigmund Freud.

In the second place, we must distinguish between responsible psychological investigation and mere foolery. What does the phrase psychological investigation permit, or appear to permit?

The whole question of biography—for, indeed, that is really what is under discussion here—is a fascinating one from the psychologist's point of view. The twentieth century being the age of biography presents examples galore from which to examine the phenomenon.

Why does a biographer decide to write about a certain subject? When Anton Schindler, the first biographer of Beethoven, refers to his subject as "our hero," is he trying to tell us something? Most certainly he is, and his worshipful bias is the more apparent when we learn that Schindler destroyed over two hundred of Beethoven's conversation books (which the composer used to communicate with because of his deafness) because they did not conform to the picture of "our hero" Schindler wished to paint.

Equally noteworthy at the other extreme is the Freud-Bullitt study of President Woodrow Wilson, where the authors' scarcely concealed hostility occasionally bursts forth into open view with such phrases as "he [Wilson] crept back to the White House . . ."

We can see, then, at the outset, that at its impoverished or perverted extremes, the subject of some biographers receives extravagant bias at their hands, sometimes pro and sometimes con. In either case, history's comprehension of the subject is obscured by a willful veil thrown over his life by a tampering biographer who has shown himself able and ready to suppress facts or inject his own gratuitous views.

Where, in the midst of these extremes, does responsible biographical study fit? Where objectivity is tempered by compassion, not tampered; where truth is pursued with interest, and not with preconceived notions which twist or refuse to acknowledge the facts in order to confirm the theories held by the biographer. Such responsibility, in which the biographer has examined himself and his own feelings as well as those of his subject, is rare indeed; prejudice comes more naturally, it would appear. Yet it is precisely this kind of careful double scrutiny which distinguishes literary study at its best.

The point of all of the foregoing being that what Sherlockians have to fear from the so-called psychological criticism is not the application of principles and methods that Holmes himself would be the first to approve, but the clumsy or biased application of such methods. The Master can be made to appear more than ridiculous or ludicrously sublime, depending on which pernicious extreme is adopted; but what interests us most about him is his great humanity, a humanity based on the three dimensions Watson uses to describe him. Since it is not only unreasonable but foolish to attempt stemming the evolution of criticism and study, let us approach the new literature with an open mind, as the Master himself would suggest, and examine the data placed before us in the calm light of reason. Let the studies which are either lightweight or top-heavy float or sink to their own levels.

Let it further be noted that psychological criticism or psychological biography in no way seeks to diminish the empirical achievements or activities of its subject by ascribing to such activities unconscious motivations and desires. On the contrary, neurotic impulses which are transmuted into artistic or social accomplishment are to be applauded and the more wondered at, for such a transmutation represents the most spectacular and miraculous kind of alchemy.

Thus, in commenting on Holmes, or Watson, or even in investigating Doyle himself, there is no reason for the reasonable Holmesian to become alarmed or take offense. Irresponsible commentary of any kind is always annoying, but the people of whom we speak are of such stature that the puny arrows of gratuitous iconoclasts must inevitably fall far short of their disagreeable mark. And as for responsible psychological investigation, we can only rejoice at those hitherto hidden areas and wellsprings of motivation it succeeds in illumining for us. Psychological criticism, in fact, is ultimately the greatest tribute to the reality of Holmes's and Watson's characters; the more valid it is, the more complete and complex and real those characters must be to support it. Our admiration for Holmes and Watson can only increase when we are made to realize, through the imaginative and careful studies to come, the subtle introspection they are still capable of eliciting.

The subject of this article is one which has generally been avoided, even by the most adventurous of Sherlockian scholars. Not, we believe, out of a false delicacy, but because it has seemed difficult, perhaps impossible, to extract, from Holmes's many references to a Divine Power and a Divine Purpose, his personal religious belief. But we find ourselves today in one of the most religion-oriented societies of the last two thousand years; the epicenter of an explosion of religious sentiment, which, whatever its relation to the traditional, established religions, must have, as its inevitable result, a re-religionizing of society. In these circumstances, it becomes ever more important to know where, in the matter of religious belief, Holmes stood. In this article, the author—himself a licensed minister—presents us with the first serious attempt to analyze Holmes's beliefs, and to answer (we think successfully) the question ...

Did Holmes
Believe in God?

≥

DAVID PEARSON

≥

"You must study him, then," Stamford said,
as he bade me goodbye. "You'll find him a knotty
problem though. I'll wager he learns more about
you than you about him."
—A Study in Scarlet

. . . while those fateful eyes still strained to pierce
the veil.
—The Valley of Fear

I

The intellectual climate in the latter half of the nineteenth century was hardly favorable to orthodox faith. Darwin's theories and
the great advances in technology, as well as a continuing revo-
lutionary ferment among the have-nots, all contributed to a dis-
enchantment with, and distrust of, the established religions.
Long-cherished beliefs were being revised, and spiritual foundations were tottering. Men were increasingly bold in their attacks on
the supernatural elements of early Christian history, and such books
as Winwood Reade's *Martyrdom of Man* won numerous converts

to the ranks of skeptics and pessimists. Hardly any author of note possessed an unshakeable conviction about the divinity of Jesus Christ or of the soul's survival beyond death. Yet the majority were pitifully anxious to cling to a vague spirituality with which they could justify and reinforce their faith in human aspirations. Influential artists such as Matthew Arnold and A. H. Clough expressed despair in one breath and sought to supply bases for hope in the next. Meanwhile, the mass of men, as always, lagged centuries behind the thinkers and continued in their various degrees of unquestioning fidelity.

The above paragraph has been written with the awareness that if one wishes to enter the mind of an individual, one must first place him within his particular milieu. This was the religious milieu of Sherlock Holmes. But it is also said that a man's philosophy cannot be properly understood without knowledge of his intellectual inheritance from his parents. If this be true, it is a great pity that we know so little about the parents of Holmes. We can probably risk the assumption that his early domestic life was fairly typical of mid-Victorian families in the upper middle class. Therefore, we may conjecture that young Sherlock matured within a conventional Protestant home—most likely lukewarm Anglican—with possible undertones of Catholicism derived from his half-French mother. (At least twice during his career we know of cases pursued in the interests of the Vatican.) Considering the relative frequency of his Biblical quotations or allusions, it is reasonable to suggest that he received training in the Scriptures at an early age.

However, further supposition as to sect would be hazardous, except for admitting the extreme unlikelihood of a nonconformist background. Nonconformity scarcely seems a credible creed for such an independent thinker as the youthful Holmes had become by the time of his first case. As he described himself at the time to Watson in "The *Gloria Scott*," he was "always fond of moping in my rooms and working out my own little methods of thought." Because so many nonconformists were notoriously dogmatic and inflexible in their attitudes and opinions, their children were not encouraged to question Holy Writ or to think things through for themselves. Thus, Holmes, with his free spirit of inquiry, was not likely to have been reared in so claustrophobic an environment.

Then, too, since emotion has always been the dynamics of evangelical movements, his passion for reason and distrust of emotion make our vote against a nonconformist Holmes even more of a certainty. (Besides, in "A Scandal in Bohemia," he disguised himself as "an amiable and simple-minded Nonconformist clergyman," which does not imply profound respect for that particular cut of cloth!)

2

When attempting to discover clues to Holmes's belief in God, one is immediately struck by how rarely religion plays a part in his documented career. True, he often quotes—or rather paraphrases—the Scriptures; and although at the conclusion of "The Crooked Man" he claims a "rusty" knowledge of the Bible, he is quick enough to recognize an allusion to the David-Bathsheba-Uriah triangle and employ it as a key to unlocking the Aldershot mystery. But he never seems to attend church services, and he detects as readily on the Sabbath as on other days of the week. In fact, his ignorance of the marriage ceremony in the Church of England is an important aspect of the plot in "A Scandal in Bohemia." Surface hints of any religious inclination or interest, let alone outright orthodoxy, are few and far between. This is not to say that Holmes seems irreligious. Rather, it would appear that to him religion might be listed among those items which Watson—who later, of course, modified his opinions—considered to be immaterial to the Master's work. When Watson is horrified to discover Holmes's ignorance of the Copernican system, Holmes becomes quite impatient: "You say that we go round the sun. If we went round the moon it would not make a pennyworth of difference to me or to my work." And Watson goes on to include "Knowledge of Philosophy—Nil" among his new friend's "limits" for the same reason that he includes Astronomy: vague speculations about "other worlds" are of no value or use in the art of detection. Time and again, especially in the earliest tales of the Canon, we are reminded of what Stamford called Holmes's "passion for definite and exact knowledge." Such a description hardly applies to theology. There is nothing definite and exact about the "science of God," and Christianity would scarcely be called a faith if it were also knowledge. So at the outset, at least, "Did Holmes believe in God?" appears an irrelevance that "would not make a pennyworth of difference."

Nevertheless, pressing on, one is forced to a revision of opinion, even as was Watson about his analysis of the Master's presumed limits. All men in all eras are "religious" in the broadest sense of the word. For present purposes, let us take religion to mean the attitude of individuals in community toward the powers which they conceive as having ultimate control over their destinies and interests. These powers may be benevolent or malignant; they may be fickle; they may be personal or impersonal; they may be called Fate or Providence, Nature or God, Universal Law or the Cosmic Force; they may be Ideas and Movements; and they may simply be individual predilections or governing passions. In searching the Canon, it is possible to identify several "powers," forces, or ideas sacred to Sherlock Holmes. Although they would not be easy to systematize into a creed, they definitely are insights into Holmes, the religious animal. Therefore, if we are not yet ready to render verdict on his belief in God, we may at least consider his other beliefs.

3

In what did Holmes believe—some might cynically add, "besides himself?"

First of all, he had great faith in analytical reasoning and logic. His bent was always toward the scientific and the rational. The cardinal tenet in his religion was respect for the truth. He cherished empirical knowledge. He was a reader of Darwin, whom he quotes in *A Study in Scarlet*. He wrote a celebrated monograph on "Ears." He was enthusiastic about the Bertillon system of measurements. He appreciated the "settled order of Nature," as he calls it in "The Solitary Cyclist," and valued few things as highly as having a workable system or method. In "The *Gloria Scott*" we hear him speak of "those habits of observation and inference which I had already formed into a system." In "The Musgrave Ritual" Watson tells us that "in his methods of thought he was the neatest and most methodical of mankind." And in *The*

Sign of Four, chafing against Watson's embellishment of *A Study in Scarlet* with crude sensationalism, he insists: "The only point in the case which deserved mention was the curious analytical reasoning from effects to causes, by which I succeeded in unraveling it." He (or is it Watson again?) would have us believe him to be a mere thinking machine; certainly from descriptions in the earliest stories this view could be almost justified.

Reasoning from effects to causes was Holmes's professional art and crowning achievement. To accomplish this chain he must have facts. In "The Man With the Twisted Lip" we are told that he would not rest for days on end while wrestling with a problem, "rearranging his facts, looking at it from every point of view until he had either fathomed it or convinced himself that his data were insufficient." When asked to explain a cryptic note in "A Scandal in Bohemia," he replies: "I have no data yet. It is a capital mistake to theorize before one has data. Insensibly one begins to twist facts to suit theories, instead of theories to suit facts." Watson opens "The Five Orange Pips" by explaining that he has not recorded certain cases of Holmes because their explanations were "founded rather upon conjecture and surmise than on that absolute logical proof which was so dear to him." And as example of yet one more instance of this passion, this bit of conversation from *The Hound of the Baskervilles:*

"We are coming into the region of guess-work," said Dr. Mortimer.

"Say, rather, [said Holmes] into the region where we balance probabilities and choose the most likely. It is the scientific use of the imagination, but we have always some material basis on which to start our speculations."

Empirical knowledge, facts, logic, reason—here, clearly, is Holmes the scientist, having, like a true intellectual child of his age, no patience with anything smacking of the supernatural. In more than one adventure he showers scorn on superstition. Concerning the existence of a "Sussex Vampire" he wryly remarks: "But are we to give attention to such things? . . . The world is big enough for us. No ghosts need apply." Regarding "The Devil's Foot" mystery he says, "I fear that if the matter is beyond humanity, then it is certainly beyond me." And, in the spirit of all those who offer rational explanations of Biblical miracles, he silences Watson's accusation in *The Hound of the Baskervilles* as follows:

HOLMES: If the devil did desire to have a hand in the affairs of men—
WATSON: Then you are yourself inclining to the supernatural explanation.
HOLMES: The devil's agents may be of flesh and blood, may they not?

All of this indicates pretty clearly that if Sherlock Holmes had a religion, it would need to be logical and rational in order to satisfy his intellectual conscience. Assuming that he did, in fact, consider the universe an orderly one, it would be interesting to know whether or not he would, after his fashion, deduce that all effects in nature testify to a first cause. For instance, would he not reason that man's mental superiority could not possibly be expected to derive from some accident in chaos? Unfortunately, we shall never know for sure.

4

A second thing in which Holmes strongly believed was moral law. Christianity has no monopoly on moral and ethical values, so we cannot thereby prove his orthodoxy. But he certainly possessed as keen a passion for being on the "right side" as ever man could boast, Christian or no. And he held a firm conviction that right inevitably triumphs and wrong is punished. In "The Resident Patient" he is an advocate of "the sword of justice"; in "The Problem of Thor Bridge" it is actually "the God of justice" whose assistance he claims. In "The Illustrious Client" he almost preaches in his zeal: "The wages of sin, Watson—the wages of sin! . . . Sooner or later it will always come." When Dr. Grimesby Roylott of "The Speckled Band" (surely one of the most unforgettable villains in the entire Canon) meets his horrible death by the very means which he intended for others, Holmes's nemesis approaches Old Testament self-righteousness when he says with grim satisfaction, "Violence does, in truth, recoil upon the violent, and the schemer falls into the pit which he digs for another."

The presence of good and evil in the world was real to Holmes. His remark about the "devil's agents" indicates this. He refers to Charles Augustus Milverton as being "as cunning as the Evil

One." And as much as he respected science, a scientist without a moral conscience—such as Moriarty—was anathema to him. (In this sense we can see that Holmes would never substitute science for God.) That curious and disputed case called "The Creeping Man" contains a choice bit of Holmesian moral philosophy occasioned by an attempt at rejuvenation which backfires horribly:

"When one tries to rise above Nature one is liable to fall below it. The highest type of man may revert to the animal if he leaves the straight road of destiny. . . . Consider, Watson, that the material, the sensual, the worldly would all prolong their worthless lives. The spiritual would not avoid the call to something higher. It would be the survival of the least fit. [A Darwinian echo.] What sort of cesspool may not our poor world become?"

Watson's estimate of Holmes as "the best and wisest man" is partly a moral judgment. The Master would hardly be so well loved among all the great literary figures were he not so *good*. The very nature of his profession, as well as his intense personal pride, his kindness, courtesy and warm humanity, his sympathy with the downtrodden—all help to line him up in the ranks of Right. Anticipating his possible demise in the Alps, he tells Watson: "If my record were closed tonight I could survey it with equanimity. The air of London is the sweeter for my presence. In over a thousand cases I am not aware that I have ever used my powers upon the wrong side." So once more we can affirm that Holmes believed in moral law and the supremacy of good over evil.

5

Closely connected with the foregoing argument, it is also safe to say that Holmes believed in human progress. His faith in the future was a tough one. We cannot know on what he based such optimism, but we do have some evidence that he approved of the wide-sweeping social reforms in the England of his day. In "The Naval Treaty" he waxes most enthusiastic about the board-schools, referring to them as "lighthouses" and "beacons of the future . . . out of which will spring the wiser, better England." Obviously he was concerned with the betterment of mankind, and just as any creed (for him) would necessarily be an intellectual one, so any gospel would be a social one. A religion that did not

Where Holmes *could* have prayed. The interior of St. Bartholomew-the-Great, the "parish church" of St. Bartholomew's Hospital ("Bart's"), in whose "Path. Lab." Holmes and Watson first met. *Conrad Research Library.*

place reliance on human reason and work for human advancement would not appeal.

On at least one occasion the Master indicated a hope in benevolent purposes working through history. In "His Last Bow," Watson metaphorically sets the scene for that "most terrible August in the history of the world" by speaking of "God's curse" on man's degeneracy. However, at the end of the story, the aging Holmes counters this view in one of the most poetic and moving passages in the entire Canon:

"Good old Watson! You are the one fixed point in a changing age. There's an east wind coming all the same, such a wind as never blew on England yet. It will be cold and bitter, Watson, and a good many of us may wither before its blast. But it's God's own wind none the less, and a cleaner, better, stronger land will lie in the sunshine when the storm has cleared."

Where Holmes could have prayed even more conveniently: St. Paul's Portman Square, which stood at the south end of Baker Street. It has recently been demolished. *Contrad Research Library.*

Here we see that Holmes does not flinch from the prospect of personal suffering or death. He is realistic about life, and understands that the way to salvation lies through countless trials and perils. But that a kind of salvation is ultimate, be it only in human terms and on the human scene, he never doubts. Man is rational. Logic will triumph. Good will result.

6

Thus far what we have said does not really show that Sherlock Holmes had the slightest interest in the greatest mystery of all. Is there documented proof of his attitude toward the infinite? Despite first impressions, the answer is definitely yes, a great deal of proof, some of it revealing a positive side to his philosophy and some of it a negative. Let us begin with the negative.

Several times in the Canon we hear the Hardyesque voice of futility and despair coming from the Master's lips. Witness the following:

From "The Boscombe Valley Mystery"

"Why does Fate play such tricks with poor helpless worms?"

From "The Veiled Lodger"

"Poor girl!" he said. "Poor girl! The ways of Fate are indeed hard to understand. If there is not some compensation hereafter, then the world is a cruel jest."

From "The Retired Colourman"

"But is not all life pathetic and futile? Is not his [Josiah Amberley's] a microcosm of the whole? We reach. We grasp. And what is left in our hands at the end? A shadow. Or worse than a shadow—misery."

From "The Cardboard Box"

"What is the meaning of it, Watson?" said Holmes, solemnly, as he laid down the paper. "What object is served by this circle of misery and violence and fear? It must tend to some end, or else our universe is ruled by chance, which is unthinkable. But what end? There is the great standing problem to which human reason is as far from an answer as ever."

This is the voice of the times. It is Hardy and Arnold and Clough all over again. If it were not so somber and gloomy, one could call it a shaking of the human fist at the universe. We would like to know when Holmes first encountered Winwood Reade's *Martyrdom of Man*. Perhaps it was while in the university or even earlier. Nevertheless, in *The Sign of Four* he strongly recommends this pessimistic book to Watson. Greatly acclaimed in its day, Reade's attack on religious beliefs contains an indictment of the most cherished belief of all—the immortality of the soul. Therefore, we would also like to know to what extent Sherlock Holmes agreed with him. For him to have been so enthusiastic in the first place argues that he must have admired the thought processes of the celebrated controversialist and found his conclusions stimulating. Incidentally, in chapter ten of the same novel he paraphrases Reade on one point—i.e., whereas it is impossible to predict what individuals will do, the great number of men "remain constant" and predictable in their behavior. Obviously, knowing this is a tremendous asset to a consulting detective. The discussion is occasioned by Watson's suggestion that man is a. "soul concealed in an animal." Holmes agrees that there may well be an "immortal spark" in people, regardless of their position on the social ladder; but he admits that, after all, we are a "strange enigma." Our place in the scheme of things is a mystery in itself, and our destiny is a blind one. So much for the negative Holmes.

7

To find the positive Holmes let us review evidences of three characteristics: a) his sense of wonder, whimsicality, and humility; b) his essentially open-minded attitude; and c) his suspicion of a benevolent creation. To take the first, Holmes says in "The Mazarin Stone," "Life is full of whimsical happenings, Watson." In "The Blue Carbuncle" he refers to "only one of those whimsical little incidents which will happen when you have four million human beings all jostling each other within the span of a few square miles." And the opening of "A Case of Identity" contains his personal belief that truth is stranger than any fiction, rendering unnecessary Watson's constant proneness to romanticize the cases. Holmes might be indulging in a bit of whimsicality in *The Valley of Fear* when he calls himself "a believer in the genius loci." The pagan idea of deities presiding over a particular place is, of course, the reference; certainly modern psychics are gifted with the ability to "read the atmosphere" of, for instance, a room in which a crime has been committed. Whether or not the Master truly possessed this gift, whether or not he was simply being whimsical, the allusion is an interesting one.

We need not wonder about his attitude toward his art. In "The Copper Beeches" he describes it as a "thing beyond myself." He claims no personal credit for that which he cannot comprehend. His spirit is, in fact, the spirit of the devout scientist who realizes the limits of his knowledge and faces the infinite in deep humility. In *The Sign of Four,* Holmes has this to say:

"How small we feel, with our petty ambitions and strivings, in the presence of the great elemental forces of Nature! . . . [J. P. Richter] makes a curious but profound remark. It is that the chief proof of man's greatness lies in his perception of his own smallness. It argues, you see, a power of comparison and of appreciation which is in itself a proof of nobility."

In similar spirit did the author of the eighth Psalm express his wonder about man's place in creation.

Second, when we consider how broad- and open-minded a man was Sherlock Holmes, we are made aware that he would never ultimately give in or give up. He would not close the books on the mystery of life. In "The Red Circle" he says, "Education never ends, Watson. It is a series of lessons, with the greatest for the last." When Watson, in *A Study in Scarlet,* objects to the breadth of a controversial Darwinian theory to which Holmes has alluded, the Master explains, "One's ideas must be as broad as Nature if they are to interpret Nature." No one could ever accuse him of believing in a God too small! To Holmes the imagination is boundless, as he makes plain in *The Valley of Fear:*

". . . there should be no combination of events for which the wit of man cannot conceive an explanation. Simply as a mental exercise, without any assertion that it is true, let us indicate a possible line of thought. It is, I admit, mere imagination, but how often is imagination the author of truth."

Not for him the motto of so many undergraduates: "Don't confuse me with the facts. My mind is already made up!" It would hardly be in keeping with his free spirit of inquiry for Holmes to be satisfied for very long with such a simple way out as futility.

Third, what about his "suspicion of a benevolent creation"?
There is in "The Naval Treaty" what might be called the only
truly religious soliloquy in the entire Canon, the only recorded
instance of Holmes's definite and certain attitude toward that
which we earlier suspected of being "immaterial" to his work.
Although Watson (in "The Cardboard Box") credited him with
no appreciation of nature, we find Holmes, in philosophical mood,
interrupting his detection to admire a moss rose:

"There is nothing in which deduction is so necessary as in religion,"
said he, leaning with his back against the shutters. "It can be built up as
an exact science by the reasoner. Our highest assurance of the goodness
of Providence seems to me to rest in the flowers. All other things, our
powers, our desires, our food, are really necessary for our existence in
the first instance. But this rose is an extra. Its smell and its color are an
embellishment of life, not a condition of it. It is only goodness which
gives extras, and so I say again that we have much to hope from the
flowers."

Possibly Holmes was remembering Jesus's lesson drawn from the
lilies. Nevertheless, his remarks cannot reasonably be forced into
an orthodox mold. When he speaks of a "goodness which gives
extras," he may or may not have in mind the personal God of
Christianity. But at least there is a positive assurance here, and a
reasonable ground for hope. In this one passage the Master comes
nearest to revealing his private formula for belief, founded, as one
would expect, upon empirical observation and a certain logic—
reasoning backward from effects to causes. The stiff-necked skeptics might call it wishful thinking, but surely it is as sensible as
many other theories, and perhaps more so than most.

8

What about philosophical development? Unfortunately, tracing
any sort of growth in Holmes is virtually impossible because of the
nature of the tales, where the principal business is, of course,
detection and entertainment. They were not intended to be philosophical or theological documents, and we have already seen that
even the slightest allusions to such matters are extremely scattered
and incidental. If one ascribes traditionally accepted years to the
cases cited, he will find that—so far as anyone can tell—the mind

of the Master remained basically consistent in its outlook. Sometimes, after he has appeared to be moving toward the hopelessness of determinism, he expresses himself in a way that implies a solidly grounded hope. His cardinal principles are unchanging, and if he seems to become more human and emotional in later cases, it is only because of Watson's limited understanding in the earliest ones. Naturally, so intelligent and broad-minded a man was never too far along to welcome new ideas; but by the time we meet him as a young student in "The *Gloria Scott*" he is already very much the spiritual "father" to the aging fifth-columnist in "His Last Bow."

9

To summarize, we have seen that Holmes believed strongly in such concepts as reason, logic, moral law, and human progress. When considering creation, he displayed a sense of wonder and humility, and his conversation sometimes suggested that the universe must have a basis of intelligence—even a benevolent one, from whom or what we might hope much. But what about God? Can we now answer the query of our title? We are as ready now as we shall ever be. The fact of the matter is that Holmes rarely uses the word. Dozens of characters, including Watson, call upon God's name, particularly in the heightened emotion of an oath. However, Holmes almost never does. In this writer's opinion, the three principal occasions on which he refers to "God" are:

1) when he is relating his miraculous escape at the Reichenbach Falls, and attributes it to "the blessing of God";

2) When, in "The Disappearance of Lady Frances Carfax," he wonders what has happened to "the brains God has given me"; and

3) in the famous quotation from "His Last Bow" discussed earlier, in which he speaks of "God's own wind" bringing in a better England.

In all three instances the expression is vaguely, perhaps even popularly, used, and could just as easily be taken to mean Fate or Providence or Nature, terms he employs much more frequently, after all. This is perhaps more true of the first quotation, which implies that the powers that be are fickle. It is a common enough saying, as is the second one. In the third there is a strong suggestion of benevolent purposes working behind the scenes in human history, but the God of the orthodox Christian should not be taken for granted here. To say the least, the evidence for assuming that a personal, anthropomorphic deity is meant in this quotation is inconclusive.

Again, one cannot help but experience frustration that the world's greatest solver of mysteries left us no possible solution to the greatest mystery of all. Although he maintained that religion "can be built up as an exact science by the reasoner," we search in vain for his monograph on God. What a work that would have been! How impoverished is human thought without it! *Or did he find his data insufficient?*

In conclusion, those who attempt to pigeonhole the Master into a particular creed or sect are hardly justified by the writings. His free, inquiring spirit could never be bound by dogma—it would be analogous to trying to bottle sunlight. The very most this writer can attribute to him in terms of religious outlook is that of the liberal deist, a man imaginative, independent, and open-minded to the end, daring to hope—even expect—brighter tomorrows, willing to trust in floral (and other) evidences of a benevolent intelligence or design, yet psychologically prepared for ultimate disappointment if it come. Most of all, he envisions a Holmes of valiant stoicism, reminding Mrs. Ronder when she asks of what use is her life: "How can you tell? The example of patient suffering is in itself the most precious of all lessons to an impatient world."

It is to be hoped there will be "some compensation hereafter"; that the universe is not "ruled by chance." But one can imagine Sherlock Holmes in his Sussex twilight, serenely dividing his hours between "philosophy and agriculture," often quoting to himself a scriptural passage which appears, paraphrased, no fewer than three times in the Canon. That passage is Luke 21:19, taken from Christ's counsel concerning the Last Days: "In your patience possess ye your souls." Perhaps this verse, after all, should be the Master's epitaph.

The parodies, crude or subtle, of Sherlock Holmes may now be of a respectable antiquity: they began to appear not long after the first appearance of the Master himself. Who hasn't heard of—and, indeed, laughed at—such comic paper characters as Sheerluck Bones or his more polished modern successor (still going strong), Schlock Homes? But that imitation which is the sincerest flattery had another—and now less known—manifestation: a mass-produced Sherlock Holmes series of adventures which reached European best-sellerdom before World War I. Here two Sherlockian scholars (one Canadian, the other Austrian) describe the origin, circulation, and success of this immense plagio-corpus, and come to the conclusion that . . .

This Is Not *Our* Sherlock!

PART I

DONALD A. REDMOND

That the earliest English-language parodies and pastiches using the character of Sherlock Holmes appeared in the 1890s, almost immediately upon Holmes's becoming a national figure, is well known to most avid readers. That an extensive literature of Sherlock Holmes, not as parody but as straightforward non-Canonical adventures of the great detective, began to appear soon after the turn of the century in the major languages of Europe must be much less well known—especially as none of this plagio-corpus appears to be available in translation. Its extent is immense. One German series alone comprises more than 230 tales, each of some 25,000 words—a total of 5,750,000 words compared to the 660,000 of the entire Canon. Lachat mentions at least four such series and "at least three hundred" tales appearing between 1907 and 1930.[1] This in addition to tales written originally in Spanish and Portuguese!

The Metropolitan Toronto Central Library holds an extensive but far from complete file of the Spanish and Portuguese "plagiates,"* acquired in the fine collection purchased from Harold Mortlake Ltd. Many of them are translations of the German series *Aus den Geheimakten des Weltdetektivs,* the originals of which were made more available by the Olms Press reprinting of fifteen tales in 1973.[2]

Foltin's introduction to this reprint volume is the source of much of the following detail. He dates the *Geheimakten* between 1907 and 1911–12, one of innumerable *Trivialliteratur* series churned out by such firms as the Verlagshaus für Volksliteratur und Kunst (Publishing House for Popular Literature and Art) using anonymous hack writers. Luckily it is known that one contributor to the Sherlock Holmes series was Kurt Matull (Matull-Berns). The series title of the first ten numbers was "Detective Sherlock Holmes and His World-Famous Adventures." Predictably the holders of the German rights to the Canon, Messrs. Robert Lutz, forced the removal of this title, and the series became "From the Secret Operations of the World[-Famous] Detective." Olms Press reprinted fifteen of these:

2. The Bloody Jewels
4. The Moneylender's Daughter
9. The Lady with the Canary Brilliant
15. The Slave-Dealer's Treasure
33. The Firebugs of New York
40. The Mystery of the Tower Room

---

* Despite correspondence between Dr. Krejci-Graf and Mr. Redmond—and between this scholastic-Sherlockian partnership and myself—on the admissibility, within an English text, of the word *plagiate,* I have decided to retain it. It does not exist officially in accepted English, but I think that we could well do with this word. In his article on p. 21, Jacques Barzun has brilliantly defined the meanings which differentiate parody, pastiche, and plagiarism; but there is another class of work, owing its inspiration to the ideas of other writers, that does not fall within these classifications. This class of work, to which the name plagiate may conveniently now be given, is, as it were, an extension of the original theme. Parody's function is to mock; that of pastiche to imitate without suspicion of plagiarism; plagiarism is the conversion (legal term) of another's work—characters and/or ideas—in order to pass it off as one's own. No such fraudulent intention is perceptible in the plagiates of which Redmond and Krejci-Graf write: the hundreds of para-Holmes simply went on to describe adventures that Sir Arthur Conan Doyle had not described, but which (given a great deal of half-witted credulity) he might well have written. Plagiate is the word, then!—*Ed.*

42. The Maiden-Murderer of Boston
46. A Criminal Doctor
47. The Lady with the Veil
52. Outrage at a Hamburg Cycle Track
56. The Vampire of London
57. The Drama in the Circus Angelo
71. Under Strange Compulsion
74. The Slave-Dealer of Constantinople
80. Raid on the Dresden Fair

Comparison of the titles of the first eighty-one numbers, listed in
No. 80, with the titles of the Portuguese series, of which the
Toronto library holds nearly two hundred, shows that the German
tales were translated, but in a different sequence. The lurid-
colored covers, most showing Holmes in peril of life, were re-
drawn, but a sardonic pipe-smoking profile of Holmes still appears
in the upper corner, identifiable enough even without his name
on the cover. Some tales even appear in more than one version.
No. 9 of one series, "O Roubo do Diamante Azul" (reminiscent of
"The Blue Carbuncle"), appears in another series as No. 1, "O
Roubo de Brilhante Azul."

But this is not our Sherlock. Resemblance to persons living or
dead is purely coincidental. Occasional traces of the true Holmes
flash out, as Foltin notes, but this is by and large a counterfeit
Holmes, a celluloid Tarzan swinging through papier-mâché trees,
and risking his neck by his own celerity and occasional stupidity.
The tales come close to formula; the hack is evident. It is almost
possible to predict the page on which Holmes will find the trace
of the villain, become entrapped, be rescued, and finally bring
the desperado to account.

Watson, by the way, does not appear. Young Harry Taxon, as
Foltin notes, is Holmes's *famulus* (the German usage for a graduate student assistant) or detective-in-training, as well as butler,
secretary, and errand boy added for young readers to identify
with; Lachat remarks, "if not wholly added as a stooge (*Lust-
knabe*), who behaves as masochistically true and devoted as a
Prussian orderly." In later series Harry Taxon even gets first
billing, as *Harry Taxon und sein Meister,* while another series is
simply *Weltdetektiv.* While Harry has relatively little to do, he

occasionally makes up in agility and keenness for old Watson's blithe obtuseness, and for the pseudo-Holmes's own blundering.

The Slave-Dealer's Treasure

Summary of a typical story is worthwhile. The tales frequently begin with a scene between Harry Taxon and Holmes, not unlike the Canonical prooemium in 221B Baker Street. Some indeed do begin there, but this is no Baker Street known to London: a villa with electric bells and some forerunner of television to reveal who is at the garden gate; the household presided over by the faithful Mrs. Bonnet. In this story, Holmes, immersed in the familiar litter of newspapers, is ruminating over a death notice. A client is soon announced, Notary O'Brien, whom Holmes astonishes by announcing to him his precise errand: that the will of the dead man, a quondam slave-dealer named Firmont, is missing from O'Brien's own safe. "The matter is wholly charming," declares Holmes—a nice touch of the old Holmes.

At the scene, Holmes discovers a hair from a black man entangled in the key ring on which is the safe key. The clothes of the trusted night attendant, Jamesson, who was to watch over the safe, have been fished out of the Thames. Jamesson himself, who had been found in a pool of blood, unconscious, has now disappeared; Inspector Wilson concludes he has been murdered. On page 4 (each story is complete in 32 pages) Holmes makes a photomicrograph of blood from the scene and finds it to be pig's blood. He and Harry Taxon conclude that three former accomplices of Firmont, aware that he has hidden a treasure of jewels and gold dust, have staged the theft of the will. One of the three is Jamesson, notwithstanding that he has been with O'Brien for a year; another is the black man.

At Firmont's dwelling they meet his adopted daughter, a charming quadroon child. She reveals a mortal fear of Maori, a black man and former acquaintance of Firmont. On the walls are trophies of the chase and African weapons, among which Holmes finds an arrow which, by experimenting upon a stray cur, he finds to be poisoned with curare. Shades of Mrs. Hudson's poor sick terrier! He concludes that Firmont was murdered by Maori.

Jamesson's body has now been found, and Holmes in the

morgue does the work of Spilsbury: concluding, from the new garments it bears, that the original intent was to give the impression of murder by drowning. But he finds signs of strangulation, and in the throat a piece of paper. Jamesson and Maori had fallen out, and the black had attempted to prevent his swallowing it. Holmes reconstructs the sodden paper photographically to find Firmont's message: that his daughter Zaire knows the hiding place of the treasure, the "monument of Giacomo Diabelli." Diabelli turns out to have been a popular sculptor of tombstones, and a rash of upsetting tombstones in the night ensues. Holmes and Taxon stand watch in Westminster churchyard, only to be taken themselves for grave robbers, while the true culprits escape, having meanwhile tricked Harry into relaxing his guard, and kidnaping Zaire.

In the suburb of Mortlake, in London's dockland, Holmes and Harry, disguised as Uncle Tom and his niece Jenny, fiddle and sing in local haunts of black seamen, to no avail in the search for Maori. (Holmes is constantly disguising himself in beards and outlandish costumes, even if he immediately rips off the beard to reveal his true identity.) They quaff "a mixture of sherry brandy and soda water" in the pub. Harry discovers the house in which Maori has stayed, and they let themselves in, to find it empty save for a man tied hand and foot in the cellar—"Blue Jack" Brown, whom Harry recognizes as the spurious policeman who lured Zaire away. In gratitude for his rescue, Blue Jack throws in his lot with Holmes.

Concluding that Maori has decamped for France, Holmes shifts his attention to Paris. There, disguised now as the "Marquis Montrosa," he visits the singing teacher, Professor Jules Lararque, really a white-slave dealer to whom Maori is to hand over Zaire. Blue Jack, however, reveals that Maori is going to attempt to dispose of Zaire otherwise. Holmes, now in the guise of a workman (an "unshaven French ouvrier"?), starts off for Maori's (conveniently found) address, encounters the pair on the street, and follows them to the Paris zoo. Here Maori, having drugged the girl, leaves her to fall from an elevation into the polar bears' cage—to be saved in the nick of time by Holmes.

Holmes now attempts to penetrate the Paris catacombs (not the sewers), where Blue Jack says Maori has hidden his treasure.

A. CONAN DOYLE

AVENTURAS DE SHERLOCK HOLMES

O TERROR DE LONDRES

2

A. Conan Doyle, *Aventuras de Sherlock Holmes:* "O Terror de Londres" (Colecção Policial, #2, Publicação para adultos). Portuguese translation of a German "Sherlock Holmes" story not by Doyle. *Copyright: Donald A. Redmond.*

Aventuras Extraordinarias de Sherlock Holmes: Conan Doyle: "O Bandido Negro." Portuguese plagiarism. *Copyright: Donald A. Redmond.*

Memorias íntimas del Rey de los Detectives

Una corrida de toros en Granada

Memorias íntimas del Rey de los Detectives, #39: "Una corrida de toros en Granada." "Stronger than a charging bull"—Holmes in the bull ring, in a Spanish plagiarism. *Copyright: Donald A. Redmond.*

Holmes saves an apache in a fight, is introduced to the apache gang and succeeds in entering the catacombs, only to be tricked by Maori and left to die lost in the trackless maze. Blue Jack outwits Maori at the top of the shaft to the catacombs, wrings the secret of the treasure from him and lets him drop to his death. As the catacombs become "hotter and hotter," Blue Jack penetrates them, only to be blown to bits by the booby trap which guarded the treasure. Holmes reaches the open air, to return with Harry and find the jewel chest; but poor Zaire never recovers from the drugging, and the treasure goes to charitable ends.

Pauline, Move Over

In the course of the secret adventures, Holmes is dropped out of a castle window by a mad scion of a noble family; walled up in blocks of ice by a mad doctor; threatened by a mad butcher who converts lesbians into sausage; and nailed into a wine barrel by a gang of arsonists who set the building ablaze around him. He becomes a crack shot in a circus; is knocked unconscious and set to drift over a Danube waterfall in an oarless boat, and, later in the same story, is tied up to be thrown into the Bosporus by an enraged Turk after he has posed as an old Turkish physician for some weeks.

The police are the usual misguided muddlers. The description of English judicial processes is remarkable—closely resembling French procedure, with frequent mention of "investigating magistrates," suspects being summarily incarcerated while proof is found, and even the near-use of the guillotine while red-coated soldiers stand guard. The geography of London is sometimes accurate, even if the Midland Railway from St. Pancras through the tunnel under Finchley Road and Haverstock Road (not "Haverstockfield") does not go to Southend.

There are reminiscent bits in this last story. The (First) Lord of the Admiralty begs Holmes to solve a mystery of a missing submarine; and Holmes reads on a visiting card, "Superintendent Lionel Small, Rector of Kings-Shool [sic] Boarding School for Boys rank," and is begged to solve the mystery of pupils who disappear abruptly while swimming in the Thames. As Foltin notes, the writer knows his Canon well. The lady with the veil, however, is

no lady. Like the man with the iron chin, she (he) is spotted while
Holmes (alone, or with Harry Taxon) is on a constitutional stroll
through London; and it is remarkable how often the key character, nay more the villain, is spotted by page 4. Seldom does
Holmes actually engage in ratiocination or deduction. The best
example, too brief, is in the "Outrage at a Hamburg Racetrack."

Holmes is interrupted at breakfast by an agitated visitor who
thrusts himself past Mrs. Bonnet (shades of Mrs. Hudson's ex-
postulation over abrupt visitors!). Professor Munroe, the inventor
of a new explosive, has had it stolen. The police have arrested a
man loitering outside the professor's house in Portland Place and
found in his pockets the keys to the professor's laboratory. Holmes,
calming his client, accompanies him to his "two-storied villa . . .
which lay behind a narrow front garden," a "neat little building."
Having heard that the professor's assistant had reported sick and
committed himself to a hospital, and heard the arrested suspect's
story of a man who told him to report for work at Professor
Munroe's and gave him a packet to bring, Holmes dashes away,
to return an hour later. ". . . In the previously cold, dispassionate
features of the great criminalist a noticeable excitement was reflected, such as only very special causes called forth in him. 'Quick,
Professor! Get your hat and come,' cries Holmes. 'You must accompany me on an excursion.' " The game is still afoot, as they
drive to the Golden Cross Hospital and discover that the supposedly sick assistant is not there but has substituted a doddering
old man. Holmes then explains his reasoning. As is typical, by
page 8 he has identified the criminal. The remaining complica-
tions in the story are the twists and turns by which Holmes manages to get himself into difficulties while pursuing the villain, who
successively escapes. In this particular story, the criminous Joe
Blackburne is captured on board the ship *Nordstern* (North
Star) but not before he has lit one of the new explosives, which
has a two-minute ignition time. The ship is battling through
tremendous seas, and in a bald *deus ex machina* ending, a mighty
wave extinguishes the explosive and saves Holmes and all.

Boston, New York, and Points West

The original of the "maiden-murderer of Boston" is obviously
Herman W. Mudgett, alias H. H. Holmes, *fl.* 1890s, *d.* abruptly

7 May 1896 of suspense via a rope, and who according to the Chicago *Tribune* "murdered at least six young women" in a labyrinth in his basement. There are references to this prominent character in the *Baker Street Journal*, vol. 20, pages 63 and 127 (1970), the latter quoting the *Tribune* of 27 March. Whether these were lesbians and converted into sausage is not therein mentioned, but it is not a far step to throw in a bit of Sweeney Todd of Fleet Street and meat pie infamy.

To give the "world detective" flavor, the tales take place almost as widely as Watson's experience of women, in "many nations and three separate continents." While the first tale in the Olms Press selection begins in the proper Baker Street atmosphere—

A foggy, genuine London autumn day had dawned over the mighty Babel on the Thames. The September sun labored to steal in through the windows of an elegant ground-floor bachelor dwelling in Baker Street.

(How Mrs. Hudson's airy rooms have changed!)

"The early mail already here?" asked the occupant of the rooms, a lean, tall, beardless man in his forties, with energetic features and shrewd, penetrating eyes.

—but the plot of this tale stems from Tehran. Most often, wherever the action is laid, Holmes happens conveniently to be in town—attracting crime as a light does moths. Paris, Hamburg, Boston, New York have been mentioned. The firemen on the cover of the New York tale wear brass helmets magnificently French in style. From "Gloster Castle, the former Benedictine abbey of St. Rochus," somewhere, it would seem, on the Welsh coast, the shady proprietor undertakes to drive to London in his own "cab." The Circus Angelo, which Holmes joins temporarily, is in Vienna. The case *Unter Fremden Willen* (Under Strange Compulsion) takes Holmes from "Kapstadt" to the South African "Kaffir lands." The slaver of Constantinople takes him from London to Bucharest, down the Danube, and on to the threshold of Asia. The folk festival in Dresden begins in a Berlin café and skips from Leipzig to Dresden. The Continental Bradshaw gets as much use in these tales as does the original in the Canon.

The writer has some difficulty with Scottish names, never being quite sure whether the "head of the criminal police" of London is named Gordon or McGordon, or at another time Duff or Macduff. English phrases are thrown in here and there for atmosphere —"old boy" to Harry Taxon; London "policemen" appear, but it sounds odd to have the discoverer of a crime cry, "Zu Hilfe! Die Lady ist ermordet!"—slightly reminiscent, Vincent Starrett would recall, of the broken German of Chicago's Nortseit of old. And "all right" is never in its English sense.

The German and "continental vogue," not only for the treatise on the binomial theorem, but for Sherlock Holmes and other characters whom Foltin mentions—Nick Carter, Lord Percy, otherwise Percy Stuart, and hundreds of others of putative English or American antecedent—ranks with the detective pulps of American origin as popular culture. But they are far more *romans policiers* than they are true detective stories. This Sherlock is much closer to Lecoq the bungler than to the companion of Doctor Watson. The intellectual exercise of solving the crime is not there, as Foltin points out. Indeed, only the idiot police would have difficulty finding the criminal, who is early and obvious on the scene. It is the excitement of the chase, the peril to the hero, and his larger-than-life achievements which give the thrill. Holmes is wiry of muscle; he is a crack shot who gives advice to circus professionals and beats them at rapid fire. In one story alone, that ending in Constantinople, Holmes is fluent in Hungarian, Rumanian, and Turkish, not to mention German and French— indeed, in "most of the European languages," it is casually mentioned. He reminds one slightly of Leacock's Great Detective, furiously seizing and changing disguises, not to mention galloping off in all directions.

This is not our Holmes. He cannot really be taken seriously as such; but he must be taken seriously as the major picture which popular culture in the European languages has of Holmes, and the one which by pervasiveness must well have overshadowed the Canon in Europe for the first quarter of the century. This imitation is sincere flattery indeed.

NOTES

1. Pierre Lachat, "Der Welt erster Detektiv-Berater: Sherlock Holmes, Fakten und Fiktionen," *Tages-Anzeiger Magazin* (Zürich), nr. 49 (7 Dec. 1974), pp. 28–38.

2. *Sherlock Holmes: aus den Geheimakten des Weltdetektivs*, 15 Lieferungshefte in einem Band, mit einem Vorwort von Hans-Friedrich Foltin. Hildesheim; New York: Olms Press, 1973.

This Is Not *Our* Sherlock!

❦

PART II

K A R L   K R E J C I - G R A F

❦

First I will tell you how I came to know about the pastiches, which
at that time were called *Schundhefte** (trash books), not to be
seen by parents or teachers. My father had bought the Lutz edition
of *Study in Scarlet, Sign of Four, Adventures, Memoirs,* the
Hound, and the *Return* (Leipzig, 1902–1908). The last volume
(IX) contained a preface stating "Sir Artur Conan Doyle wird
keine Sherlock Holmes-Abenteuer mehr schreiben; er hatte diesen
Enthschluss in England öffentlich bekannt gegeben, als dort die
'Tanzenden Männchen' erschienen. —Weitere Sherlock Hol-
mesgeschichten sind also von ihm nicht zu erwerten." (Sir
Arthur Conan Doyle will write no more Sherlock Holmes adven-
tures. He made this publicly known in England when "The
Dancing Men" appeared. —Accordingly, no further Sherlock
Holmes stories may be expected from him.) The volume con-
tained "The Cardboard Box," "Charles Augustus Milverton,"

---

* In England they were known as Penny Dreadfuls, Penny Bloods (i.e., Blood-
  and-Thunders), or simply as Bloods. Despite their unchallengeable morality,
  they were always confiscated and destroyed by parents and schoolmasters.
  —*Ed.*

"The Three Students," "The Missing Three-Quarter," and three non-Canonical stories. The books are still in my possession.

We lived in a small town at the frontier of Bohemia (but a town, in all probability, since the tenth century, when Heinrich der Städtegründer gave town charters to many frontier settlements; in the earliest documents of the thirteenth century, the place has already acquired the status of a chartered township). In 1908 I had to enter the *Gymnasium* (high school) at Budweis—now Ceske Budojovice, Bohemia—the nearest to my home town, and then still with the majority of its inhabitants German or German-speaking (in the following year, the Germans had dropped to a minority of 48 percent).

Now, in about the fourth year at the *Gymnasium*, it happened that I observed that one of my comrades—not very diligent, but a good comrade—frequently went to the house of one of our teachers, to clean the teacher's bicycle.

I couldn't understand this contradiction and asked him about it, being insistent when he tried to evade the question, and as others became attentive he told me, "Halts Maul, wir reden später." (Hold your tongue, we'll talk later.) Next time he went, he told me "Komm mit." In the teacher's apartment there was a dark room without windows and there was the bicycle. And in the corners were heaps of *Schundhefte:* Sherlock Holmes, Nick Carter, Nat Pinkerton, Buffalo Bill, Texas Jack, and others.

When we went away we had several under our shirts, but we were honest and brought them back next time and exchanged them for others. Also, there was a bookshop where one could buy used copies and exchange three old ones for two new (that is, old ones which we had not yet read), and these we used to exchange; but I want to say that we never misused the teacher's trust and brought back everything we had borrowed. Of course he confiscated the *Hefte* when he found a pupil reading during lectures, and he well knew why we came to clean his bicycle, but never a word was said about what was clear to both sides. Besides, he was the best liked of all our teachers; he didn't need to raise his voice, but during his lectures there was a quite uncustomary silence. My sister had him too (she later became a teacher). After having danced through one night, he came next morning into the classroom half-seas over (and girls are much more ready to mock or deride), hung his top hat on a nail which was not there, bowed to the blackboard instead of the class, sat down and began his lecture, and the class listened without a sound, as quiet as little mice.

This was the way I became acquainted with the *Geheimakten des Weltdetektivs*. I must have read a hundred of the stories, and I can assure you they were not plagiates but pastiches. There was no Dr. Watson but a Harry Taxon, and the series was continued under the title *Harry Taxon und sein Meister,* of which I have read only a few. I don't remember titles, but in the Sherlock Holmes series was one title *Der Kanariendiamant,* but at that time *Maza* (1921) had not yet appeared (my acquaintance with the stories extends from about 1911 to the beginning of 1914, when my parents were recommended to take me away or I would be kicked out). There was one issue where the cover picture showed two centaurs depicted in white gypsum or marble, a bearded one brandishing a spear against a young one who is only partly stone—the head being that of Harry Taxon about to be wrapped up in gypsum. There was another story where a girl sang a song: a mother was killed by her son at the request of his lover, and he was bringing the heart to her. He stumbled on the way and fell, and the heart softly whispered, "Hast du dir Weh getan, mein Kind?" (Have you hurt yourself, my child?) Such are the bits I remember. Where did Olms Press get their copies? I have people searching the flea markets for copies, and I go there myself when I can, but nothing turns up. I have asked many old friends, and through them and my former schoolboys' club I have tried to get schoolboys interested in the search, but so far without result. But I will say there was no sex, no Western-style brutality (but there was none of that in Bret Harte), and no more superstition than in today's serious literature.

I have heard that there was a Swedish series of such pastiches.

To commit a sacrilege: these pastiches—i.e., the better ones, as there were great differences in interest if not in style (of which I was no judge at that time)—are not worse than a lot of stories in *His Last Bow* and *The Case Book*. It is a pity that Doyle did not stop writing the Holmes stories after he had promised it.

Re plagiates: We would have called *plagiate* something that used not only the names but even the plot (or part of it) of another work. We would have regarded a title like *Der Kanariendiamant*

THIS IS NOT OUR SHERLOCK!   [243

as a plagiate (plagiarism) on "The Mazarin Stone," yet in this case *Der Kanariendiamant* is older than *Maza*. I would have detected immediately if in the *Geheimakten* which I read there had been a duplication of the plots of Conan Doyle. I think Lichtenstein,* writing in German, uses the word plagiate rather loosely. Of course, using the name Sherlock Holmes in the title of the series would have constituted a plagiarism, just as was the use of the name H. Clauren as author in *Der Mann im Mond,* a persiflage written by W. Hauff. My good old dictionary (1871) defines *Plagiate* "wenn ein Schriftsteller die Gedanken, Phrasen etc. eines anderen (gleichsam dessen Kinder) entwendet und für die seinigen ausgibt." (When a writer purloins the thoughts, phrases, etc. of another [as it were his children] and passes them off as his own.) But the *Schundhefte* were only using the name of Holmes and the fact that he was a detective; there is no similarity in the stories. I am no lawyer, but I think that even the use of the name would not have been indictable as plagiarism, but an infringement of a trade name. Proof of this seems to be that the series could be continued under another title. I think that the use of the word *plagio-corpus* is correct, as *plagios* means depending, borrowing. But plagiarism (*Plagiate*) has a definite meaning in law, different from *Nachdruck,* which means a reprint, legal or pirated. But these are matters for the law. . . .

---

* Alfred Lichtenstein, *Der Kriminalroman: eine literarische und forensisch-medizinische Studie mit Anhang: Sherlock Holmes zum Fall Hau* (München: Reinhardt, 1908), calls the producers of the *Geheimakten* "tapfer plagiierende Verfasser" (boldly plagiarizing authors), p. 47.

Two Sherlockians wrote to me—oddly enough, both from Canada —about Samuel Rosenberg's book, Naked Is the Best Disguise, *which must, for a long time, enjoy the unchallenged title as the most original work ever to have been written on Sherlock Holmes and Conan Doyle. One correspondent said, "Rosenberg . . . has done a fine job of literary detective work. . . . Without necessarily subscribing to all his conclusions, he has certainly untwined a number of the complexities of Doyle." The other correspondent said, ". . . I haven't yet decided whether the whole thing is a gigantic 'put-on,' or a serious piece of scholarly research. Nonetheless, a delightfully entertaining book." Thousands of readers, both sides of the Atlantic, have been enchanted and/or infuriated by Rosenberg's totally unprecedented approach to his sacred subject, which may now be seen (for all its originality) to conform to a newer school of criticism: in which the search for the author is made within the unsaid, the cryptic, the analogical, the coded— conscious and subconscious—what really (or so the theory goes) tells us all about both himself and his creation. In the meantime, encouraged by sales and praise ("I see the book made the Book-of- the-Month Club . . ."), and undeterred by the outraged cries of protest, Rosenberg has gone confidently (and outrageously) ahead with the development of his search for "the related and unrelated mythological sources that lie hidden-revealed below the beguiling surface of the Sherlock Holmes adventures." What he has since discovered, Mr. Rosenberg tell us in . . .*

Some Notes on the Conan Doyle Syndrome and Allegory in "The Adventure of the Red Circle"

⊠

SAMUEL ROSENBERG

⊠

> A man's life of any worth is a continual allegory
> . . . his works are the comment.
> —John Keats, *Letters*

> *Syndrome,* n, a group of related things, events, or
> actions. From *syn* (together) and *drome* (to run).
> —*Random House Dictionary*

The allegorical Conan Doyle Syndrome (sin-drome) and the related and unrelated mythological sources that lie hidden-revealed below the beguiling surface of the Sherlock Holmes adventures were discovered serendipitously: they were found while I was looking for more book-title allusions like the clearly Dionysian *Origin of Tree Worship* in "The Adventure of the Empty House" —allusions which might also allude to ex-Professor Friedrich Nietzsche,* upon whom I believe Doyle based both his *evil superman* ex-Professor Moriarty and his *good superman* Sherlock Holmes. (Another far better known model for Holmes-as-detective was, of course, the remarkable Dr. Joseph Bell, Doyle's teacher at the Edinburgh Medical School.)

---

* Nietzsche, self-proclaimed Dionysian, who even called himself "Dionysus" when he became insane, wrote a book with a similar title. It was *The Origin of Tragedy* (in the cult of Dionysus), later published as *The Birth of Tragedy.*

My method of search for the Nietzsche-Dionysus clues was a simple one: Whenever a book was mentioned, I first read the book, something about its author in reference and critical works, and then wrote a detailed synoptic analysis of the story and scene in which the book was mentioned. Soon, after this procedure was repeated in more than twenty stories, a most surprising phenomenon loomed up out of *The Complete Sherlock Holmes:* the existence in the stories of previously unknown layers of meaning or allegory. My accumulated notes and analyses revealed that in almost every story I'd dissected, the mention of the printed or written word in any form—books as objects, book titles, quotations from or references to any literary work, magazine articles, newspaper items, "agony columns," signs, advertisements, diaries (especially "lust diaries"), letters, manuscripts, words scribbled on paper or upon the wall (even in blood), "read" in the dust of floors, or even in the expressions of faces—was usually accompanied by a compulsive or automatic allusion to some form of forbidden sexual expression, either heterosexual or homosexual, or both.

These below-surface compulsive allusions, in turn, were frequently associated with images of draconian punishment inflicted on the sex offenders and, deviously, to the unrelated punishment of large numbers of people in such cities as Sodom and Gomorrah, Khartoum or Jericho, or in the American or English civil wars.

Astonished by the discovery of this rigid constellation of word, sex, and punishment images revolving secretly behind the lustrous façades of so many of Doyle's "simple detective stories," I continued my study of these exciting obsessive idea-and-image clusters, and found that they usually appeared in tandem with other obsessive elements, all of which are irrelevant to the stories in which Doyle had implanted them.

It was now obvious that this observed pattern was far from random. It was a syndrome of compulsively linked images, ideas, persons, objects, and actions which functioned like any other medical or philosophical syndrome: if any single element of the constellation appeared, I could now accurately predict that every other element of the constellation would, like "Mary's little lamb," be sure to follow.

Yes, Conan Doyle did indeed think in "syndromic" terms. In

"The Five Orange Pips," Doyle, speaking through his "puppet" Holmes, says:

"The ideal reasoner would, when he had once been shown a single fact in all its bearings, deduce from it not only the chain of events which led up to it, but also the results which would follow from it. As Cuvier could correctly describe the whole animal from the contemplation of a single bone, so *the observer who has thoroughly understood one link in a series of incidents would be able to state all the others, both before and after.*" [Emphasis added.]

This "sin-drome," so-called because of its central theme of illicit love or sexuality linked to a set of uniquely Doylean images and ideas, is expressed in many stories with the following elements:

(A) After using his superlative reasoning powers to penetrate the mystery brought him, Sherlock Holmes frequently anticipates the criminal's plan of action and goes to the scene of the crime. In other cases he sets a trap for the suspected malefactor.

(B) There, with Watson and sometimes others (or alone), Holmes frequently conducts a vigil at night or in a dark room awaiting the

(C) arrival of an unknown person (or one known only to Holmes), or of a dangerous criminal or murderer.

(D) In more than twenty stories a remarkable Doylean event occurs. Before or after (sometimes before and after) the arrival of the unknown person or the man of violence, one or more references to the printed or written word will be made (books, book titles, etc.), usually by Sherlock, which evoke the already mentioned references to acts of forbidden sexuality. This syndromic link then triggers a reference to some form of drastic punishment to "sinning" individuals and/or to the punishment of large numbers of people in a collective situation or war.

(E) When the "unknown" or "violent" person does finally appear after the long vigil in the dark, another uniquely Doylean surprise will occur: there is a sudden reversal, confusion, or switching of the sexes. Instead of the expected male, a female appears, or a man dressed as a woman. Or he will prove to be weak and/or effeminate. Thus in *A Study in Scarlet,* after a suspenseful night vigil, instead of the expected murderer, a little old lady appears, but "she" proves to be a young man in perfect female disguise. Conversely, readers of "The Yellow Face" will recall the "hideous man" who is seen on "a very dark night" in the second-story window of a rural cottage, who turns out to be a pretty "little coal-black negress" who has been wearing a mask. Similarly, in "A Scandal in Bohemia," Irene Adler plays a *scene at night* with Holmes in which she is dressed as a "young man," and fools him completely. Soon, as we shall see, a similar set of sexual metamorphoses will occur in "The Adventure of the Red Circle."

Conan Doyle's continued compulsive use of transvestite characters is truly extraordinary. His first transvestite appears in *A Study in Scarlet,* the first Sherlockian story published in 1887, but the last transvestite may be seen in his last Holmesian adventure, "Shoscombe Old Place," published exactly forty years later. I call that a compulsion! And while we're at it, let's not forget "The Mazarin Stone," in which Sherlock himself tells Watson gleefully that while he was disguised as "an old lady" and shadowing the nefarious woman-killer, Count Negretto Sylvius, he dropped his parasol, and the Count picked it up and courteously handed it to him.

Sometimes the "confusion or switching of the sexes" is expressed by Doyle in verbal terms, by the manipulation of names, or by the use of allusions to literary works in which transvestism plays an important part. Thus, in *A Study in Scarlet,* we find that when Dr. Watson is left alone for a few hours while Holmes is off foolishly chasing the transvestite actor—"old lady," Watson spent his time reading Henry Murger's *Scènes de la Vie Bohème.* That book, later adapted for the opera as *La Bohème,* is best remembered for its *Charley's Aunt* sequence in which Rodolphe is imprisoned by his uncle and forced to wear an oriental woman's harem clothing, complete with petticoats.

Also, as readers of "The Red-headed League" may remember, after Holmes and his companions wait in the "pitch-dark" cellar of the bank to arrest the decidedly effeminate thieves John Clay and Duncan Ross, Sherlock Holmes ends his recapitulation of the mystery with a seemingly irrelevant reference to the bisexual George Sand, the world-famous author who scandalized the "straight" world by appearing in men's clothing and with a big cigar clenched between her teeth. The name George Sand is coupled by Holmes with that of Gustave Flaubert, author of "scandalous heterosexual novels." Like so many other Sherlock Holmes stories, "The Red-headed League" is syndromic from beginning to end.

(F) In many stories a hand-to-hand combat will follow the arrival of the awaited criminal or villain. Alone, or with the help of others, Sherlock will overpower him and then turn him over to Scotland Yard for formal arrest and punishment. But, in the few stories where the "unknown person" proves to be a female, as in "Yellow Face," "Golden Pince-Nez," "Scandal in Bohemia," or "The Red Circle" (discussed in the pages that follow), there is no hand-to-hand combat, and the woman usually goes unpunished by the law.

(G) Perhaps the most important element in the Conan Doyle Syndrome and allegory: In every story, Sherlock Holmes remains aloof from all the human problems and passions as a completely sublimated "reasoning machine" and bounty hunter. He is the unquestioning, incorruptible guardian of the Victorian criminal and moral codes. As such his unvarying role is that of detector, preventer, judge and punisher of every deceptive, larcenous, or immoral act, including those that are sexually deviant.

> "I wrote no *letter*."
> "The cunning demons! And you?"
> "I came in answer to *your letter*."
> "Lucia, I wrote no *letter*."
> "They have trapped us with the same bait."
> —Conan Doyle, *Adventures of Gérard*

I do not call it the "Sherlock Holmes Syndrome," because Conan Doyle displays the same set of mutually enchained images, ideas, and story elements in his novel *Uncle Bernac* and in his *Brigadier Gérard* novels.

In *How the Brigadier Lost His Ear,* a Freudian gem, we find the heterosexual "crime," the linked printed or written word (quoted above), the drastic punishment of the lovers, and the uniquely Doylean images of individual and mass punishment and death linked to the acts of forbidden sexuality. We also find two people waiting in a pitch-dark room for an expected man of violence; and then, we have a predictable surprising switching of the sexes and transvestism.

Brigadier Gérard, a swashbuckling womanizer in Napoleon's army, loses his ear during the French occupation of Milan. Enraged by Gérard's conquest of Lucia, the Doge's granddaughter, the defeated men of Milan use the syndromic device of forged letters to trick, capture, and imprison the fornicating pair. Gérard is sentenced to death; Lucia is sentenced to losing an ear for her sexual crime.

But, during the night before his execution, Gérard breaks into the adjoining cell, where he learns of her impending mutilation. While they are waiting in the pitch-dark cell for the expected man of violence, Gérard has a brilliant idea: he will accept her punishment. To do so, he shoves Lucia into his cell, puts on her cloak (transvestism) and then waits in her bed.

Fulfilling the Doylean scheme, the executioner turns out to be soft-hearted and compassionate and, believing in that dark room (he doesn't light his lantern because he cannot bear to look at the beautiful women he must mutilate) that Gérard is Lucia, he cuts off part of Gérard's ear. Then, just before the switching or confusion of the sexes is about to be discovered, Napoleon's soldiers arrive to rescue Lucia and Gérard. The French soldiers then complete the syndromic requirement of mass murder linked to the other elements already stated by killing all the Milanese sexual avengers.

One superb example of the Conan Doyle Syndrome in a Sherlock Holmes adventure: in "His Last Bow," we recall, the German master spy Von Bork is given a "small blue book . . . printed in golden letters, *Practical Handbook of Bee Culture*"—instead of the volume of British naval secrets by the disguised Sherlock, acting as a double agent.

Like every other book mentioned syndromically by Doyle's characters, this bee book, written by Sherlock Holmes and bearing the subtitle *With Some Observations upon the Segregation of the Queen*, fulfills Doyle's strange compulsion to associate sexual intercourse with the death of a sexual partner. After a queen bee is impregnated by the drone on their all-too-brief honeymoon, she kills him in a manner revealed in the ancient Greek myth cited by Robert Graves: "Aphrodite Urania ('Queen of the mountain') or Erycina (of the heather) was the nymph-goddess of midsummer.

She destroyed the sacred king, who mated with her on a mountain top, as the queen-bee destroys the drone: by tearing out his sex organs."

I'm sure the reader now familiar with the sin-drome has recognized that the required automatic metaphor of the murder of great masses of men tied "irrelevantly" to the sexual act of bees and men is conveyed by the fact that the book Von Bork thought he was going to get contained military secrets he would have used to kill thousands of British sailors, soldiers and civilians during the continuing war between Germany and Great Britain.

Conan Doyle's direct awareness and use of a book, in this case a manuscript "lust diary," as the trigger for his sin-drome is openly exhibited on an entirely conscious basis in "The Adventure of the Illustrious Client." First we read the melodramatic climax in which the wronged Kitty Winter throws sulphuric acid into the face of the blackmailer Baron Gruner, permanently blinding and disfiguring him. After witnessing this awful scene, Holmes and Watson return to their flat to discuss the case, and once again a book is linked directly and indirectly to punishment for sexual "sins" and then to "murder." (When asked if he had ever heard of Baron Gruner, Holmes answers, "You mean the Austrian murderer?") During the "wrap-up" discussion of the case, Sherlock says:

"The wages of sin, Watson, the wages of sin. Sooner or later, it will always come. God knows, there was sin enough," he added, taking up a brown volume from the table. "Here is the book the [acid-throwing] woman talked of. If this will not break the marriage [of Gruner to Miss de Merville], nothing could. But it will, Watson, it will, for no self-respecting woman could stand it."
    "Is it his love diary?"
    "Or his lust diary. Call it what you will."

The familiar phrase, "the wages of sin (is death)," used by the great revealer Holmes comes from the New Testament's Epistle to the Romans (6:23) and follows a long catalogue of mankind's sins, including fornication, covetousness, murder, malignity, deceit, treachery, hatred of God, and so on. But a follow-up paragraph gives greater importance to the "sin of men who, leaving a natural use of women, burned in their lust for one another." Once again, in the mind of the omnivorous reader Doyle, who remembered nearly every word he ever read, a book is linked to a second book which links together most of the units of his syndrome of sin and draconian punishment.

Conan Doyle's Literary Use of the Legendary Past

Several decades before such great literary masters as Thomas Mann, James Joyce, T. S. Eliot, and André Gide recognized the undiminished relevance of the ancient myths, legends, and Biblical chronicles to modern man—who constantly re-enacts the ancient dramas—Conan Doyle anticipated the modern mythic literary mode, and rewrote many ancient dramas in the modern secular parables called detective stories.

In his "The Crooked Man," as one example, Doyle copied his story of Barclay (a treacherous and lecherous soldier who gets a wife by sending her "true love" to certain death in battle) from the celebrated Biblical story of King David, Uriah, and Bathsheba. Clever Doyle then has his great detective confess his copying for him.

At the end of the story during the inevitable explanation by Holmes to his admiring friend and narrator, Watson, he refers to the name "David" shouted by Mrs. Barclay several times during the overheard quarrel that led to her husband's death and says:

"There's one thing . . . If the husband's name was James, and the other was Henry, what was this talk about 'David'? That one word, Watson, should have told the whole story had I been the ideal reasoner which you are so fond of depicting. . . . It was evidently a form of reproach."

"Reproach?"

"Yes, [King] David strayed occasionally, you know, and on one occasion in the same direction as Sergeant James Barclay. You remember the small affair of Uriah and Bathsheba? My Biblical knowledge is a trifle rusty, I fear, but you will find the story in the first or second [book] of Samuel."

Once again, a book [of Samuel] is selected because it contains many of the elements of the Conan Doyle Syndrome: illicit sex, murder of an innocent man, all in the context of a war in which a great many men on both sides were killed.

This *Punch* cartoon of Sir Conan Doyle, in painful and inescapable bondage to his creation, Sherlock Holmes (i.e., if Mr. Rosenberg's theory is correct, Conan Doyle himself), was published in 1926, four years before Conan Doyle's death. The brilliant drawing is by the *Punch* star artist Sir Bernard Partridge. *Contrad Research Library.*

Greek Mythology in "The Adventure of the Red Circle"

Conan Doyle's use of Greek mythology in the writing of his modern detective stories was first noticed by me in "The Final Problem." When Sherlock Holmes first tells Dr. Watson and the reader about the existence of his great nemesis Professor Moriarty, he uses words and images that indicate Doyle was thinking of the Greek myth in which the heroic Theseus, with the help of Ariadne's celebrated thread, penetrates the Minoan labyrinth to kill the youth-devouring Minotaur and escape.

After describing the "king-devil"* Moriarty as the "Napoleon of crime . . . the organizer of half that is evil in this great city," Sherlock, in a burst of imagery that clearly recalls Theseus, Ariadne, the Minoan labyrinth, and the Minotaur, says:

For years I endeavored to break through the veil that shrouded [him], and at last the time came when *I seized the thread, and followed it until it led me, after a thousand cunning windings, to ex-Professor Moriarty, of mathematical celebrity!* [Emphasis added.]

But the very first reference to the Theseus-Minotaur saga is on display in *A Study in Scarlet,* published six years earlier. There, in another story about a hero who pursues a monster through half the world, the chase finally ends in London, where the avenger (Hope) gets a job as hansom cab driver so that he can track down and pursue the monster (Drebber) through the streets of the metropolis. In telling his story, he invokes the image of the greatest of all labyrinths, or mazes, the one built by Dædalus to house the Minotaur: "The hardest job was to learn my way about [London], *for of all the mazes that were ever contrived, this city is the most confusing.*" (Emphasis added.)

But Jefferson Hope, latter-day Theseus, does manage to penetrate the London street-maze to find and kill his own personal Minotaur; when he does finally kill him, he does so at "Number 3, Lauriston Gardens, which," writes Conan Doyle, "had an ill-omened and minatory look." Of course, the words "minatory" and "Minotaur-y" have different meanings, but I'm sure the reader will agree they certainly look alike.

---

* In *The Valley of Fear,* Moriarty is called a "king-devil."

Theseus, Danae, and Gorgo-Medusa in "The Red Circle"

But first, before we show how Doyle based his story upon the ancient Greek myth, let us, together, reread the surface or façade narrative of "The Red Circle." It begins with Sherlock Holmes's listening attentively to Mrs. Warren, a very frightened lodging-house landlady. She tells him that ten days earlier she had rented her third-floor room to a foreigner who insisted on total privacy. No one was to enter the room for any reason, and meals and a copy of the [London] *Daily Gazette* were to be left on a tray before the door. The lodger had also received a front-door key; he had not been seen since then, though he could be heard pacing back and forth constantly.

When Sherlock sees how agitated Mrs. Warren is, he agrees to try to ferret out the mysterious lodger and find out what he is up to. When she leaves, Sherlock begins his investigation by carefully reading his own file of the *Daily Gazette*. At once, in the midst of all the typically erotic and other items in the paper's "agony columns," he finds one that he guesses is connected with Mrs. Warren's invisible lodger. Someone who signs himself *G* has inserted a message to "someone else" saying that light signals will be beamed from a certain house, using a simple code. (Note to fellow syndrome-watchers: these references to a newspaper and its "agony columns," as well as to the light-signaled messages, are indeed syndromic and will, as we shall see, trigger the additional references to unbridled sexuality that leads to the murder of individuals in a context of organized assassination of many others. Also, there will appear the inevitable switching and confusion of the sexes after a long vigil in a dark room. In short, "The Red Circle" is yet another example of Doyle's remarkable imaginational compulsiveness.)

At half-past twelve that day, Holmes and Watson go to Mrs. Warren's house to begin the unraveling of the mystery. The landlady takes charge and hides them in a dark room opposite the room of the mysterious lodger. With the door of their hiding place slightly ajar, Holmes and Watson stare fixedly into a large mirror in their room, an arrangement that permits them to see the opposite door while they remain invisible. Then, by prearrangement, food and the newspaper are left on a tray in front of the lodger's door. Soon, as the hyperattentive Holmes watches the reflected image in Mrs. Warren's mirror, "there was the creaking of a turned key, the handle revolved . . . and I caught a glimpse of a dark, beautiful, horrified face glaring . . ." (The alert reader has noted that the Doylean syndrome is at work here: after waiting in a dark room for the expected mysterious, unknown man, Holmes and Watson once again are surprised to see a woman instead. And, again, the image cluster includes the mention of a newspaper left before the door. But this is only the beginning of one of the most fascinating applications of Doyle's mysterious fixations.)

As predictable by the foregoing, the very next scene provides new syndromic clues. Minutes later, out on the street before the lodging house, Holmes spots the exact house mentioned in the morning newspaper as the station to be used for signaling the woman concealed in Mrs. Warren's top floor.

That night they return to the lodging house to take up another night vigil in "the darkened sitting-room." Finally, after a long wait, they see someone flashing signals from the house across the street.

Using the code as stated in the morning *Daily Gazette*, Holmes reads aloud the flashed message consisting of two Italian words, Attenta! (Attention!) and Pericolo! (Danger!). At once, Sherlock and his companion run to the "signal station," and, in the company of Inspector Gregson and the American sleuth Leverton, they race up to the third floor. There they find a gigantic, brutally ugly man dead on the floor in a widening pool of blood—with a knife protruding from his throat.

Leverton immediately identifies the corpse as "Black Gorgiano," a Mafia chieftain from Naples and New York, and the mystery deepens: Who is this man, and what is his connection to the beautiful woman hidden these last ten days in the room across the street? To find out, the brilliant Holmes lights the candle used for signaling and passes it back and forth across the window. Moments later, Mrs. Warren's lodger appears breathlessly. When she sees the dead man on the floor, she thinks it's her husband Gennaro, but when she sees that it is Black Gorgiano, she dances around the room with joy.

When she returns from orbit, the beautiful lodger (Emilia

Lucca) and the assembled group return to her room, where she explains it all.

She and her husband Gennaro were Neapolitans who had left Naples for New York City because of her father's opposition to their marriage. In New York, Gennaro found a good job and a happy life in permanent exile. All went well until one day Gennaro brought home his fellow countryman Gorgiano, a mythic monster in human form. Says Emilia:

"He was grotesque, gigantic, and terrifying . . . his voice was like thunder . . . his thoughts, emotions, his passions . . . monstrous. He talked or rather roared with such energy that one could only sit and listen, cowed with the mighty stream of words . . . his eyes blazed at you and held you at his mercy."

Later, Emilia Lucca adds:

"His *terrible, wild-beast eyes were always turned on me.* . . . One night his secret came out—the love of a brute—a savage. He pushed his way in, seized me with his mighty arms, hugged me in his bear's embrace, covered me with kisses, and implored me to come away with him." [Emphasis added.]

At that moment, she says, Gennaro came home, heard her scream, and tried to kill Gorgiano. But the monstrous Mafioso knocked Gennaro senseless and left the house.

Finally, after Gorgiano tried to get Gennaro to kill his employer and friend, Emilia and Gennaro fled [like Orestes from the Furies] across the Atlantic, where Gennaro contacted Mrs. Warren and then substituted Emilia as the "mysterious lodger." He had then taken the room across the street as the signaling station. Earlier he had signaled his wife, but both Holmes and Gorgiano had read the message. Gorgiano had reached Gennaro's room before Holmes arrived and had been killed by the desperate husband.

After hearing this lurid tale, Holmes, Leverton, and Gregson agree that it is a case of "justifiable homicide" and predict that Gennaro will be freed to resume his happy life with his beautiful wife.

Emilia Lucca as the Mythological Danae, Mother of Perseus

In order to show how exactly Conan Doyle rewrote the well-known mythological story of Perseus, his mother Danae, and the terrible Medusa, we shall review the legend step by step, beginning with the first part of Danae's role in it. (As we proceed, I will show how Doyle rewrote it.)

When the Delphic oracle told the Argive King Acrisius that any son born to his daughter Danae was predestined to kill him, Acrisius sentenced Danae to solitary confinement in a tower where no impregnating male could ever find her. According to one version of the myth, she had already had an incestuous affair with her uncle Proetus, and her father was taking no chances.

But when the raunchy Zeus, whose favorite Olympic sport was the seduction of mortal women, heard about her plight, he transformed himself into a beam of light, flashed through a tiny hole in the tower and impregnated her. The child born of this amazing 186,000-mile-a-second copulation was the great hero Perseus, who later "accidentally" killed Acrisius, thereby fulfilling the oracular prophecy. (Note: this legendary tale is staged in the Mediterranean, arena of all Greek and Roman mythology.)

In "The Red Circle" we find many similarities with the above portion of the Perseus myth. They indicate that the well-read, total-recall, ingenious Doyle simply rewrote the mythic tale in a modern secularized form.

1. The general geographic arena remains the same, but is shifted by Doyle from Argos, near Athens, to the not too distant Naples, Italy.

2. The relationship between Danae and Acrisius may be simply stated: he refused to let her get married or sleep with any man. In "The Red Circle" we have this same situation explicitly stated by Emilia. She had fled to life in permanent exile with Gennaro because her father "opposed the marriage." A minor point, but definitely part of the story copied by Doyle.

3. Like Danae, concealed in a secret tower where no intrusive male can find and copulate with her, Emilia Lucca is secretly confined in the top story, or tower, of a London lodging house where, it is hoped, the would-be rapist Gorgiano cannot find her and get between her legs. To keep her safe, even her husband doesn't visit Emilia Lucca. So, again like Danae, Emilia doesn't enjoy any sexual intercourse while imprisoned.

4. The ingenious rewriter Doyle, thinking of the sexually potent beam of light of the Danae myth (the transformed Zeus) that

enters the tower-prison and Danae's womb, uses the exact same device brought up to date. He has Gennaro, Emilia's husband (and therefore sexual partner), send her coded messages with a candle beam. These beams of light enter Zeus-like into her otherwise impenetrable secret chamber, and inform her of the sexual peril posed by the raunchy Gorgiano now in the immediate neighborhood. Gorgiano is about to break into the London equivalent of the Argive tower.

Michael Harrison has reminded me that, in the context of light as sexual substance revealed here, the lighted "candle" used to penetrate the eye and mind of the imprisoned Emilia-Danae is an obvious phallic symbol. I agree with Harrison and suggest that, when Sherlock Holmes flashes the candle beams of light which make Emilia-Danae come running to him in the murder chamber, he has taken over the symbolical role of Zeus-the-copulator and husband Gennaro, the licensed sexual partner. That Doyle thought of a member of the Holmes family as Zeus (Jupiter to Romans) is verified in the earlier "Adventure of the Bruce-Partington Plans" (1908) in which Sherlock says of his brother Mycroft's descent from his Olympian heights: "But *Jupiter* is descending today." (Emphasis added.)

But this use of fire (lighted candle) is not the only example of a Sherlockian substitutive symbolical sex in the Canon. In "A Scandal in Bohemia," Holmes stages a completely orgasmal Freudian scene when he has a very phallic fire rocket thrown into Irene Adler's "room" (womb). Says the pre-Freudian Holmes: "A *married woman grabs for her baby;* an *unmarried woman reaches for her jewel box.*" He then relates that Irene Adler "responded beautifully. The photograph is in a *recess* [vagina or womb] behind a *sliding panel* just above the *right bell-pull* [clitoris?]." (Emphasis added.)

In this cloacal recess Miss Adler had hidden the photographic proof of her sexual relations with the gullible King of Bohemia. Yes, "A Scandal in Bohemia" is Freudian all the way.

Perseus, Gorgo-Medusa, and Sherlock Holmes

Now part two of the Danae-Perseus myth as it relates to "The Red Circle": When Acrisius learns that Danae has given birth to a son, he refuses to believe that Perseus was immaculately conceived by a Zeusian "beam of light," and blames his brother Proetus who had previously lain with her. But, still mindful of the Delphic warning, he has Danae and Perseus locked into a large chest and has it set adrift on the Mediterranean. Eventually, guided by Zeus, the chest washes ashore on the island of Seriphos, where King Polydectes grants mother and child permanent asylum. This coincides exactly with Doyle's story of the woman who, because her father disapproves of her marriage, sets sail from Naples across the Mediterranean and the Atlantic to take up a permanent home in exile.

When Perseus attains manhood and learns that Polydectes is about to force his mother Danae into marriage, he bravely—and rashly—offers to seek out, kill, and bring back the head of the terrible Gorgo-Medusa if Polydectes will marry someone else.

Believing that, like all the others who had perished in the attempt, Perseus will never return alive from battle with the "snakylocked female monster" whose terrible gaze and face turn men to stone, Polydectes quickly agrees, and the foolhardy Perseus begins his apparently suicidal mission.

But fortunately for him, the great Athena, Perseus's sister, is sent by father Zeus to make sure that the young hero accomplishes his very dangerous mission. Athena had reasons of her own for helping Perseus. When Medusa was a young goddess she had offended Athena by using the temple of Athena for sexual intercourse with Poseidon. It was Athena who reacted to this desecration by transforming Medusa into a monster with long tusks, snake-hair, and a face with terrible eyes that turned men to stone. Now, still unforgiving, she wished to help her brother Perseus as her instrument for the final destruction of Medusa.

To accomplish this, she first takes Perseus to a picture gallery where accurate portraits of the three Gorgon sisters are on display. There, exactly like a scene in a James Bond or commando-training film, she briefs him accurately on their facial differences so that he will attack only the mortal Gorgo (Greek for Medusa) and not her two immortal sisters, Stheno and Euryale. She warns him never to look directly at Gorgo-Medusa but only at her reflection in the mirrorlike shield she gives him.

Then, following Athena's precise instructions, Perseus seeks out the Stygian nymphs, who give him winged sandals, a magical bag for carrying Gorgo-Medusa's lopped-off head, and a cap of darkness that will help him see everything but remain invisible.

In a far-off land Perseus finds the three terrible sisters sound asleep, surrounded by vast numbers of men and beasts they have turned into statues. Then, with the careful use of the magical mirror-shield, he gazes at the right Gorgon, and, with his sword guided by Athena, he cuts off the head of Medusa and flies off, hotly pursued by the surviving sisters. But they cannot see him in his cap of darkness, and give up the chase.

Here are the exact similarities between the ancient myth of Perseus and his confrontation with Gorgo-Medusa and Conan Doyle's rewritten version:

The Perseus myth: Athena voluntarily briefs the hero Perseus in all the details of his perilous mission.

The Red Circle: Mrs. Warren voluntarily briefs the hero Sherlock Holmes in the details of his possibly dangerous investigation.

The Perseus myth: Athena tells Perseus where he can obtain the cap of darkness which enables him to see others while he himself remains invisible.

The Red Circle: Mrs. Warren suggests the use of her storage room, a pitch-dark room where Holmes can see others while remaining invisible himself.

The Perseus myth: Athena gives Perseus a mirror-shield which enables him to see the dread female Gorgo-Medusa indirectly.

The Red Circle: In the dark room (cap of darkness) provided by Mrs. Warren, there hangs her mirror, which permits Sherlock Holmes to look at the unknown female indirectly.

The Perseus myth: Gorgo-Medusa is always described as having terrifying, horrible eyes and face.

The Red Circle: When Holmes and Watson catch their first glimpse of the unknown stranger from their "cap of darkness" hiding place and by means of the mirror, she is described as having "a dark, beautiful, horrified face."

In every other Sherlock Holmes adventure I can think of, it is always Sherlock alone who devises the strategy, techniques and instruments, and who stage-manages the inevitable denouement. But in "The Red Circle" it is Mrs. Warren who brings the case to him and persuades him to take it. It is she who suggests the strategy for viewing the mysterious lodger, and who provides him with the metaphorical "cap of darkness" (dark room) and the Athena-like mirror. In fact, Holmes takes a rather passive role throughout, and really doesn't solve this mystery at all. Both he and the reader learn most of the story from Mrs. Warren, from Detective Leverton, and then finally from Emilia Lucca. All of the actions of the story, with the exception of Holmes's signaling to bring Mrs. Lucca to the murder chamber, are initiated by the two Gs—Gorgiano and Gennaro. And Holmes never does get to see the murderer Gennaro in the time limits of Watson's narration.

> "I was struck by the snaky locks of grizzled hair
> which curled out from under his old straw hat."
> —Dr. Watson, in "The Retired Colourman"

Despite the fact that Gorgiano is an excessively heterosexual male, his name (and his ultimate fate) closely resembles that of Gorgo, the female monster slain by Perseus. The name and sex switching in "The Red Circle" follows a now-familiar pattern, since it is preceded by the mention of the syndromic messages "printed" with beams of candlelight. In the original myth we saw the Zeusian beams of light enter the secret Argive tower and impregnate the woman hidden within. Here, through the mysterious transformations within the psyche of Doyle, we witness beams of light which, when flashed to the top floor of a London house, lead a man to his death.

In her essay, "Gorgo and the Origins of Fear," Thalia Feldman derives the word *gorgo* from the Sanskrit root which she defines as "a gurgling, guttural sound, sometimes human, sometimes animal, perhaps closest to a growling beast."*

The word *gorgo* also suggests gorge, to eat with a bestial appetite; for sensual pleasure as well as food. *Gorge* is also the throat. It also reminds one of the very strong Italian cheese *Gorgonzola*,

---

* This paragraph is quoted from Hazel Barnes's excellent summary and analyses of the various theories about Medusa. See her *The Meddling Gods*.

which the early non-Italian comedians like Chaplin found irre-
sistibly funny. If we put all the word associations of *Gorgiano*
together we have "a very smelly, evil-eyed, rabidly-oversexed,
rather ridiculous character who is the spittin' image of Mack
Swain, the comic monster in the early Chaplin comedies."

But Doyle's Gorgiano is also depicted as a very serious, threatening monster with the facial characteristics of Gorgo-Medusa.
Emilia Lucca identifies Gorgiano with Gorgo when she relates
how she was almost turned to stone herself by his "terrible, glaring, wild-beast eyes" that were turned on her. And Gorgiano dies
nearly as Gorgo-Medusa did. The evil goddess was decapitated,
but Gorgiano dies when his jugular vein is severed by the knife
left sticking in his throat.

Another similarity: Many Greek vases and paintings depict
Gorgo-Medusa as a Fury who relentlessly pursued, caught, and
killed those who offended the gods. Gorgiano is described by
Emilia Lucca as the perfect human Fury, who, like the Furies
that chased Orestes across the Sicilian strait, chased the Luccas
from New York to London and finally tracked them to Mrs.
Warren's lodging house.

Curious about Doyle's transformation of the rampantly heterosexual Gorgiano into the male equivalent of Gorgo-Medusa, I
looked for and found another unmistakable example in "The
Adventure of the Retired Colourman." He is the evil Josiah
Amberley, who jealously murdered his young wife and her lover
in a gas chamber. Josiah is described (in the words quoted above)
in Medusan terms: "I was *struck by the snaky locks of grizzled
hair* which curled out from under his old straw hat." (Emphasis
added.)

Yet another Doylean set of "male Medusa" images is melodra-
matically exhibited in the final scene of "The Speckled Band"
(1892). After Sherlock Holmes savagely drives the lethal snake
back through the ventilator into the adjoining room, a "most
horrible cry" is heard. Watson and Holmes enter the room and
find the snake-killed Grimesby Roylott, who had previously killed
his stepdaughter Julia Stoner with the same snake. (The name
Stoner suggests one who has been turned to stone by a snake-haired
Medusa.)

Dr. Watson's description of the dead villain, is clearly based upon that of the mythological dead Medusa whose every strand of hair is a deadly snake: "... his eyes were fixed in a dreadful, rigid stare. ... He made neither sound nor motion ... and *there reared from among his hair ... a loathsome serpent.*" (Emphasis added.)

The sight of Roylott found dead with open "dreadful, rigid stare," and gazing at the snake about to strike him, is duplicated thirty-two years later by Doyle in "The Problem of Thor Bridge" (1922). In this brief, tantalizing stunner, Watson refers to "Isadora Persano ... who was found stark staring mad with a matchbox in front of him which contained a remarkable worm said to be unknown to science." A "worm" is a "serpent," says the *Oxford Unabridged Dictionary,* which cites dozens of "worm-serpent" examples from Beowulf onward. So it would seem that, small as it was, the "remarkable worm" unknown to science (but not to mythology) was sufficiently Medusan to kill the mind of Isadora (*sic*) Persano. Some psychoanalysts believe that Medusa, the beautiful woman who had phallic snakes for hair, was, for the Greeks, an agreed-upon symbol of petrifying hermaphroditism. The male-female name chosen by Conan Doyle for the hapless "journalist-duelist" seems to be suitably hermaphroditic.

> Approach the chamber [of death], and destroy your sight with a new Gorgon. See, and then speak for yourselves.
> —Macduff in *Macbeth,* 2.3.68

Three hundred years before Doyle felt compelled to switch the sex of his own Gorgo-Medusa (Gorgiano) from female to male, his idol William Shakespeare also gave his *Antony and Cleopatra* audiences two precise references to a masculinized or sexually ambivalent Medusa, who is linked to illicit copulation, lover's suicide, and the death of large masses of men in war.

The first Medusan reference is made when her messenger returns from Rome with the terrible news that her great lover Antony is married to Octavia. Upon hearing this, the man-killing Cleopatra "turns to stone," as the saying goes, and, enraged, likens the messenger to a "Fury crowned with snakes" (Medusa was, as we have said, frequently depicted in ancient art as a Fury). Then, assuming the role of Perseus for a moment, Cleopatra draws a knife and wields it in a decapitating manner. The frightened messenger runs for his life.

Later, minutes before she suicidally puts the famous snake to her breast, she repeats the Medusa metaphor, ambivalently, by saying of Antony:

> Though he be painted one way like a Gorgon,
> The other way's a Mars.
>
> [2. 5. 116–17]

The quotation above, from *Macbeth,* also refers to a male Medusa. Macduff's "new Gorgon" refers quite clearly to the sight of King Duncan, just stabbed to death by Lady Macbeth. The Gorgon image here suggests that Lady Macbeth slashed King Duncan's head, almost severing it.

(Saint) Gennaro Lucca

When the Neapolitan Emilia Lucca enters her husband's room in response to Sherlock's faked light signals, she arrives fearing the worst. Again using words that remind one of the face of Medusa, Doyle writes, "Slowly she advanced, her face pale and drawn with frightful apprehension, her eyes fixed and staring, her terrified gaze riveted on the dark figure on the floor."

"You have killed him!" she muttered. "Oh, *Dio mio,* you have killed him!" But then she takes another look at the dead man lying in the ever-widening pool of blood, and she goes into what used to be called transports of delight:

She sprang into the air with a cry of joy. Round and round the room she danced, her hands clapping, her dark eyes gleaming with delighted wonder, and a thousand pretty Italian exclamations pouring from her lips. It was terrible and amazing to see such a woman so convulsed with joy at such a sight.

As I read this, I thought: First Emilia thinks that the dead man is Gennaro, but when she sees that it is Gorgiano lying in his own blood, she becomes ecstatically happy . . . now what does all this remind me of?

Then I remembered. Some years ago, while on a photography assignment in Naples, I attended the annual exhibition of St.

Gennaro's congealed blood at the Naples Cathedral. Tens of thousands of excited Neapolitans jammed the church, all praying that their patron saint's blood would liquefy. And when it did, the entire crowd screamed with joy. Reacting exactly as Emilia, belle of Naples, did. They danced and sang and uttered a million "pretty Italian exclamations of delight." And, like Dr. Watson, "I thought it was terrible and amazing" to see such people "so convulsed with joy at such a sight."

When "Mr. Leverton . . . the hero of the Long Island Cave Mystery" (there are no caves in Long Island, where I live) first sees the corpse of the "monstrous" Gorgiano, he adds to the mythic nature of "The Red Circle" by exclaiming: *"By George! It's Black Gorgiano himself!"* (Emphasis added.)

Here again the amazingly persistent Doyle gives us another mythological reference that is highly relevant to the story, since it refers to St. George, the patron saint of England. St. George is always shown iconographically as the heroic slayer of the fire-breathing dragon about to toast, rape, and eat the sacrificial virgin maiden.

The exclamation "By George," says the *Oxford Unabridged Dictionary,* quietly, is the final evolved form of the ancient English battle cry "St. George!" or "By St. George!" After the Protestant Reformation, when the English discarded most other saints, the indispensable patron saint of England was held over and used exclamatorily as "By George!"

Thus we see that the assiduous mythographer Doyle, who certainly knew what the OED knows, did indeed regard his Gorgiano as a mythic monster who was to be killed by a modern Perseus and vocally recognized as a dragon which had been prevented from devouring (sexually) the delightful Neapolitan dish named Emilia Lucca.

Emilia Lucca as St. Lucia (Lucy)

Though the beautiful Mrs. Lucca says that she was "born in Posillipi, near Naples," her last name derives from the city of Lucca, in Northern Italy, and from the martyred early Christian St. Lucia, or Lucy. An Italian encyclopedia says that the name *Lucca* is based on the word *Luca,* or *Luce,* meaning *light.* I mention this because I've found that the variations of the name St. Lucia, also based on the word light, hold a special mythic significance in the Sherlock Holmes adventures, particularly "The Red Circle" and *A Study in Scarlet*.

As the protectress of all Catholics who suffer from eye diseases, Lucia is also the patron saint of Catholic eye doctors, including Dr. Conan Doyle, a lapsed Catholic and former ophthalmologist. When we keep these facts in mind and learn more about St. Lucia (Lucy), we also gain insight into the myth or allegory that is half-concealed behind the façade of the entertaining Sherlockian adventures.

Yes, I do believe that the name Emilia *Lucca,* fugitive from the unbridled sexual lust of Gorgiano, was chosen by Doyle with conscious mythogenic intent.

St. Lucia was the Sicilian girl martyred during the fourth century persecutions of Diocletian because she vowed to remain a holy virgin. Her rejected pagan suitor denounced her as a secret underground Christian, and she was sentenced to serve as a brothel slave. But through prayer she became miraculously immovable. Then, to make herself too ugly and pitiable to serve as a whore, she tore out her eyes. A second miracle restored her sight, but she was finally murdered with a large knife thrust into her jugular vein. St. Lucia is usually depicted holding her two eyes in a dish and/or with a knife protruding from her throat.

(There is an anticlimactic, naïve, or black-humor note in my *Dictionary of Saints:* "St. Lucia is also the patron saint of sore throats.")

I believe that Doyle, compulsive repeater of imagery in many stories, was thinking of the martyred St. Lucia (Lucy) when he wrote the scene in which human-monster-dragon-Gorgo-Gorgiano, would-be rapist of the saintly Mrs. Lucca (Lucia), is himself found dead with a "knife projecting from his broad, brown, upturned neck."

Conan Doyle seems to have had the martyred St. Lucia (Lucy) in mind for a very long time. Twenty-four years before "The Red Circle" appeared (1911), Doyle published his first Sherlockian adventure, *A Study in Scarlet,* in which his first Lucy (Ferrier) is a secret Christian living among the "pagan" Mormons in Utah. Like the later Mrs. Lucca, Lucy is martyred by a sex-mad, polygamous Mormon who also killed her stepfather John Ferrier in an action personally directed by Brigham Young.

In this disgracefully ignorant and prejudiced anti-Mormon story, Lucy dies of a "broken heart" after she has been forced to the brothel-like "harem" of Enoch J. Drebber.

Like the later sexual-monster Gorgiano, found dead with a knife stuck in his throat, Drebber is also executed privately in a scene that also recalls the death of the legendary St. Lucia. Lucy Ferrier's avenging lover, Jefferson Hope, holds a knife to Drebber's throat, reminds him of his rape of the innocent Lucy, and forces him to drink an instantly fatal poison.

The inspiration to perform an act may often be gentle, and even seemingly irrelevant. Gibbon tells us that it was in listening to the evening bells sounding across the Campagna and hearing the chanting of the monks that it came to him to write of the decline and fall of the Roman Empire. Struck by the fact that he found no fewer than fifteen Canonical mentions of, or references to, red Indians, the author of this article decided to go further and deeper into the possible, and possibly intimate, experiences that Holmes had had of the Noble Savage. More, the careful scrutiny of all these references seemed to indicate that Watson may have shared the experience of knowing a red Indian (or red Indians). Talking of Holmes, Watson observes in "The Naval Treaty" that "He had, when he so willed, the utter immobility of countenance of a red Indian." Watson can't have been referring to the utter immobility of a cigar-store Indian—such images were not a commonplace of Victorian England. So, Watson must be referring to a real Red Indian. Mr. Bennett Shaw has opened up a new and important aspect of Sherlockian research in considering the facts and hypotheses of the relationship between . . .

Sherlock and
the American Indian

※

JOHN BENNETT SHAW

※

John H. Watson, M.D., as portrayed by Nigel Bruce in the Rathbone films, was a bumbler and a dullard. This is most unfortunate
for the millions who have not read the Holmesian Canon but who
views these films again and again. They have a false conception of
the author of the Sherlock Holmes cases. Watson was a reasonably
intelligent fellow, trained by his medical studies and by his association with Holmes to observe and to apply logic in reaching
conclusions. Further, we all know that he could and did (at least
fifty-six times) write fine tales that are both exciting and absorbing.

Yet one reads with amazement that Watson, in *A Study in
Scarlet,* assessed Holmes and found that his limits were many, that
the minuses outnumbered the pluses. This summation was both
inaccurate and very illogical. There are some who feel that Holmes
was "putting Watson on." Perhaps, or possibly the fact that he,
Watson, had recently moved to Baker Street to room with the
Great Detective could be his excuse. At best he was foolish to try
this at this time, for he made judgments about his associate that
were grossly wrong. The very idea that Holmes's knowledge about
literature, philosophy, and politics were given as "nil" astounds

one. Rather when one really views the mind and heart of Holmes one could simply assess him as a Renaissance man. As Dakin says, ". . . his information on the widest range of subjects including those rated so low by Watson was far greater than first appeared to his friend." Holmes read about, talked about, and at times wrote about such subjects as international politics, philosophy, music, classical European, English and American literature, astronomy, miracle plays, medieval pottery, comparative religion, and anthropology.

For the purpose of this essay I am especially interested in Holmes's knowledge of America and, more specifically, of the Red Man (i.e., the American Indian). Reference to America occurs in at least eleven of the adventures, and in six of these, American happenings or characters play a major part in the plot. Even making allowance for the fact that Holmes owned and used a copy of *The American Encyclopaedia,* one must conclude that he had a rather extensive knowledge of the United States geographically, historically, politically, and linguistically. Note especially

the importance of this latter knowledge, the linguistic, in solving the mystery in "The Three Garridebs." I agree with both Shaler and Baring-Gould that Sherlock Holmes could not have known so much about America, nor would he have been able to use this knowledge with such familiar ease, unless he had lived in the States for some time, and that long before the stint when, as "Altamont," he lived and worked there in 1912.

As I have been a resident of the American Southwest for all of my life, I have been especially interested in the several references in the Watsonian Canon to the American Indian and to his specific environment. As nearly as I can determine, the Red Man and his milieu are mentioned fifteen times. I would include such references as the two to buffalo, to war path, to hunting ground, and the like; and I would even include the use of the "apaches in the Montmartre district" ("The Illustrious Client"), for this name derived from that of the warlike American Indian tribe. Specifically named tribes are Blackfeet (*A Study in Scarlet*), Pawnees (*A Study in Scarlet,* twice), Apaches in their natural state ("The Noble Bachelor"), and in the Continental usage of the name as mentioned above. Further, the word "redskins" is used (*A Study in Scarlet*), as is "red Indian" ("The Naval Treaty"); also, a real live Indian, presumably a guide, who unfortunately when mentioned is no longer alive, is named "Indian Pete" (*A Study in Scarlet*), and the term "Indians" is used (*The Sign of Four*). And in the same adventure Holmes says, "No, then, where are we to find our savage? South America, I hazard." This is not properly a reference to the Indian about whom we write, but it does show that savagery and Indians were linked in Holmes's mind. Also in the case "The Five Orange Pips" is a reference to a man who as a young man emigrated to Florida and became a planter, and there can be no doubt that he came into frequent contact with Choctaws and Seminoles, for these tribes owned the land in Florida, or thought they did. As I have indicated above, both Holmes and Watson used terms that referred directly to the Indian environment: such as hunting ground ("The Red Circle"), wild west ("The Three Garridebs"), war path (*The Sign of Four*), and braves (*A Study in Scarlet*).

From all this evidence, I would conclude that in terms of history and anthropology and, perhaps, linguistics, Holmes was most con-

Comments upon these quotations in written and phonetic Cherokee.

(1) Gꓢ RꞭꞋⱤꙄꓷ Bꚍ Ꙅꓴ Ꮣ ꓢWKꓢ
wa-ga e-li-e-s-di yv-hna-s-sa tla ga-la-tso-de

ᎫG ꓷꙄꓷꞋꙆ ꙄhꓢWꝏ
tsu-nah-di-s-di-yi ya-ni-ga-ta-ha.

(2) Dh Ɪh ꝋZ EꞪꞀ ᎫꝋWꙄꓢ
a-ni qua-ni na-no gu-na-ge tsu-na-la-s-ga

ꝋꞋꙄꓢRh hWꓢ DꞮꙄꓷ
u-ni-s-ga-e-ni tsi-ta-ga a-li-s-di

(3) Ɪꓓ DꙄꙆG ꓢVDSꓥꔯDVVꔯR
qui-da a-s-gi-nah qa-to-a-du-ne-he-e tse-to-he-e

(4) DhBꝋꙄD4 DꓥVꔯ i4Z ꓥꙆhꙄꝏꙆ
a-ni-yv-wi-ya a-se a-ne-to-he v-se-no di-da-ni-yi-s-gi

Ꮣ DSGꞝꙄꓷ BꞀGꞌꝋꙆꙆGꓥ.
tla a-da-lo-ho-hi-s-di-ye-gi yu-na-da-s-da-wa-di

(5) ꞪꞐGꞌ VꞝꞀ ꝋꞐꞋ DꓥꞪ
na-he-yu tse-ge-se u-yo a-ne-hi

DBꝋꙄ ꞀVꓢꞭꙆꞀ.
a-yv-wi-ya ge-tse-ga-li-s-ge

(6) D4Ꙅ ᎫꓢꞪꞝ DꙷBꞮ DꓥꞪ DhBꙄꝏD4
a-se-ka tsu-ga-na-wv a-ma-ye-li a-ne-hi a-ni-yv-wė-ya a-se

ꝋhꓥᎫꓥ ꞀꞀ AꙷꝮ DhGWY
u-ni-ne-gu-hi ge-se go-we-lv a-ni-tsa-la-gi

ꮮꞮꙄY AꮣꙄꓷ ꓥꞪꞀꝋh
tla-v-s-gi go-hu-s-di di-na-da-dv-ni

(7) ꓕD DꙄꝋꙄ ꞀꞮꝋꝋꞪ ꮮZG ꝋꙷꙆꙄꓷ
hi-a a-s-ka-ya nu-da-nv-du-na da-no-wa u-we-nv-s-di

ꓔGꞌꓢꞭ ꓥꞀꝋꝋRT.
i-yu-du-li di-ge-nv-sv i

(8) DꔯꓥꞀ ꓔꓢꙷꓕꙄꓷ ꓔEꙙZ AꙷꝮꓕT.
a-he-di-ge i-ga-we-i-s-ti i-gv-yi-no go-we-lv-i

(9) D4ꙶ DhGꝋW SꝏꞮꓢ.
a-se-dv a-ni-tsa-ka-ta du-ha-da-de

(10) Ꮣ D4ꙶC ꓔꓢ ꓥꞪCꓔ BꞀꞀ DhDꞮV
tla a-se u-tli i-ga di-na-tli-i ye-ge-se a-ni-a-qua-tse

D4ZꞀDꙶꝏꓢꞀꓥ ꓥꓥꙷꞭꓔꝏYꝋhꝋꞮꓔ.
a-se-no-ge-a-se u-s-ga-se ti di-go-we-li-i-s-gi u-ni-ka-he-i

(11) ᏔᎢ Ꮝ ᏠᎠᎴ ᎤᎦᏔᏍ ᎠᏂᏍᏆᎠᏱ.
hna-qua-le tla-a-se u-tli-i-qa a-ni-ga-ta-hi-yi-qi

(12) ᏅᎠ ᎤᎦᏔ ᎠᎦᏴᏟ ᎭᏁᏏ ᏗᎦᏗᏸ ᎨᏎ Ꭲ.
nv-a u-ka-ta a-ga-yv-li yo-ne-ga di-ga-ti yi ge-se i

(13) ᎢᏗᏴᏫᏯ ᎠᏂᎨᏯ ᏗᏗᎰᎯ.
i-di-yv-wi-ya a-ni-ge-ya di-di-yo-hi

(14) ᎢᎦᏓᏠᎲ ᎡᎳᏗᏓ ᎡᎬᏂᎭ.ᏍᎤᎩ ᎾᎯᎷᏅᎾ
i-ga-da-tlo-hv e-la-di-tla e-gv-ni-ha ga-to-hv nu-na-da-hv-dv-na

ᎠᏂᎦᎸᏥ ᎠᏂᏴᏫᏯ ᏙᏙᏎ?
a-ni-ga-lv-tsi a ni yv wi ya do-do-se

(15) ᏝᏛ ᎤᏟ ᎬᏚᏎᏕ ᎭᎯᏳᏤᎨᏎ ᏙᏆᎴᎷ
ha-dv u-tli yu-s-ka-se-de na-hi-yu-tse-ge-se to-qua-le-lu

ᏩᏴᏏ Ꭲ ᏧᎾᎾᎦ Ꮄ Ꮧ Ꭲ Ꭴ Ꮯ ᏄᏂᏏᎧᏎᏙ Ꭲ.
wa-yv-s - i tsu-na-na-ga le ti i   u tli nu-ni-s-ka-se-to-i

Translation into English of the foregoing Cherokee comments.

(1) Like all cattle, buffalo were not housebroken.
(2) Those Pawnee and Blackfeet were always chicken. (Literally, as an example: "The Pawnee and Blackfeet are a scary chicken-like".)
(3) What was that renegade Pete doing there anyway?
(4) There were probably a lot of Indians there, but like Sherlock Holmes, when they followed one must not expect to know it.
(5) Even then the poor Indians are taking the rap.
(6) It could be, the South American Indian might have been this savage; but, for the record, we Cherokees are _not_ related.
(7) This guy would be simple to go on the war-path in our country.
(8) A hell of a lot nicer way of putting it than in quotation number one.
(9) Very likely he planted Choctaws.
(10) It is debatable that the Apaches were such great warriors, but they sure have a good press-agent.
(11) And then again, they were not so smart.
(12) Old stoney face was usually the white agent.
(13) Us Indians are usually girl hunters.
(14) This is hitting below the belt - why call these crazy French bastards Indians?
(15) It was no wilder than now - these drive-in movies are really where the action is.

Questions and answers about the Sherlockian "Red Indian" references —in the Cherokee language, as referred to in Mr. Bennett Shaw's article. *Artwork from Mr. J. Bennett Shaw.*

a	e	i	o	u
ga	ge	gi	go	gu
ha	he	hi	ho	hu
la	le	li	lo	lu
ma	me	mi	mo	mu
na	ne	ni	no	nu
gwa	gwe	gwi	gwo	gwu
sa	se	si	so	su
da	de	di	do	du
dla	dle	dli	dlo	dlu
dza	dze	dzi	dzo	dzu
wa	we	wi	wo	wu
ya	ye	yi	yo	yu
ö	gö	hö	lö	nö
gwö	sö	dö	dlö	dzö
wö	yö	ka	hna	nah
s	ta	te	ti	tla

The Cherokee syllabary of eighty-five characters, invented, as the "most developed script ever created by an American native" (Dr. David Diringer), by the Cherokee Sequoya or Sikwaya (or John Gist/Guest) in 1821. Guest-Sequoya's syllabary—for which your Editor's research has provided the most astonishing source—has maintained its position as the "classic" Cherokee script despite two later attempts (1890) to introduce "more rational" scripts.

versant with what was known about these subjects at that time. He surely had read widely, and had talked about and listened and remembered much about these and other factual subjects. Indeed all this makes the most convincing argument, as advanced by Shaler and Baring-Gould, that Holmes lived in America long before these cases happened and were recorded by Dr. Watson.

As for Holmes's knowledge of history, Whitfield J. Bell expressed it well if a bit enthusiastically: "Certainly to have judged Holmes's knowledge of history as 'nil' would have been as undiscerning as Watson's estimation of Holmes's literary attainments. The fact simply is that in history Holmes was a student and a

Ted Walker's impression of Sherlock's solution of a "three-pipe problem" when the Master is on Indian territory. *Drawing from Mr. John Bennett Shaw, BSI.*

scholar who might have honored the faculty of arts at any university." The ease with which Holmes laces the Watsonian narrative with Indian names and facts and word usages certainly implies a considerable knowledge of the nineteenth-century American Indian, and this, coupled with other anthropological opinions, leads me to conclude that he had read and studied the origins and habitat of the American Indian. I am not alone in the opinion that Holmes was very knowledgeable in anthropology, for others have written on this. As Wilton Marion Krogman says, "Among the fields in which he showed considerable knowledge was anthropology. Primarily, his interests were concerned with what we today classify as physical anthropology, but he knew archeology and ethnography as well." He did, indeed.

Before I close this research effort I want to give a brief account of a project that I undertook in 1967. I had carefully gone through the Canon and had listed fifteen quotations that referred to the Red Man, or the American Indian. I took these quotations to a member of that race, a literate and talented Cherokee, and asked him to translate these into the Cherokee language and to write them in the Cherokee script which was devised by that great scholar of the Cherokees, Sequoyah, and then to write the phonetic reading of his translation and, if he wished, to comment in English. He did, and the writing is beautiful; the comments fresh, direct, and honest. As an example I will use the two quotations from "The Noble Bachelor" that speak of the Apaches: "After that came a long newspaper story about how a miner's camp had been attacked by Apache Indians and there was my Frank's name among the killed." The Cherokee version of this was:

ᏓᎠᏎᎤᏟ ᎢᎦ ᏗᎾᏟᎢ ᏰᎨᏎ ᎠᏂᎠᏉᏤ
tla a-se u-tli i-ga di-na-tli-i ye-ge-se a-ni-a-qua-tse
ᎠᏎᏃᎨᎠᏎ ᎤᏍᎦᏎᏘ ᏗᎪᏪᎵᎢᏍᎩ ᎤᏂᎧᎮᎢ
a-se-no-ge-a-se u-s-ga-se ti di-go-we-li-i-s-gi u-ni-ka-he-i

And the comment was: "It is debatable that the Apaches were such good warriors, but they sure had a good press-agent."

And the second quotation: "Frank had been a prisoner among the Apaches, had escaped . . ." In Cherokee this read:

ᏂᎧᏍ ᏢᎠᏎ ᎤᏟᎢᎦ ᎠᏂᎦᏔᎯᏱᎩ.
hna-qua-le   tla-a-se   u-tli-i-qa   a-ni-ga-ta-hi-yi-qi

And the comment was: "And then again, they were not so smart."

And lastly, from *A Study in Scarlet:* "There are no inhabitants of this land of despair. A band of Pawnees or of Blackfeet may occasionally traverse it in order to reach other hunting-grounds, but the hardiest of the braves are glad to lose sight of those awesome plains and to find themselves once more upon their prairies."
And the Cherokee:

ᎠᏂ ᏩᏂ ᎾᏃ ᎬᎾᎨ ᏧᎾᎳᏍᎦ
a-ni qua-ni na-no gu-na-ge tsu-na-la-s-ga
ᎤᏂᏍᎦᎡᏂ ᏥᏔᎦ ᎠᎵᏍᏗ
u-ni-s-ga-e-ni tsi-ta-ga a-li-s-di

And the comment: " 'Those Pawnees and Blackfeet were always chicken [meaning cowardly],' and a more literal translation of the comment would be, 'The Pawnees and Blackfeet are scary chicken-like.' "

I must disagree with my Cherokee friend, for, from the evidence, I think Mr. Holmes had a broader knowledge of the American Indian than he. For, after all, Holmes was "best and wisest."

BIBLIOGRAPHY

Baring-Gould, William S. *The Annotated Sherlock Holmes.* New York: Clarkson N. Potter, Inc. 1967.
——*Sherlock Holmes of Baker Street.* New York: Clarkson N. Potter, Inc., 1962.
Bell, Whitfield J. "Holmes and History." *The Baker Street Journal* [O.S.], October 1947, vol. 2, no. 4, pp. 447–456.
Dakin, D. Martin. *A Sherlock Holmes Commentary.* London: David & Charles: Newton Abbot, 1972.
De Waal, Ronald Burt. *The World Bibliography of Sherlock Holmes and Dr. Watson.* Boston: New York Graphic Society, 1974.
Hardwick, Michael, and Hardwick, Mollie. *The Sherlock Holmes Companion.* London: John Murray, 1962.

Harrison, Michael. *The World of Sherlock Holmes.* London: Frederick Muller Ltd., 1973.

Krogman, Wilton Marion. "Sherlock Holmes as an Anthropologist." *The Scientific Monthly,* March 1955, vol. 80, no. 3, pp. 155–162.

Redmond, Donald A., ed. *Bigelow on Holmes.* Toronto: Metropolitan Toronto Library, 1974.

Shaler, Louise. "A Study in Scarlet in the Utah Territory." *Sherlock Holmes Journal,* Winter 1972, vol. 11, no. 1, pp. 9–15.

Not a few of the many Sherlockian commentators, the Editor in-cluded, have busied themselves with examining the social status (even to the construction of the pedigree) of those notable persons who enrolled themselves in the tally of Sherlock Holmes's clientele. Yet, with the exception of providing a biographical background to that "Napoleon of Crime," Professor James Moriarty, no compara-ble Sherlockian scholarship has busied itself with investigating the background of Holmes's enemies. Obviously, Holmes compiled his own dossier (or "blotter") on all persons having, or likely to have, to do with him: extracts from this rather haphazard index are quoted several times in the Canon. In any case, it is clear that Holmes used his invaluable reference book only as an aide-mémoire—he already knew the names memorialized in its hastily scrawled pages. But do we? Watson, recording Holmes's muttered —and brutally truncated—extracts from the master file, gives only the briefest details. Enough to tell us, we know, that Holmes was instantly in possession of all the essential biographical facts, but only enough, alas! to whet our appetite for more. To close an in-formational gap too long left open, here then is the first full-length biographical note of one of Holmes's enemies; indeed, next to Moriarty, Holmes's principal enemy. Here, based on that fa-mous index, is the background of an out-and-out villain:

The Colonel of the Matter

The Early Career of Colonel Sebastian Moran

NICHOLAS UTECHIN

A baby born out of wedlock . . . a thirteen-year-old at Eton . . . a newly commissioned subaltern in one of Her Majesty's infantry regiments . . . a battle-hardened veteran crawling down a drain after a wounded tiger . . . finally second-in-command to the Napoleon of Crime. And his end? Well, justice calls out for the gallows, but then Colonel Sebastian Moran always was a slippery customer.[1]

The early years of Sebastian Moran have hitherto been a closed book. Sherlock Holmes, in his index of criminal biographies, gives a terse description of the man's background:

"Moran, Sebastian, Colonel. Unemployed. Formerly 1st Bengalore Pioneers. Born London, 1840. Son of Sir Augustus Moran, C.B., once British Minister to Persia. Educated Eton and Oxford. Served in Jowaki Campaign, Afghan Campaign, Charasiab (dispatches), Sharpur, and Cabul. Author of *Heavy Game of the Western Himalayas,* 1881; *Three Months in the Jungle,* 1884. Address Conduit Street. Clubs: The Anglo-Indian, the Tankerville, the Bagatelle Card Club.[2]

We also have some idea of his position in the criminal hierarchy built up by Professor Moriarty: a man worth £6,000 a year for his counsel and his ability with firearms. Above all, we have Dr. Watson's superb description of Moran at the instant of capture:

It was a tremendously virile and yet sinister face which was turned toward us. With the brow of a philosopher above and the jaw of a sensualist below, the man must have started with great capacities for good or for evil. But one could not look upon his cruel blue eyes, with their drooping cynical lids, or upon the fierce aggressive nose and the threatening, deep-lined brow, without reading Nature's plainest danger signals.[3]

Can you not see the man yourself? Is he not brought alive before your very eyes?

But that is Colonel Sebastian Moran as he was in early April of 1894. He was fifty-four then, a man for whom the good times were over, reduced to making a living by cheating at cards. With the death of Moriarty three years before in the "boiling cauldron" of the Reichenbach Falls, his power and influence, his very reason for living, all had passed away. Half a century before, though, things had been different indeed.

When, in 1840, Sebastian Augustus Malcolm Edward McNeill was born in London, he was endowed with many of nature's advantages. True, he was illegitimate, but he never lost the love of his influential father until the end; and the downward path he trod in later life was one of his own choosing, rather than one mapped out from the start.

His father was Sir John McNeill of Colonsay.[4] Born in 1795, the third of three sons, Sir John had studied medicine at Edinburgh, graduating in 1814. Two years later he became assistant surgeon with The Honourable The East India Company's establishment in Bombay. But McNeill was not to devote his career to medicine and the ailments of Englishmen far from their homes. Instead he chose diplomacy, and in 1835, having been political assistant to the Company's envoy in Persia, he was appointed secretary of the special British embassy to Teheran under Henry Ellis. He was a man of great promise and, unlike so many, quickly fulfilled the high hopes that were held of him. A year later, on 25 May 1836, John McNeill was made Envoy and Minister Plenipotentiary to the Shah of Persia. By 1841 he had been created a G.C.B. (Civil Order) by a grateful Queen and her Prime Minister; after all, it was due almost entirely to Sir John that a treaty of commerce between Britain and Persia was concluded in October of that year.

Domestically, Sir John was less fortunate and less happy. Immediately after graduation in 1814, he had married Innes Robinson; by her he had one daughter, Innes, born two years later. But his young wife died that same year, perhaps even in childbirth, and for nine years McNeill remained a widower. Then, on New Year's Day in 1823, he was married a second time, to Elizabeth Wilson; and see the catalogue of tragedies that befell four of the five children born of this union:

> Margaret, born 1824, dies 3 October 1826
> Hester Mary, born 12 March 1826, dies early 1834
> John Robert, born June 1830, "did not live more than a year"
> Elizabeth Jane, born 30 March 1832, dies February 1834
> Margaret Ferooza, born 5 January 1834

No surviving sons—in those far-off pre-Victorian days when lineage and the continuation of the family name were so important. And McNeill, with a brother who was to become Lord Justice General and Lord President of the Court of Session in Scotland, had indeed a family tradition to uphold and continue. Maybe he thought that more permissive times might come with the advent of a young queen; perhaps he merely longed for a surviving male child; whatever the reason, we believe that Sir John met and, in 1840, had an illegitimate child by a Frenchwoman, of whom the only thing we know is her surname, Mourant. That child was to become Colonel Sebastian Moran.

We can discover nothing about the first decade of Sebastian McNeill's life. To be a child born out of wedlock was to be put in a difficult position. Of course he did not live with his father—how could he? Probably he spent his early years out of the country, with his French mother. But Sir John, even while he was in Persia, did not forget his son, and we can be sure that there was always enough money available for the boy's education, and even the chance of an occasional paternal meeting. Illegitimate though he was, to Sir John McNeill, Sebastian was his son, and as such was due as many as possible of the opportunities a legitimate child would have had. That is why, in 1853, we find recorded in the Eton College List[5] the name of Malcolm McNeill: he was in the

Fourth Form, Remove F, at that most prestigious of English schools. Why he was entered in the roll as Malcolm is unclear, but since this is only the first of several examples of Sebastian having his surname changed or using different Christian names, we must assume that his father was protecting himself by disguising the child's exact identity.

By the time the next Election of boys at Eton was held, in 1856, Sebastian was no longer there—his name does not appear. Although he may well have wanted to stay on and reap the benefits that inevitably accrue to an old Etonian, what he saw and did in the year 1855 must have had an immeasurable effect on him. At the beginning of that year, Sir John McNeill and Colonel Alexander Tulloch were sent to the Crimea by the British government: their mission was to report on the arrangements and management of the commissariat department. They were also to look into the administrative officers' method of keeping accounts and to investigate the causes of delays in unloading and distributing clothing and other stores which had been sent to Balaclava. The two men were on the peninsula for almost a year, and we believe that Sir John took his fifteen-year-old son with him. This was Sebastian's first encounter with the adult world—he saw the privations to which men sometimes had to accustom themselves. On the other hand, the boy was fascinated by what he saw of the British army: although of course he was not present, he read of the stirring Charge of the Light Brigade on 25 October 1854, when six hundred cavalrymen charged straight into the face of massed Russian artillery; and it was at this time that the idea of going into the army may first have occurred to him.

Sir John and Sebastian returned to England at the end of the year, and by January 1856 the McNeill and Tulloch report was ready. Sebastian, however, must have returned to his schooling, this time on a private tuition basis. Two more years were enough to insure that he was ready for the university; and his father's unseen influence made it certain that when he wished to go to Wadham College, in the University of Oxford, the chance was not denied him. There, in the University Calendar for 1859[6] (reporting events which took place the previous year), we see the name of Edward Mourant, entered as having come up to Wadham in the Michaelmas Term. Again to avoid embarrassment for his well-

known and much-respected father, Sebastian had agreed to continue his education under yet another combination of names, this
time adopting his mother's surname and making use of his own
last Christian name.

What Edward Mourant studied at Wadham is not known;
twenty-five years later his son was to read mathematics at Oxford,
but one cannot assume that the child followed in his father's footsteps. We do know, however, that he did not take an Honours
degree, for, although the Calendar for 1862 records that Edward
Mourant took his degree on 6 June 1861, his name is not listed
under any subject, nor is the class of degree he obtained given.
Whatever it was that he studied must have interested Sebastian,
however, in that he took the trouble to take his M.A. almost exactly
a year later, on 26 June 1862. Does this mean that he was con-
templating an academic career at this stage? Perhaps. One cannot
say more.

So, what to do? A highly educated twenty-two-year-old with the
whole world open before him, and only the disadvantage of illegitimacy to hold him back. The cloistered university life might
have appealed; one gets the impression, at least from his later life,
that the church would never have exerted much influence on
Sebastian; a diplomatic career was clearly closed to him because of
his illegitimacy and his father; a legal career could have been a
possibility. Sebastian Moran remembered what he had seen a few
years before in the Crimea, and forthwith he decided to go into the
regular army. With the money that must have been available to
him, he could doubtless have purchased a commission without difficulty;[7] but the young man adhered to the maxim that what is
worth doing is worth doing properly, and he decided to study
hard and be coached for entry into the army. Searching through
the directories of available and qualified army coaches, he came
across a certain name—that of a man recently come down to London after having somewhat sullied his reputation at a university in
the North of England. That man was Professor James Moriarty.

It will be remembered that Sherlock Holmes, when discussing
Moran with Watson after the affair of "The Empty House," said
that when the Colonel left India, Moriarty had "sought him out"—
the wording is important, for it implies previous knowledge of
the man on Moriarty's part, not simply of his reputation. At what

other stage could Moran and Moriarty have been in contact than in this early part of their careers, when neither had yet decided to go into crime? The coach seeking pupils, the fresh university graduate seeking a military career: surely it was obvious and inevitable?[8] The two came together; and in 1864 Mourant was commissioned as a subaltern in the 19th Foot.

Eighteen sixty-four was an important year for Mourant in other ways, too. In that year he married, and a son, Walter Isidore (who was to read mathematics at Merton College, Oxford, twenty years later),[9] was born the next year. The identity of his wife remains a mystery, and one which it would be fascinating to penetrate.

Although Sir John McNeill was now sixty-nine and retired, and could no longer be seriously affected by the discovery of an illegitimate son, Sebastian joined his regiment, still using the name of Mourant—indeed, he was never to use his real name, McNeill, again. And he used yet another Christian name: in the Army List for 1881, after the Second Afghan War, we encounter the name Augustus Mourant in the roll for the 19th Foot—by then he had risen to the rank of major.[10] In passing, it might be pointed out that Sherlock Holmes used the name Augustus to cover the true identity of Moran's father when he read Watson the biography in his scrapbook of criminals.

In those days, over a hundred years ago, it was entirely possible that it could take seventeen years to rise from second lieutenant to major. Over the years between being commissioned and fighting in the Afghan War, when we can again pick up his trail, Augustus Mourant served his Queen and country wherever his regiment was sent, or wherever he was seconded. The years 1868–69 saw the British expedition to Abyssinia (later Ethiopia) under Sir Robert Napier, with action being seen twice, at the battle of Arogee and the storming of Magdala. Four years later, Mourant may have been part of the force under the command of Sir Garnet Wolseley which was sent to British West Africa to throw out the fetish-worshiping Ashanti tribesmen from a British-protected area of the Cape Coast. The small force of a little over two thousand men fought two hard battles but emerged victorious. The campaign is of some Sherlockian interest in its own right, whether or not Mourant was involved: one of the two newspaper correspondents who accompanied the soldiers was Winwood Reade—he was later to write *The Martyrdom of Man,* a book which Holmes recommended to Watson as "one of the most remarkable books ever penned."[11]

Sir John would have been happy to see his son in the country of his next posting, India. Over half a century previously, the young John McNeill had worked for The East India Company; now, at the end of the seventies, his son was out there, serving in the foremost part of the British Empire. During his four years of service in India, Mourant saw little action; he was able instead to devote himself to two new hobbies, big-game hunting and card playing. It is quite possible that he had done some shooting during his vacations from Oxford; indeed, the young Sebastian may have fired a musket when a fifteen-year-old in the Crimea. Whether or not he had shot before, Mourant rapidly established himself as a fine shot—Holmes was later to credit him with being the "best heavy-game shot our Eastern Empire ever produced."[12] A trip to the Northwest frontier gave Mourant the opportunities, knowledge, and expertise he was to utilize in 1881 when, as Sebastian Moran, he wrote his book, *Heavy Game of the Western Himalayas.* As for card playing, you have to be a very good card player to become a good enough cardsharp to make your living by it.

In 1878 the Second Afghan War erupted, and Mourant saw his

finest hours in military service. The 19th Foot was not involved, but because of his special knowledge of the area and prowess with firearms, Mourant was loaned to the Indian Army. Holmes maintained that he was in the Bengalore Pioneers—clearly the name has been disguised, but the Pioneers of the Corps of Madras Sappers and Miners (The Queen's Own) has been suggested elsewhere,[13] and I see no reason to dispute this. The high spot of Mourant's military career came at Charasia, where, fighting the army of Amir Yakub Khan, he acted so gallantly that he was mentioned in dispatches.

And then, suddenly, it was all over. The British finally established their right to have a permanent mission in Afghanistan, and the war ended. As we have seen, the Army List for 1881 shows that Augustus Mourant was a major; shortly afterward, he was promoted to colonel, but he left the army within a few months. Mourant was a man of action: with the fighting over, he was not about to return to the safe Richmond depot of the 19th Foot back in England. He decided to stay out in the East and go where adventure took him. And with the rank of colonel, and therefore a respected and gallant member of Her Majesty's Armed Forces, Augustus Mourant left the army. He changed his life-style and

finally, irrevocably, changed his name, merely taking the Anglicized form of his surname: Mourant to Moran. He returned to India, where he had ample opportunity to make good use of his ability as a shot. Holmes refers to Moran as "the old shikari": a shikari was usually a *native* hunter or guide, but Moran might in fact have demeaned himself to this role because of the opportunities thereby afforded to cheat rich jungle hunters.

For it was during these three years, from 1881 to 1884, that Moran turned from an officer and gentleman to a criminal and ruthless murderer. Why he did this, how it came about, is unexplained and inexplicable. Could it be that the ruthless personality of James Moriarty, with which Moran had come into contact all those years earlier, had exerted some unseen influence? Perhaps his years in the army had given Moran a warped sense of the value of human life. Or might this extraordinary change have come about through a hitherto genuinely unfelt, or suppressed, resentment over his illegitimacy (here we are stepping on Freudian ground, and must be very, very circumspect)? Clearly Sherlock Holmes himself had difficulty in fathoming the cause for Sebastian Moran's fall from moral rectitude:

"There are some trees, Watson, which grow to a certain height and then suddenly develop some unsightly eccentricity. You will see it often in humans. I have a theory that the individual represents in his development the whole procession of his ancestors, and that such a sudden turn for good or evil stands for some strong influence which came into the line of his pedigree. The person becomes, as it were, the epitome of the history of his own family. . . . Well, I don't insist upon it."

That was how Holmes tried to account for it after Moran's capture—and yet it hardly holds water in the case of the McNeill of Colonsay family; should we therefore examine Moran's family on his Continental mother's side? That aspect of the problem I leave to someone else, and wish him the very best of luck.

Moran did nothing actually illegal in India, but, as Holmes deftly put it, "without any open scandal, he still made India too hot to hold him." The change in his son's character was enough, though, to affect the health of Sir John McNeill; and as he died in 1883, in Cannes, we can only assume that his demise was brought on by a broken heart. The change in his character was serious enough that when Moran returned to England at some point in 1884, Professor Moriarty sought him out specifically and asked him to join his gang. We know the rest of the story.

In October 1884, Colonel Sebastian Moran's son, Walter Isidore Moran, now nineteen, went up to Merton College, Oxford. What path in life did *he* choose to take?

NOTES

1. In his recent book *The Return of Moriarty,* John Gardner maintains that Moran was poisoned by order of Professor Moriarty in April 1894 because of liberties taken during the Professor's absence.

2. "The Empty House": in the margin to this entry, Holmes has added, "The second most dangerous man in London."

3. "The Empty House."

4. All information on Sir John McNeill of Colonsay (1795–1883) has been taken from the *Dictionary of National Biography* and from *Sir John McNeill —A Memoir,* by Florence MacAlister. I am also indebted to my friend Robert Hutchinson, of Glasgow, for vital assistance.

5. *The Eton College Lists,* 2nd series, comprising the years between 1853 and 1892. Compiled for the Old Etonian Association by Henry Edward Chatwynd-Stapylton, 1900.

6. *The Oxford University Calendar 1859, corrected to December 31, 1858.* Oxford: John Henry and James Parker, Broad Street, 1859.

7. Again, for some military details, I am indebted to Brigadier Peter Young.

8. This fits in with my dating of Moriarty's career, as published in "Professor James Moriarty, 1836–1891," *Baker Street Journal* (New Series), vol. 24, no. 2.

9. *The Oxford University Calendar 1885.* Walter Isidore Moran was a Postmaster at Merton: "No person is eligible to a Postmastership who has exceeded the age of 19 on the day of election." Walter was exactly nineteen.

10. The Army List, *Whittaker's Almanack,* 1881.

11. *The Sign of Four.*

12. "The Empty House."

13. "Dr. Watson and the British Army," *Baker Street Journal* (Old Series), vol. 2, no. 3, Mrs. Brighton Sellars. Both Mrs. Sellars and Edgar W. Smith ("The Old Shikari," *The Best of the Pips*) chart the course of the Second Afghan War.

In his article in this anthology, Professor Jacques Barzun discusses criticism in its most general sense; here, the author homes in on one highly specialized aspect of criticism—that of assessing the factual authenticity and all-round probability of some Sherlockian plots. It has been accepted for many decades that exaggeration— and, indeed, plain error—is as much a basic component of the stories in the Canon as (may we say this?) the presence of Holmes and Watson. What of it? That Watson (or the Agent) overloaded the plain statement of fact in the interest of catching the reader's attention, and of persuading the reader that what was described was true, is no argument against the honesty of the description. Far from it, as only calculating liars speak and write as from a dishonestly conceived script. Watson wrote as he remembered—and if his remembrance was always colored by his loyalty to, and abounding admiration for, his eminent friend, surely we may peel away the layer of iridescent exaggeration with which Watson coats the kernel of truth, and see the actual facts beneath the ribboned decoration? In this article, a Sherlockian critic gently strives to seek the truth beneath the wrapping, as he presents . . .

A Critique
of the Biologic Plots
# of Sherlock Holmes

※

EDWARD J. VAN LIERE

※

> "It is with a heavy heart that I take up my pen
> to write these . . . words. . . ."
> —"The Final Problem"

No less a person than Oliver Wendell Holmes, the poet-physician, remarked that critics were made from the chips of creative writers. He had nothing good to say of them, and generally refused to read critical reviews of his own writings.

Now critics are apt to be unpopular people, and often have only a small circle of friends, a circle which may become smaller with the passing years. One reason for this is that these unreasonable folk question matters which we all wish to believe. Not many people like to have their cherished beliefs destroyed. They want to believe the legend of Sleepy Hollow and that of William Tell. They shudder when a psychiatrist hints that Jeanne d'Arc might have been psychotic, since she heard voices. In religious beliefs they are fundamentalists and are pained when a modern Biblical scholar attempts to give scientific explanations for some of the miracles related in the Old Testament.

Many of these well-meaning and often charming people may be highly critical of the actions of their neighbors or even the manners of their own children, but their critical sense sinks beneath the threshold when their cherished beliefs are assailed.

On the whole, I am in sympathy with these good people and am myself a firm believer in old traditions. I like to think, for example, that Robin Hood and his band led comfortable and carefree lives in beautiful forests and did not suffer from the cold and damp climate of England. I like to believe furthermore that the so-called gay nineties actually were gay and that there was no unhappiness, poverty, or disease. Although I know these illusions are not true, they die hard. Since I am a firm believer in traditions, it is with considerable reluctance that I criticize the "sacred writings." On the other hand, the scientific training of a lifetime makes it difficult to refrain from calling attention to biologic errors. With this somewhat inadequate and lame apology I don my critical cap.

Since I am a professional physiologist, the story of "The Adventure of the Creeping Man" has especially interested me. Professor Presbury, around whom the plot revolves, was portrayed as a scientist of international repute. When this famous physiologist began to do strange things, such as walking on all fours, scaling virtually vertical walls, and swinging through the trees like an ape, he naturally caused grave concern to his only daughter Edith and his close friends and associates. Furthermore, the professor's faithful wolfhound, Roy, lately had several times tried to bite him. Matters came to such a pass that Sherlock Holmes was asked to make an investigation.

Professor Presbury, a man in his early sixties, had fallen madly in love with a very young girl, the daughter of one of his colleagues. As Holmes remarked to Watson: "The real source lies, of course, in that untimely love affair which gave our impetuous professor the idea that he could only gain his wish by turning himself into a younger man." Sherlock Holmes discovered that the professor in his desire to regain his youth had connived with an Austrian scientist who was studying the effects on man of the administration of serum obtained from certain monkeys. The serum Professor Presbury received had been taken from the langur, ". . . the great black-faced monkey of the Himalayan Slopes, biggest and most human of climbing monkeys."

The story is of distinct interest, because it uses the theme of rejuvenation. About the time this story appeared, there was a great deal of interest in the possibility of rejuvenation. Testicular

glands from various animals (goats and monkeys) were trans-
planted in man; in some instances only extracts of these glands
were injected. The work of Steinach and of Voronoff, European
physiologists, had received wide publicity. The real pioneer in the
study of rejuvenation was, of course, Brown-Séquard, who reported
the results of his work in 1889. This brilliant French physiologist
had administered subcutaneously to himself the extract of ground-
up testicles of dogs and guinea pigs. He firmly believed that the
injection of these extracts made him feel younger and that he was
far less fatigued at the end of the day. The Sherlock Holmes story
does not say whether Professor Presbury's ardor for the young
girl with whom he was in love was increased; rather, emphasis is
laid on the changes in the professor's personality and his reversion
to the manner of apes.

There is, of course, no scientific basis for this story. It is rank
nonsense, but it does make an interesting yarn. The danger is that
those individuals who are not familiar with biology might gain
the impression that, when injected into human beings, extracts
from apelike animals could produce some of the effects so vividly
described in this tale. It may be that in the years to come certain

One of the world's most
historic meetings—"You
have been in Afghanistan, I
perceive?" The place: the
then new "Path. Lab." at
"Bart's"; the date: Tues-
day, 4 January 1881—with
Holmes hard at work on a
"biologic plot." *Drawing
by kind permission of the
Editor of* Sherlockiana,
*journal of the Danish
Baker Street Irregulars.*

advances may be made in the direction outlined in the story, but most certainly they have as yet not been accomplished. As for the ethics involved in rejuvenation of human beings, one is inclined to agree with Holmes when he remarks to Watson: "There is danger there—a very real danger to humanity. Consider, Watson, that the material, the sensual, the worldly would all prolong their worthless lives. . . . It would be the survival of the least fit. What sort of cesspool may not our poor world become?"

In "The Adventure of the Devil's Foot" Dr. Watson describes the dramatic death of two individuals and the dementia of two others, all of whom unknowingly inhaled the fumes of the burned powder of a rare plant, devil's foot root *(Radix pedis diaboli)*. The effects of this agent, according to Dr. Watson, were alarming indeed: "All three of them, the dead woman and the two demented men, retained upon their faces an expression of the utmost horror—a convulsion of terror, which was dreadful to look upon." In point of fact, both Sherlock Holmes and Dr. Watson nearly lost their own lives when they experimentally inhaled the fumes of the drug. Dr. Watson writes:

I had hardly settled in my chair before I was conscious of a thick, musky odor, subtle and nauseous . . . my brain and my imagination were beyond all control. . . . I broke through that cloud of despair and had a glimpse of Holmes's face, white, rigid, and drawn with horror— . . . I dashed from my chair, threw my arms round Holmes, and together we lurched through the door . . . and had thrown ourselves down upon the grass plot. . . .

It appears that the drug was a most potent agent indeed, and Sherlock Holmes admitted to Dr. Watson that their experiment was unjustifiable.

Whether such a drug exists as Dr. Watson delineated is quite doubtful. He describes it as a ". . . reddish brown, snuff-like powder" and depicts its pharmacologic actions as follows, ". . . stimulates those brain centers which control the emotions of fear . . ." I have failed to find in the pharmacologic or toxologic literature a drug which produces a mental condition in man or animals such as is narrated in the tale told by Watson. Moreover, a casual questioning of some of my medical colleagues who are more familiar than I with the toxicological properties of exotic plants has not yielded the specific information I sought. It is significant that Dr.

Watson himself was not familiar with this preparation, for Dr. Sterndale, the famous African explorer, who was in possession of some of the powder, addressed these remarks to Dr. Watson. "It is no reflection upon your professional knowledge, for I believe that, save for one sample in a laboratory in Buda, there is no other specimen in Europe. It has not yet found its way either into the pharmacopoeia or into the literature in toxicology."

The logical conclusion must be drawn that the biologic plot does not rest upon a solid foundation. The story as related by Dr. Watson, however, makes an entertaining, albeit gruesome, tale.

The story, "The Adventure of the Speckled Band," is remembered and well regarded by many readers of Sherlock Holmes tales. Unfortunately, however, from the biologic point of view it is open to criticism. The author of this present essay is not a herpetologist—indeed, he dislikes snakes and knows but little about them—but he believes that attention should be called to certain scientific errors in this story.

The reader will remember that Dr. Roylott used a snake, "a swamp adder, the deadliest snake in India," to murder a stepdaughter because he wanted her money. Roylott had trained the adder to go through the ventilator, which had an opening in the girl's room, and had suspended a bell-rope over the victim's bed so the snake could descend the rope and bite her. The snake was then called back up the rope and out of the ventilator by a low clear whistle and was rewarded by being allowed to drink a saucer of milk.

Holmes had discovered the fiendish plot and saved the life of the second stepdaughter by warning her not to sleep in her room at night. Arrangements were made so that Holmes and Watson would occupy her room and await events. When the snake came down the rope, Holmes attacked it with a cane he was carrying and drove it back into the ventilator. The maddened snake returned to the room where Roylott was keeping vigil. A little later, when Holmes and Watson entered Roylott's room, they found him dead; he had been bitten by the snake.

The story flows along very well, but it seems that the following criticisms can justifiably be made. As I understand it, snakes cannot climb up and down a rope; furthermore, snakes are deaf (they are supposed, however, to have a sense of vibration); and, lastly, they do not care for milk. If all or any of these criticisms are true, the story pretty much falls apart, which is a pity, for the tale is ingenious, well told, and, as previously mentioned, enjoyed by many readers.

The reader may recall that Sherlock Holmes himself wrote the story of "The Adventure of the Lion's Mane." Holmes, at the time he wrote it, was in retirement and was living in the Sussex Downs, not far from the place where the tragedy occurred. The death of a person as well as that of a dog was caused by the poisonous sting of the Lion's Mane (*Cyanea capillata*). It was called the Lion's Mane because the jellyfish resembled a mass of tangled hair which looked as if it might have been procured from the mane of a lion.

The story overemphasizes the lethal effects of the sting of the huge jellyfish. It is generally believed that *Cyanea capillata* cannot cause the death of a person. The cœlenterate which Holmes probably had in mind presumably belonged to the genus *Physalis,* commonly known as the Portuguese man-of-war. It is known that the sting of this cœlenterate may produce dangerous clinical symptoms in man, and it is possible that death may result if the symptoms are complicated by anaphylactic shock.

To make "The Adventure of the Lion's Mane" a success, it probably was necessary that a man be killed by *Cyanea capillata*. An author cannot be blamed for taking such a privilege. McPherson, who was the victim, although a fine athlete and an expert swimmer, suffered from a chronic cardiac ailment which had been caused by an attack of rheumatic fever. The shock produced by the tentacles of the jellyfish, together with the excitement and concomitant physical exertion, might have caused the fatality. If we accept this interpretation, contact with *Cyanea capillata* might have been the indirect rather than the direct cause of McPherson's death.

Holmes, in order to bolster his case, calls attention to a book written by J. G. Wood, *Out of Doors,* which gives an account of a person who had come in contact with *Cyanea capillata* and who had suffered a very unpleasant experience. I do wish to make it clear that there is no doubt in my mind but that the genus *Cyanea capillata* is capable of producing great discomfort to a swimmer and possibly even some danger. *Cyanea artica* is described in a standard textbook of biology as a creature which may measure six feet in diameter and bear tentacles reaching the astonishing length of 130 feet.

It would have been well had Holmes rested his case with the death of McPherson. Had he done so, I would not have found too much to criticize. According to the story, however, McPherson's dog, an Airedale terrier, a few days later met the same fate as his master. It was unfortunate that Holmes found it necessary in his story to have a dog killed by *Cyanea capillata*. A dog's body is well covered with hair, especially an Airedale's, and only an insignificant portion of its skin is actually exposed. It seems incredible that this animal could have been fatally injured by *Cyanea capillata*. In this instance the brilliant Holmes was quite wrong. It might be facetiously suggested that if Holmes was intent upon having a dog killed by *Cyanea capillata* he should have chosen a Chihuahua, the Mexican hairless dog.

"Silver Blaze" is not one of the author's favorite Sherlock Holmes stories. I know nothing about horse racing* but do like horses. My criticism of the plot is a theoretical one, since it concerns equine psychology. Silver Blaze was portrayed as a magnificent race horse. ". . . he was the first favorite for the Wessex Cup." We can well believe that Colonel Ross, the horse's owner, was much upset when, one morning a few days before the all-important race, he found his prize horse had disappeared. Someone had taken Silver Blaze from his stable during the night. Moreover, his trusted (*sic*) trainer, John Straker, was found dead on the moor, presumably brutally murdered.

Colonel Ross lost no time in getting in touch with Sherlock Holmes. The great detective came up from London and rose to his usual heights. First, he found Silver Blaze in sufficient time for him to be entered in the race; second, he showed conclusively that the horse had been responsible for Straker's death. Holmes showed that Straker, who had the reputation of being ". . . a zealous and honest servant," was after all a scoundrel of the first water. He had obtained a very delicate knife, such as is used to operate on a cataract of the eye, with the idea of cutting a tendon of the race horse so that he would be lamed. In the words of Holmes,

---

* Neither, obviously, did Dr. Watson—*Ed.*

". . . it is possible to make a slight nick upon the tendon of the horse's ham and do it subcutaneously, so as to leave no trace."

Straker was a villain, no doubt of that, and deserved punishment, but whether he deserved death is another matter. We admire Silver Blaze's high spirit and his spunk, but in my judgment the weak part of the plot is that Silver Blaze had no real justification to kill his trainer. Let us examine the record.

On their return to London, Holmes related the following to Colonel Ross and Dr. Watson: "Once in the hollow he [Straker] had got behind the horse and had struck a light; but the creature, frightened at the sudden glare, and with the strange instinct of animals, feeling that some mischief was intended, had lashed out, and the steel shoe had struck Straker full on the forehead." If Holmes had stated that at the first prick of the knife the nervous, high-strung race horse had kicked his trainer to death, he would have disarmed criticism. But mind you, the trainer had not touched the animal with the cataract knife or harmed him in any way. The horse apparently had a feeling of impending danger and killed his trainer, who had worked with him for a long time. Now I like horses and grant that they have a fair degree of animal intelligence, but I cannot see why Silver Blaze committed this murder. Perhaps I do not understand equine psychology.

Finally, it has been said that a dog knows instinctively whether a person likes him, presumably by the odor the person exudes. This may be true; I do not know. But if it is, perhaps a horse can in the same fashion tell a foe from a friend. I will let the reader puzzle over this and reach his own conclusion.

The biologic plots we have criticized have all dealt with either man or animals, and nothing has been said about botany. We wish to make an allusion to the latter field. Dr. Watson loved the plant life of early spring, and many delightful references to it are found in his stories; he also on occasion mentions autumn foliage. The criticism we have in mind concerns the orchids which blossom on the moor.

It will be remembered that in *The Hound of the Baskervilles* Dr. Watson plucked an orchid for Mrs. Stapleton. This presumably occurred approximately during the middle of October. Unfortunately, it has been found that the only orchid which meets the case is *Orchis prætormissa,* which flowers only in August and not in October. The question might be raised, of course, whether the orchid Dr. Watson plucked grew in a sheltered spot and happened to bloom very late in the season. Such things have been known to happen.

In this essay I have been, at times at least, rather critical, but in most instances my judgment tells me that my criticisms of the biologic plots were justified. It is painful indeed, as previously mentioned, for a person who is scientifically trained to let biologic errors go unchallenged. At times I may have been unfair; for example in "The Adventure of the Devil's Foot" I may not have pursued my research far enough or in the proper direction. Furthermore, my interpretation of equine psychology in "Silver Blaze" may have been faulty, and in "The Adventure of the Speckled Band," my knowledge of snakes may have been quite inadequate. I probably have made other errors.

Be all that as it may, my one hope is that my critical comments will in no way lessen any reader's interest in the fascinating Sherlock Holmes tales—that would be unforgivable. I agree wholeheartedly with Christopher Morley when he states in his introduction in *The Complete Sherlock Holmes*, ". . . we remain untroubled by any naïveté of plot; it is the character of the immortal pair that we relish." My real purpose for writing this criticism is not only to point out certain biologic errors but to stir up interest in these fine tales as well. After all, an effective way to arouse interest in a subject is to call attention to matters which may be controversial or point out possible errors. I have tried to do both.

Finally, before the reader judges me too harshly for attacking the sacred writings, let me make myself perfectly clear. I am quite sincere when I write that no one should criticize too seriously the Sherlock Holmes tales for taking certain liberties with biologic matters, or for that matter with nonbiologic matters. Let us be reasonably tolerant and allow such an imaginative and gifted writer as Dr. Watson a liberal poetic license. If a rather extravagant phrase or two be permitted, let us not subject the beauty of the orchid to the flame of the analytic blowpipe or attempt to measure the fragrance of the rose with an olfactometer. I rest my case. Hurrah for Sherlock Holmes! Hurrah for Dr. Watson! Hurrah for the Sherlock Holmes tales!

Aside from his passionately expressed wish for the closest union between Britain and the United States—a wish which, in all essentials, seems to have been granted—Holmes of the Canon appears a strangely nonpolitical man. But, since the time when the only thing to interest Holmes in the British Foreign Secretary was the disturbing fact that Lord Holdhurst was wearing mended boots, the Great Sleuth seems to have acquired some mild political awareness—though not at the loss of that mildly ironical view which always characterized his keen and all-seeing regard. Rarely today is Holmes depicted in both the domestic and the topical scene: this article so presents him. Though strictly for the British, the episode in the House of Commons bar may be held to have an interest for other peoples, seeing how well known both Westminster and its Palace are. And, of course, bureaucratic inefficiency and stupidity are not, alas! confined to the British system of government. That the excavating of this ill-designed car park under the mother of Parliaments destroyed the irreplaceable remains of at least three of its splendid medieval predecessors is a horror not mentioned in . . .

Sherlock Holmes
and the Invisible Car Park

꙰

ALAN WATKINS

꙰

It was a seasonable November day, with the rain cascading on to New Palace Yard like a veritable monsoon, when my friend Sherlock Holmes and I drew up in our cab outside the Palace of Westminster. I observed that the cabbie did not convey us to the members' entrance inside the Yard, as was the custom (for the constable on duty, knowing my friend's reputation, would wave us through with a friendly wink), but instead drew up outside the railings. I inquired the reason for this change.

"Why, sir," replied the fellow, "it is more than my business is worth to go in there; for, once in, I should never get out. Just you take a look."

I did as I was asked, and an astonishing sight met my eyes. The surface of the Yard, instead of accommodating motor cars, was churned into a gray mud. Enormous cranes were whirring like dervishes, air drills were pounding like tom-toms, and scattered around the compound stood huge pipes sufficient to contain a platoon.

"They have struck oil, I take it?" said I to my friend as we picked our way across the morass.

"Nothing so fortunate," he replied. "They are constructing an underground car park."

"How on earth do you deduce that?" I asked in amazement.

"Why, my dear fellow," he declared, "I read of it in *Hansard*.*
Next to the Law Reports, the agony column, and the occasional monograph on inorganic chemistry, it is my favorite reading matter—an invaluable source of information."

"You astonish me," I replied.

"The facts of the case are tolerably clear," continued Holmes. "I brought you here so that you might see the devastation for yourself. If you come into the Strangers' Bar, we may importune a friendly local and take a glass of Federation ale together. There I will tell you the full story, although the locals may add a few details. We can never have too many facts. The conclusions will then follow as surely as night follows day."

As we seated ourselves in a snug corner of the bar, glasses before us, my friend gestured to a man whom he addressed as Mr. Orme. The fellow had a frank and open countenance and honest blue eyes. I took him for a northerner making his way in the world. Holmes inquired his opinion of the car park.

"I know nothing of it, sir," was his reply, "except that construction is under way. None of us was told anything of the affair until it was too late. I am sure, however, it is a crying scandal, and a waste of public funds which could well be put to other objects. But our understanding here is that the Services Committee threatened to resign *en bloc* unless the project were carried through."

Holmes thanked the man for his assistance and turned to me.

"You see how it is?" said he.

"Not completely," I replied. "For instance, what is the Services Committee?"

"It is the committee," explained my friend, "which controls the conditions of work and leisure at Westminster. Seven years ago, on 9th April 1968, to be precise, the committee recommended that an underground car park should be constructed."

"I assume, therefore," said I, "that the matter was given the fullest consideration."

---

* For the benefit of non-British readers, *Hansard* is the name of the official daily report of Parliamentary proceedings.—*Ed.*

"On the contrary," replied my friend; "the recommendation occupies one short sentence of a short paragraph in an already slender report dealing with the new buildings yet to be constructed, and whose design has still to be decided. I will read the relevant sentence: 'It would also be possible to provide a new car park underneath New Palace Yard at an additional cost of perhaps £250,000, and your committee recommends this.' "

"So the car park precedes the buildings, which are, so to speak, in the air?" said I.

"You are very quick today," replied my friend. "That would indeed seem to be the case."

Uneasy as always at the spectacle of our legislators' being sub-

No traffic problems when one travels like this: Her Majesty Queen Elizabeth II, on her way to "open Parliament," passes the site of the Invisible Car Park. *Contrad Research Library.*

jected to ridicule or unjust criticism, I interposed: "But the cost seems very reasonable, considering the magnitude of the undertaking."

"Wait until you have heard the end of my story," advised Holmes. "In the report to the Services Committee of 8th June 1971, the estimated cost had progressed to £1.3m.; in its report of 9th May 1972, to just under £2m. The former leader of the House, a Mr. Carr, has most recently given an estimate of *over* £2m."

My friend broke off and said: "May I borrow your cuff?" I thrust out my arm, and Holmes performed a calculation with a speed of which only he is capable. Ten minutes later, he said: "Five hundred instead of two hundred and twenty cars, the present figure. I compute £7,000 extra per car, in addition to the running costs of the business."

Several features of this astonishing tale were puzzling to me.

"Is there to be redistribution," I inquired, "which will lead to a massive influx of MPs, necessitating greater parking facilities? Is it not the policy of all governments to eliminate the use of Central London by private vehicles? Did not the planning authorities have views upon the matter?"

My friend gave a wry chuckle, causing a Mr. Fletcher, who was sitting nearby, to start in alarm.

"The answers are simple enough," replied Holmes. "There are to be *no* additional MPs. The car park was, in fact, first suggested, not by the Services Committee, but by the Environment Department. With regard to the authorities, the sole obligation under Circular 80 on government offices (as Westminister is taken to be) is to *inform*. The Greater London Council has, I understand, made the most strenuous objections, only to be brushed aside. Further, it was informed a full seven months after the decision."

Just then a tall, frail gray figure entered the room. I took him for an accountant fallen upon hard times.

"Whoa, there, Carr!" said my friend. "What news of the underground car park?"

"I am now occupied with other matters, sir," said Carr, "and the affair has nothing to do with me. Nor did it when I was in my previous office, for I inherited the project from my predecessor, Mr. Peart. In some quarters, I believe, it is known as Fred's Folly."

Holmes turned away in disgust.

"That fellow can tell us nothing more than we know already," he said. "Now, what conclusions do *you* draw?"

"From what you tell me," I replied, "there is no good reason for building a car park. Therefore we must look for hidden motives. I suspect the Services Committee is under the control of the IRA, for an underground five-story car park would assuredly provide an excellent target for those villains."

"Ingenious," said my friend, "but it will not do. The old car park was a good enough target for the Fenians."

"Or," said I, "this may be the final solution to the back-bencher problem. They will drive their cars down, only to find themselves in the Thames."

"Why," said Holmes, "should the Services Committee resort to such a device when it already controls the Kitchen Committee, which can avail itself of poison—and sometimes does?"

I confessed myself baffled.

"Think, my dear fellow," said Holmes. "What will stand above the car park?"

"Big Ben," I replied.

"Precisely," said my friend. "The worthy Colonel Lipton has already established that the tower is tilting nine and a half inches out of true in a northwesterly direction."

"Perhaps," I hazarded, "it will become an even greater tourist attraction than at present, like the leaning tower of Pisa?"

"But what if it collapses, owing to the excavations?" said Holmes. "The blow to national spirit will be infinitely greater than that caused by the collapse of Rolls Royce. The filmmakers will be at a loss when they desire a quick shot indicating London. We are clearly dealing with desperate characters who will stop at nothing."

A uniformed attendant appeared and handed a message to my friend. He perused it impatiently, screwed it into a ball and tossed it aside, narrowly missing Dame Joan Vickers.

"Ha," he exclaimed, "it is just as I thought: a pretty pickle, and no mistake! Big Ben has shifted a further two inches. I suggest we walk rapidly across Waterloo Bridge to the Festival Hall before we find ourselves in serious danger."

The world success of the Sherlock Holmes stories, with the consequent rise of their hero to world fame, has set Sherlockian scholars a still-unsolved problem: the problem of explaining the absolute success of Sherlock Holmes, especially in comparison with the relative non-success (one would never call it failure) of his numerous, often more brilliant, more attractive, rivals. This, for Sherlockians—as was noted in the Preface—is a problem whose solution must *be attempted; and here, once again, is an aspirant for the honor of being the first to solve it. Whether or not the philosopher-criminologist succeeds in his praiseworthy effort is a decision which must be left to the judgment of the individual reader. But rarely can there have been so novel, so convincing an approach to the analysis of that character that the author of this article sees as . . .*

The Flawed Superman

☒

COLIN WILSON

☒

When Dr. Conan Doyle moved to Southsea, a suburb of Portsmouth, in July 1882, he was twenty-three years old and had no hard-and-fast plans for the future. He rented a house for £40 a year, screwed his brass plate to the door, and sat back to wait for patients. For many weeks none appeared, so he whiled away the time writing stories. In fact, he had already had a few published—at about three guineas* each—and many more rejected. His penchant was for tales of bizarre adventures set in Africa or the Arctic (he had visited both places as a ship's doctor); the style was influenced by Bret Harte, and had a touch of facetiousness. And some time that autumn he began a story: "In the month of December 1873, the British ship *Dei Gratia* steered into Gibraltar, having in tow a derelict brigantine *Marie Celeste,* which had been picked up in latitude 38° 40′, longitude 17° 15′ W."

For a short sentence, this contains a remarkable number of inaccuracies. The year was actually 1872; the *Dei Gratia* did not tow

---

* Three guineas (£3 3s. 0d.) was then equivalent to a few cents over $15.—*Ed.*

the *Marie Celeste*—the latter came under its own sail, and arrived a day later than the *Dei Gratia;* the latitude and longitude are wrong; and the ship was called plain English Mary, not Marie. Still, "J. Habakuk Jephson's Statement" is, after all, intended to be fiction. This was not made clear to the readers of the *Cornhill Magazine,* when it appeared in January 1884, for the *Cornhill* had a policy of publishing stories anonymously. J. Habakuk Jephson's statement, to the effect that the *Mary Celeste* had been taken over by a kind of Black Power leader with a hatred of whites, was accepted as fact by most readers. And, most notably, by Her Majesty's Advocate-General at Gibraltar, Mr. Solly Flood, who had been chief investigator in the *Mary Celeste* case; the indignant Mr. Flood launched a telegram to the Central News Agency denouncing J. Habakuk Jephson as a fraud and a liar. The statement was given wide publicity, and the incident set Doyle's feet on the road to fame; at least, the *Cornhill* was now willing to publish most of his stories at thirty guineas a time.

Doyle took note of the lesson of the *Mary Celeste* story; he developed the "factual" manner. "September 11th—Lat. 81° 40′ N.; long. 2°E. Still lying-to amid enormous ice-fields . . ." begins "The Captain of the *Polestar.*" While, in "A Physiologist's Wife" and "The Great Keinplatz Experiment," he took as his central characters a type that had always fascinated him: the abstracted intellectual. "Professor von Baumgarten was tall and thin, with a hatchet face and steel-gray eyes, which were singularly bright and penetrating."

It was in 1886, two years after he had become a regular contributor to the *Cornhill,* that Doyle came upon the detective stories of Emile Gaboriau, a French writer of sensational mysteries. In France, the police are regarded with suspicion and dislike; therefore Gaboriau could not make his detective hero a policeman; instead, he introduced a retired pawnbroker as the investigator; Tabaret's knowledge of human beings, gained from years behind the counter, serves him well in *L'Affaire Lerouge.* Tabaret is accompanied by an ex-offender, now a policeman, named Lecoq. (Obviously Lecoq's heart is in the right place, because he has been a crook.) As an ex-crook, Lecoq is a master of disguise. He also uses powers of deduction in the manner of Poe's Dupin.

And so, fragment by fragment, the personality of Holmes was

assembled. As everyone knows, his first appearance, in *A Study in Scarlet,* was a failure; Doyle had to sell it outright for £25. *The Sign of Four,* commissioned three years later by the American *Lippincott's Magazine,* was hardly more successful. Fame arrived belatedly with the publication of the first two Sherlock Holmes short stories in the *Strand* in the summer of 1891; Doyle received £35 each for the first half dozen. By the time he had allowed himself to be persuaded to start writing *The Memoirs,* he was charging something closer to £100 a story. (For *The Return,* written a decade later, he received five thousand dollars a story from the American publisher.)

Now it is easy enough to understand why the short stories achieved a success that had been denied to the novels. Victorian magazines reached immense circulations. (Aldous Huxley once told me that the *Cornhill,* later edited by his father, had paid George Eliot some incredible sum—I think it was £30,000—for *Romola.*) And a good short story is undeniably easier to read than a novel. (As a boy of twelve, I read and reread the Sherlock Holmes stories, but never derived the same pleasure from the novels.) Doyle could not have had a better showcase for his great detective. Yet no one has ever quite explained why Holmes immediately became one of the most famous characters in the whole realm of fiction. The late Edgar W. Smith once attempted it in *The Baker Street Journal* (and W. S. Baring-Gould quotes it in his *Annotated Holmes*). He begins by pointing out that we love the Victorian atmosphere of the Holmes stories, which is obviously true; but then the Victorians themselves must have taken all this for granted. He goes on to say that Holmes personifies "our urge to trample evil and to set aright the wrongs with which the world is plagued," and compares him to Galahad and Socrates. And to me, he seems to be getting further and further away from the essence of the Sherlockian fascination.

I found myself brooding on the question a few years ago, when I succeeded in picking up a small collection of Sherlockiana from a secondhand bookseller—including Vincent Starrett's *Private Life of Sherlock Holmes;* Michael Harrison's *In the Footsteps of Sherlock Holmes;* and Baring-Gould's biography. T. S. Eliot once remarked that he read through the Holmes stories once every two years. I do the same. No one has ever written biographical books about Raffles or Father Brown or Maigret. What is it about Holmes that fills his admirers with such an appetite to go on reading about him?

A partial answer, the beginning of an answer, emerges from the account of Doyle's literary struggles. I cannot think of any other writer of the nineteenth century, with the possible exception of Balzac, with such a passion for the factual detail. It seems possible that Doyle stumbled on the trick through the writing of "J. Habakuk Jephson's Statement." In fact, this story is as romantically preposterous as anything he ever wrote, but it was taken for reality. Gaboriau was influenced by Balzac, and his books have a beguilingly factual ring, at least for the first few pages. In a story, a certain amount of fact is like grit in chicken food—it makes it more digestible and nutritious. (Rider Haggard made the same discovery when he began writing *King Solomon's Mines*.) Doyle instantly perceived the value of the method, and proceeded to employ it (with the confidence of a duck taking to water) in *A Study in Scarlet*. When Watson meets Holmes in the laboratory at Bart's (about 1881), Holmes has just discovered an infallible test for bloodstains. Such a test was not actually discovered until 1900 by Paul Uhlenhuth, and first used to convict a murderer in Germany in 1904. Like other men of genius, Doyle had the power to tune in to the spirit of the age; and at the time when he conceived Holmes, crime detection was finally achieving the status of an exact science. In the mid-1880s, Scotland Yard was brooding on whether to adopt the Bertillon system of fingerprinting as a basic method of criminal identification. As a doctor, Doyle had the necessary background for pursuing the science of medical jurisprudence. He might have applied his talents as a police surgeon or pathologist; instead, he wrote stories. But, as one reads those first two chapters of *A Study in Scarlet,* one senses that Doyle had struck a rich vein, and could easily spend the next hundred pages discussing crime, medicine, detection, the science of deduction.

The reader catches his enthusiasm. A critic once said of Balzac that no other novelist produces such an illusion of reality, of talking about the real world. This is one of the secrets of the fascination of the Holmes stories. On this level of criminal investigation and medical jurisprudence, they have the ring of authenticity. This is why readers want to go on playing the game, and reading books about Holmes and his cases, like Starrett's *Private Life of Sherlock Holmes*. I believe it may also explain why the various Holmes pastiches by Adrian Conan Doyle, John Dickson Carr, August Derleth, et al. have never caught on. They imitate the style and the mannerisms, but fail to throw in the handful of grit, the illusion of fact; you know they are inventions.

All this may help to explain the popularity of the Holmes biographies, in which the writer tries to sort out Watson's muddled dates; but it hardly begins to explain the fascination of the character of the Great Detective. This is an altogether more complex matter. But you can see the essence of the trick in the passage about the ex-Commissionnaire. Watson, vaguely irritated by Holmes's air of intellectual superiority, points to a man on the other side of the street and wonders what he is looking for: "You mean the retired sergeant of Marines?" says Holmes. A few minutes later the man delivers a letter to them.

Here was an opportunity of taking the conceit out of him. He little thought of this when he made that random shot.

"May I ask, my lad," I said, in the blandest voice, "what your trade might be?"

"Commissionnaire, sir," he said gruffly. "Uniform away for repairs."

"And you were?" I asked, with a slightly malicious glance at my companion.

"A sergeant, sir, Royal Marine Light Infantry, sir. . . ."

And there you have it; Holmes the cool and infallible; Holmes the superman who is never wrong.

Doyle knew that this was what his readers wanted: the satisfaction of an "infallibility fantasy." With the story teller's instinct, he uses the same situation again and again, knowing that his readers will never tire of it, as children never tire of seeing the clown walk into the custard pie. To increase the effect, Watson plays the stooge to an extent that is slightly unbelievable. When a man is really telling a story against himself, he does it with a self-deprecating grin, and tries to soften the effect: "Naturally, I assumed this was mere brag and bounce." Watson tells such stories as if he were his own worst enemy. In the opening chapter of *The Sign of Four*, the whole scene is repeated with embellishments. He begins by "raising his eyebrows" when Holmes describes himself as the only unofficial consulting detective (although Holmes has told him as much in *A Study of Scarlet*), gets irritable when Holmes criticizes the earlier case history, and then becomes angry when Holmes tells him the story of his alcoholic brother from the marks in his watch case. The reaction is overdone. A real man would say: "But that is remarkable, Holmes. Are you *sure* you knew nothing about my brother beforehand?" Watson limps "impatiently about the room with considerable bitterness in his heart," and snorts: "This is unworthy of you, Holmes," accusing him of chicanery. And so, when Holmes explains how he made the deduction, the impact is doubled.

For most readers, these opening sections—in which Holmes demonstrates the science of deduction—are the best part of the story. Of course, we enjoy it as Holmes and Watson rattle off in a cab to catch the 2:15 from Waterloo; but we have to admit that there is an air of sameness about the cases—the attractive girls in distress, the bullying villains who bend pokers (which Holmes immediately straightens again), the sinister figure from the past who comes back to take revenge. (I have never worked out how many of the stories depend on this device, but it must be at least a quarter.) But in the opening pages of the stories, Doyle is at his most inventive, and his most realistic. These are the pages that make us want to go on reading about Holmes's life and background. Why? Because we like to be assured that Holmes is a real person; that is an important part of the pleasure. That basic *effect* —the hero once more proving himself infallible—is the effect of the fairy tale. Children love to identify themselves with heroes who possess all kinds of interesting devices for overcoming danger —magic hats that make you invisible when you turn them around, tinder boxes that grant your wishes. They love to identify with brave but perfectly ordinary little tailors who pose as conquerors and somehow manage to get away with it. As we get older, the fairy tales fail to satisfy, because we now know that the world is more difficult and demanding than that. Realistic novelists like Flaubert, Balzac, Stendhal make a virtue of this, and tell us stories of weak heroes who are finally defeated. But we don't really like their tales of defeat, for there is something in us that hungers for triumph and conquest. So if a writer is kind enough to tell us an apparently realistic story in which the hero triumphs like the brave little tailor, our gratitude is immense. Like children, we read and reread the fantasy, blissfully identifying, and reveling in the details that assure us that all this is real.

When I read *Tom Sawyer* to my nine-year-old son the other day, it struck me that Mark Twain is using the same device. I had forgotten why I read *Tom Sawyer* over and over again as a child. Now it came back. It is because Twain describes the daydreams and fantasies of a small boy with remarkable accuracy—so you accept them all as real—and yet makes sure that Tom is always the winner. Like Holmes, Tom manipulates other people; with a piece of penetrating psychology, he persuades his friends to whitewash a fence on a hot Saturday morning when they'd normally be swimming in the river. He runs away from home and attends his own funeral. He triumphs over a grown-up enemy, Injun Joe. Twain even had the courage to make Tom get the girl, when most boys' writers carefully excluded romance from their stories (thus leaving out of account a subject that preoccupies most small boys).

It is interesting to note that Twain's attempt to repeat his success in *Huckleberry Finn* was a total flop, at least as far as most juvenile readers are concerned. Even the idea of telling the story in Huck's own language is a bore. The schoolboy wants his hero's adventures to be dignified with the language of literature, not recounted in schoolboy slang. He doesn't even mind if the language is sometimes a little too literary and difficult; he likes the writer to assume he has intelligence, and he likes the feeling that the wish-fulfillment fantasy has unplumbed depths for later exploration. Again, we are touching on the fascination of the Holmes stories.

But in order to grasp the full significance of Holmes, I believe we have to see him in an altogether broader perspective. At the risk of seeming too abstract and metaphysical, let me try to explain what I mean.

The novel as we know it came into existence in the year 1740, with Samuel Richardson's *Pamela*. There had been novels before this, but they tended to be either fairy tales or picaresque "true narrations." What Richardson did was to create a highly elaborate daydream about a servant girl who resists all her master's attempts to seduce her, and ends by marrying him. I doubt whether many readers had ever identified with Don Quixote or Gil Blas; but every male could identify with the lustful Mr. B, and every female with the virtuous Pamela. *Pamela* was a magic carpet to another world—a world of the imagination; at the same time, the sheer mass of its physical and psychological detail convinced the reader of its reality.

Within a decade of the publication of *Pamela,* England had become "a nation of readers" (in Dr. Johnson's phrase). Nowadays we take entertainment for granted; it is difficult to realize what a revolution took place as a result of Richardson's invention. It was as widespread as the tobacco revolution of the Elizabethan age; but to get an idea of its significance, you would have to imagine that Sir Walter Raleigh brought back marijuana fròm the New World, and that all Europe became pot smokers. This taste for escaping into worlds of fantasy swept across Europe, and literature gained an importance that it had never possessed in any previous age. Rousseau's *New Heloise* was so popular that libraries lent it out by the hour. Scott's novels made sums of money that would be the envy of a modern property tycoon. So did those of Dumas and Hugo, Dickens and Trollope. Reading was a mass-addiction. Middle-class Victorians flocked to Thomas Cook to take them on tours of foreign lands; *every* class of Victorian flocked to the novelists to take them on tours of the imagination. *Pamela* could well have been one of the most decisive steps in the evolution of man since the invention of the wheel.

The trouble is that after that splendid start, the novel began to find itself in difficulties. Serious novelists like Balzac and Flaubert continued to pursue the line of realism developed by Richardson. But they no longer had the old universal appeal of Richardson and Scott, because they were no longer satisfying the wish-fulfillment fantasy. Everybody agreed that Balzac was a greater novelist than Dumas; but for every one who admired *Père Goriot* or *Lost Illusions,* a hundred read *The Three Musketeers* and *The Count of Monte Cristo* (surely one of the great wish-fulfillment fantasies of all time). Even Dickens made the same discovery; *Hard Times* and *Bleak House* are greater novels than *Pickwick Papers* and *Nicholas Nickleby,* but they were never half so popular; they are too "real," and they lack the element of the wish-fulfillment fantasy.

And so, in the second half of the nineteenth century, literature split into two camps: realists and fantasists. On the one hand you had the Dickens of *Bleak House,* Ibsen and his disciples, Gissing, Zola, Dostoevsky; on the other, Dumas, Stevenson, Haggard, Marie Corelli, and dozens of now-forgotten writers of romances and historical dramas.

From the beginning, Conan Doyle recognized himself as a member of the second group. One critic thought that "J. Habakuk Jephson's Statement" was by Stevenson. Doyle regarded his Holmes stories as entertainments, not to be taken too seriously; he felt that his finest work was to be found in *Micah Clark, The White Company,* and other historical novels. But even if, like Winston Churchill, you happen to be an admirer of the historical novels, you cannot help noticing that they are basically escapist fantasies, in which the modern Londoner turns back nostalgically to the days of chivalry, when Robin Hood lurked in the greenwood and crusaders rode around on white chargers. (I remember, a few years ago, seeing a newspaper photograph of Adrian Conan Doyle dressed in armor, carrying a bow and arrow; the accompanying story explained that he hoped to start some kind of movement for the revival of the medieval virtues and martial arts. For the same reason, some modern American businessmen spend their vacations dressed in cowboy gear and reconstruct the gunfight at O.K. Corral.)

Holmes, on the other hand, has his feet planted firmly on the hard pavements of nineteenth-century London. He is a connoisseur of "every horror perpetrated in the century." He is a scientist, and often speaks the dry, abstract language of science. And while this great tide of Victorian London swirls around him, with its crime and violence and misery, he holds aloof in his room in Baker Street, surveying it all with the eye of a philosopher. Most emphatically, he possesses what T. S. Eliot called "a sense of his own age."

It is rather interesting to watch the way that his character develops. The famous list at the beginning of *A Study in Scarlet* emphasizes his ignorance of many subjects, including literature, philosophy, astronomy, and politics. He tells Watson that he doesn't know whether the earth goes around the sun or vice versa, and now that Watson has told him, will forget it as quickly as possible. Yet in *The Sign of Four* he recommends Watson to read "one of the most remarkable [books] ever penned," Winwood Reade's *Martyrdom of Man,* a work of historical philosophy. And later in this novel he discourses on miracle plays, medieval pottery, Stradivarius violins, the Buddhism of Ceylon, and the warships of the future, "handling each as though he had made a special study of it." In other stories we learn that he is the author of a monograph on the motets of Lassus, loves the opera, knows something of painting ("my grandmother, who was the sister of Vernet, the French artist . . .") and is a connoisseur of food and wine. ("I have oysters and a brace of grouse, with something a little choice in white wines"—the latter possibly a Montrachet, which makes its appearance in "The Veiled Lodger.") Doyle's original idea was to make Holmes a rather limited character, like Fleming's James Bond; but he found himself unable to stick to this resolution, and Holmes emerges finally as a kind of "universal man," with an encyclopedic knowledge on every subject, as well as remarkable physical powers. (The prize fighter in *The Sign of Four* assures him that he could have aimed high if he had chosen to become a professional boxer.)

Holmes's character develops in another significant way. In the early work he is definitely an esthete; he says things "querulously" and "languidly," his cheeks burn with unhealthy red spots, he injects himself with morphine and cocaine and lies around for days on the settee "with a dreamy, vacant expression in his eyes." His power of imaginative projection is highly developed; in "The Beryl Coronet" he tells Watson that, while his mind has been in Devonshire, his body has, "I regret to observe, consumed in my absence two large pots of coffee and an incredible amount of tobacco." Huysmans's novel *A Rebours* appeared in 1884, two years before Doyle conceived Sherlock Holmes; its hero, Des Esseintes, also lives a kind of monastic existence in his luxurious rooms, attempting to live a life of the mind and the senses, and behaving as if the outside world could be ignored. In 1889 Doyle had dinner with the editor of *Lippincott's Magazine,* who asked him to write another Holmes novel (*The Sign of Four*). Oscar Wilde was also present and agreed to write *The Picture of Dorian Gray*. It seems possible that they discussed Huysmans's novel; at any event, it plays an important part in Dorian Gray's evolution.

"He had, when he so willed, the utter immobility of a Red Indian." At the site of a building demolished by an explosion—the year is 1895—the Flawed Superman, "utterly immobile," ignores the photographer, whose whole interest is in Holmes. *From a photograph by Thomas Fall, 9 & 10 Baker Street W. Contrad Research Library.*

Certainly, the Holmes of the early stories has much in common with the esthetic, world-rejecting heroes of the 1880s and 1890s.

Now this is far more significant than it seems. The esthetic hero was a highly interesting phenomenon. He was created by Samuel Richardson, in the person of Lovelace, the demonic seducer of Clarissa Harlowe. Lovelace declared that he cared for nothing but "his own imperial will." He is the proud aristocrat who declines to admit the force of necessity. The romantics developed this new kind of hero; Schiller's most famous character, Karl Moor in *The Robbers*, declares that man was made for freedom, and that laws were made to be broken by great men. Byron developed the idea; his heroes are gloomy, romantic, proud, sinful, contemptuous of public opinion. Nineteenth-century Russian literature is full of such men. But Des Esseintes, like Dorian Gray and Gilbert's Bunthorne, represents the decadence of the Byronic hero. He ends as a nervous wreck. The world he despises has the last word. Dorian Gray's single-minded pursuit of pleasure ends by destroying him. The novel was violently attacked. Wilde's defenders pointed out that Dorian's self-destruction made it a highly moral tale. But Wilde was not concerned with morality and Mrs. Grundy. Dorian had to die because that was the artistically logical conclusion of his premises. Villiers de L'Isle-Adam, in his famous play *Axel*, makes his hero express total world-rejection in the magnificent line: "Live? Our servants can do that for us." And the hero and heroine then commit suicide. There was no other logical course for them to take. More than thirty years later, the writers of the "lost generation"—Eliot, Pound, Joyce, Hemingway—were trapped in the same web. *The Great Gatsby* is a daydream about a man who is rich enough to make the world conform to his desires. Like Wilde and Dorian Gray, Fitzgerald was a self-destroyer.

In Sherlock Holmes, Doyle created his own esthetic hero. With his dressing gown, violin, and hypodermic syringe, Holmes is a second cousin of Des Esseintes. When Watson protests, in the name of common sense, against the use of cocaine, Holmes replies, "I cannot live without brainwork. What else is there to live for? Stand at the window here. Was ever such a dreary, dismal, unprofitable world? See how the yellow fog swirls down the street and drifts across the dun-colored houses. What could be more hopelessly prosaic and material?" You almost expect him to add,

"Live? Our servants can do that for us." But, unlike Des Esseintes, Holmes has good reasons for going out into the fog. Crime fascinates him, as it did Baudelaire and Dostoevsky. ("Everything in the world exudes crime," said Baudelaire.) But he derives his greatest delight from pitting his wits against criminals. He has not turned his back on the world outside; on the contrary, he regards himself as a last court of appeal.

Quite unconsciously, certainly unaware of what he was doing, Conan Doyle had solved the problem that had tormented and frustrated the novelist since Richardson. He had created a romantic hero, a man whose life is entirely the life of the mind ("I cannot live without brainwork"), yet succeeded in steering him out of the cul-de-sac of despair and defeat that destroyed so many of the best minds of the *fin de siècle* period. Moreover, it was quite logical, without any element of contrivance. When Watson meets him, Holmes is so poor that he can afford only half the rent of the rooms at 221B Baker Street (for all that, as Watson remarks, the terms were exceedingly moderate), although he is certainly not the kind of character who would enjoy sharing rooms with another man. That was around 1881. Seven years later, in 1888, Holmes was a highly successful detective with many distinguished clients (such as the King of Bohemia). It is true that, as late as "the adventure of Wisteria Lodge" (in 1890), he is complaining that his mind is like a racing engine, "tearing itself to pieces because it is not connected up with the work for which it was built." But one can have no doubt that these slack periods became more and more rare, and that by the mid-1890s Holmes was one of the busiest men in England. By the time of "The Adventure of the Bruce-Partington Plans" (around 1895), he has achieved an altogether new degree of self-control: "One of the most remarkable characteristics of Sherlock Holmes was his power of throwing his brain out of action and switching all his thoughts on to lighter things whenever he had convinced himself that he could no longer work to advantage." This is no longer the man who only three years earlier had explained that his mind was like a racing engine.

I suspect that Holmes's biographers might connect this increased maturity with the Reichenbach Falls episode and its aftermath; and I think they would probably be right. Holmes's *Wanderjahre* in Tibet and the Middle East must have allowed his personality the freedom to develop. (I say *Jahre*, although Holmes speaks of at least two years, for the death of Moriarty occurred in 1891 and the adventure of Wisteria Lodge is dated 1892.) What is more important is that the "death" of Holmes brought Doyle face to face with the implications of the character he had created. We know that he decided to kill Holmes because he was tired of inventing new mysteries for him to solve. But an author does not become tired of his characters while they still have possibilities of interesting development. Balzac becomes tired of Lucien de Rubempré, who is a weakling, but not of Rastignac or the criminal genius Vautrin. When a character reaches a certain limit, it is natural for the author to abandon him or kill him off. Shakespeare killed off Falstaff because he had got the best out of him; the "return" (in *The Merry Wives*) is a disaster. When Doyle conceived Holmes, it was simply as a fascinating eccentric who might have strolled out of the tales of Hoffmann. The atmosphere of the early stories is phantasmagoric. " 'My dear fellow,' said Sherlock Holmes, as we sat on either side of the fire in his lodgings at Baker Street, 'life is infinitely stranger than anything that the mind of man could invent. We would not dare to conceive the things which are really mere commonplaces of existence. If we could fly out of that window hand in hand, hover over this great city . . .' " etc. There is more than a touch of the *Arabian Nights* here. The reader is fascinated because, in fact, it had never struck him that there is anything very strange about London. In the early stories, Holmes is always emphasizing the fascination of the commonplace. "To the man who loves art for its own sake, it is frequently in its least important and lowliest manifestations that the keenest pleasure is to be derived," says Holmes in "The Copper Beeches." Like Poe's Dupin, he is an intellectual esthete, a man whose fastidiousness leads him to prefer the night to the day.

But, without fully recognizing what he was doing, Doyle had created a character who embodies a fragment of the superman. The only modern parallel that comes to mind is Tolkien's Gandalf, who is introduced in *The Hobbit* as a comic fairy-tale wizard, and who gradually acquires stature until he becomes the symbolic Magician of *The Lord of the Rings*. Holmes is also a kind of magician. And so, when he returned from Tibet and Persia, he had to be built up into something altogether more universal than the eccentric drug addict of the early tales. In the *Memoirs* Doyle had once tried the experiment of making Holmes fallible ("The Yellow Face"); he never tried it again. (In the earlier "Five Orange Pips" we learn there were three occasions when he was beaten by men; but Watson does not elaborate.) He also provided Holmes with a "superior" brother—but Mycroft is seldom heard of after the adventure of "The Greek Interpreter." Holmes had to be developed into something at once unique and universal. In the early days, Watson records, he had no appreciation for nature and went to the country only to pursue evildoers; in the late adventure of "The Lion's Mane," Holmes mentions how often he yearned for the "soothing life of Nature" when living in London. The eccentric esthete gradually disappears, and Holmes slowly takes on the stature of a true magician.

There were many attempts to imitate Holmes or, at least, to follow in his footsteps: Futrelle's Van Dusen, Chesterton's Father Brown, M. P. Shiel's Prince Zaleski, Bramah's Max Carrados, Freeman's Dr. Thorndyke, Agatha Christie's Poirot, Rex Stout's Nero Wolfe (based on Mycroft), Wallace's J. G. Reeder, Morrison's Martin Hewitt. My own favorite is J. G. Reeder, although I realize that many people would plump for Father Brown. When I try to define why these two characters should be so oddly satisfactory, it seems that the answer is connected with their otherworldliness. Both are harmless, innocent men whose superiority springs from their basic natural *detachment* from the affairs of the world. I personally find that more "normal" detectives, like Poirot or Martin Hewitt, are curiously unsatisfactory. It seems that Doyle's successors have mostly tried to fathom the secret of Holmes's success, and have come to the wrong conclusion. They assumed that the detective has to be "different"; so Van Dusen has Holmes's intellectuality, Poirot has his egoism, Nero Wolfe his esthetic sensitivity, and so on; then there are women detectives, blind detectives, even, I believe, a homosexual detective. (Fleming's James Bond is the nearest anyone has come so far to a sadistic detective.) Shiel's Prince Zaleski is even more of a superman than Holmes; yet he is less interesting, because the stories themselves are somehow unbelievable, slightly absurd. On the other hand, Simenon's perfectly "ordinary" Maigret is one of the most satisfying detectives since Holmes, because one is convinced by the stories. It

brings us back to the point already made: that a large part of the
fascination of Holmes is that sense of reality. Yet the tales of J. G.
Reeder and Father Brown are not notable for their realism. They
share another Holmesian characteristic, pinpointed by Watson
when he says: "He loved to lie in the very center of five millions
of people, with his filaments stretching out and running through
them, responsive to every little rumor or suspicion of unsolved
crime"; they are "outside" life. If I may intrude a personal note,
they are examples of what I would call "outsiders."

And now, it seems to me, we are beginning to approach the psychological root of this question we have set ourselves. Why *should*
the audiences of 1891 have been so ready to accept Holmes, when
the book-buying public of 1887 had been indifferent? It is not
simply that he appeared in a mass-circulation magazine, and that
short stories are easier to read than novels. Let us put the question
in another way. Why was Poe's Dupin received with relative indifference in 1842? Why was there no frantic demand for whole
volumes of Dupin stories? To our eyes, Dupin seems quite as fascinating as Holmes—one of the few fictional detectives who can
stand beside him without paling. One of the first to truly appreciate Dupin was the French poet Baudelaire; and *he* sympathized
with Dupin's asceticism, his fastidiousness, his dislike of the common daylight. Dickens created the first "detective officer" in Inspector Bucket of *Bleak House* (1852); Wilkie Collins followed
with Sergeant Cuff more than a decade later. It never seems to
have occurred to either of them that a detective should be some
kind of intellectual superman. Their detectives are as ordinary as
Maigret.

I suspect the answer lies in that slow evolution of public taste
that occurred in the nineteenth century. I say slow, but in historical terms it was like a whirlwind. Richardson taught the European mind to daydream. Intelligent men and women began to live
in the imagination in a way that had been impossible for the contemporaries of Rabelais, or even of Pepys. You feel of Rabelais,
Montaigne, Shakespeare, Cervantes, Defoe, that they are *realists;*
in spite of their genius, they were as down to earth as Julius
Caesar or Queen Elizabeth. But when you read Byron or Shelley
or Poe, you feel that they weren't entirely able to distinguish
between their imagination and the real world. They had become

so accustomed to the life of the imagination that real life had become slightly blurred. (And nowadays, when we spend so much time living vicariously through the films and television, this is even more so.) A novel is not only unreal; it is reversible; after the death of the hero, you can go back fifty pages and he is alive again. Or the author can kill him—like Holmes—and bring him back to life again, explaining it was all a mistake. It is easy for someone who has read too many novels, like Flaubert's Madame Bovary, to fall into the habit of feeling that real life is a kind of fiction—even a joke, a story, a lie. In the nineteenth century many men of genius committed suicide because they lived in a kind of double exposure in which reality and dream kept blending together and blurring each other's outlines. This was what drove De Quincey and Coleridge to laudanum and Poe to alcohol, Beddoes to suicide. Schopenhauer caught the essence of the dilemma in his title *The World as Will and Illusion;* the world was no longer one thing, but two. Friedrich Nietzsche revolted against this pessimism, asserting that "great health" can overcome anything; his "gospel of the superman" appeared, in its first complete version, in 1894. By that time Nietzsche himself was insane; he died six years later without recovering his reason.

Whether he liked it or not, European man of the nineteenth century was dragged into a new world—a world of double exposures. In the early years of the century, it affected mainly the middle and upper classes, for they were the only ones who could afford to read. By the middle of the century, the serialized novel was reaching millions more readers, and the "outsider" malaise was becoming something of an epidemic—no longer restricted, as in Byron's day, to the rich and the intelligent, but affecting, to a greater or lesser degree, everyone of unusual intelligence.

The older type of hero had demonstrated his skill in dealing with the real world—for example, Robinson Crusoe's desert island. The new intellectual climate of the nineteenth century brought the need for new heroes, men whose skill consists in their ability to conquer the world of the mind. From this point of view, Holmes was an incredible creation, an expression of the spirit of the age rather than of one man's romanticism. He is an outsider; he suffers from the romantic malaise of the century; he smokes too much and injects himself with cocaine. Yet in this world of increasing

chaos and violence, he remains a beacon of sanity. In 1888 the
Jack the Ripper murders produced a traumatic shock in English
society. There had been nothing like them before; earlier murders
had been comprehensible, motivated by fear, jealousy, greed. The
Victorian imagination was captivated by the crimes of Burke and
Hare, Thurtell and Hunt, William Corder (the "Red Barn" murderer), Constance Kent. These savage mutilations of women were
beyond their comprehension; they did not even recognize them as
sex crimes. The Ripper, with his jeering letters to the police, his
ability to evade capture, seemed to be a new kind of super criminal, a "fiend from hell." I doubt whether Conan Doyle would
have been capable of creating Professor Moriarty before 1888.
And although I can offer no proof, I have no doubt that the Ripper
was at the back of his mind when he created Moriarty. Holmes
was more than a fictional character; he was a response to a deep-
rooted psychological need of the late Victorians, a need for reassur-
ance, for belief in the efficacy of reason and for man's power to
overcome the chaos produced by this new disease of alienation.

The need is as strong today as it was in 1890, which no doubt
explains why Holmes is still so very much alive. And that thought
tempts me to explore the whole fascinating question of Holmes as
an archetypal "outsider" figure, and the precise operation of the
superman wish-fulfillment fantasy—a temptation that must be resisted, for fear of doubling the length of the present essay. But
perhaps I may be allowed one comment on the essential nature of
wish-fulfillment fantasies. It struck me the other day when I was
rereading James Thurber's delightful *Secret Life of Walter Mitty*.
Mitty is a henpecked little man living in a small and dull American
town. He compensates for the dullness—and his wife's bullying—
with fantasies in which he is always cool, heroic, dominant. . . .
Super-Mitty is always the man who keeps his head when all about
are losing theirs. He is the commander of a warship, ordering her
to be turned into the storm ("Not so fast! You're driving too
fast!" said Mrs. Mitty. "What are you driving so fast for?"). He is
the great surgeon who knows precisely what to do when an operation goes seriously wrong. ("Quiet, man!" said Mitty in a low,
cool voice.) He is the famous marksman, unjustly accused of murder by the swaggering District Attorney. ("With any known make

of gun," he said evenly, "I could have killed Gregory Fitzhurst at three hundred feet *with my left hand.*") He is the RAF's ace bomber pilot, prepared to fly a dangerous mission alone. ("The pounding of the cannon increased; there was a rat-tat-tatting of machine guns, and from somewhere came the menacing pocketa-pocketa-pocketa of the new flame throwers.") And at the end he is the great spy, defying death to the last. " 'To hell with the handkerchief,' said Walter Mitty scornfully. He took one last drag on his cigarette and snapped it away. Then, with that faint, fleeting smile playing about his lips, he faced the firing squad; erect and motionless, proud and disdainful, Walter Mitty the Undefeated, inscrutable to the last."

Our ancestors spent most of their lives dealing with physical problems; they fought, they loved, and they worked, and reality endowed them with a certain strength. Modern man finds himself in an immensely confusing world that offers no opportunity for the heroic virtues. If he wants to achieve eminence, he needs highly complex disciplines of the mind and emotions, and a great deal of luck. The trouble is that, just as the sound of the trumpet causes the sinews to stiffen, so lack of challenge induces boredom, ineptitude, and a general draining of self-confidence. We can fight this with the imagination. Now, more than at any other time in history, man needs "the strength to dream." All these daydreams of Walter Mitty are tension-inducers, and they are an important part of his resistance to the general softening effect of civilization.

Now turn to the Holmes stories. They are almost pure Walter Mitty, and I say this without any undertone of patronage. "He is the Napoleon of Crime, Watson. He is the organizer of half that is evil and of nearly all that is undetected in this great city."

Or this:

I moved my head to look at the cabinet behind me. When I turned again Sherlock Holmes was standing smiling at me across my study table. I rose to my feet, stared at him for some seconds in utter amazement, and then it appears that I must have fainted for the first and last time in my life. Certainly a gray mist swirled before my eyes, and when it cleared I found my collar-ends undone and the tingling aftertaste of brandy upon my lips. Holmes was bending over my chair, his flask in his hand.

"My dear Watson," said the well-remembered voice, "I owe you a thousand apologies. I had no idea that you would be so affected."

"Holmes!" I cried. "Is it really you?"

We smile at the paragraph when read in isolation, but I still find myself smiling with a lump in my throat as I read it in context. The Holmes stories belong among those works that we know to be full of romantic absurdities, like *The Prisoner of Zenda,* yet which still move us because they are so beautifully done.

Holmes is magnificent because he seems to be, in a sense, larger than his creator. From all we know about him, Doyle seems to have been more like Watson than Holmes. I recall a typical story told at some time by his son, with whom he was traveling on a train, and his son remarked that a certain woman was ugly. Doyle immediately slapped his face, saying: *"No* woman is ugly." The gallantry is marvelously Victorian.

Still, it must be admitted that, in the final sense, there is a dimension lacking in Holmes. And this is because there was something lacking in Doyle himself. He knew it himself. And his artistic instinct was sound when he decided to kill Holmes at the Reichenbach Falls. For Holmes is doomed to remain static; his superb qualities of character and intellect can never develop. Crime is, after all, a relatively trivial subject in itself. As Shaw's Undershaft remarks: "What you call crime is nothing: a murder here and a theft there, a blow now and a curse then: what do they matter? they are only the accidents and illnesses of life: there are not fifty genuine professional criminals in London." Undershaft goes on: "But there are millions of poor people, abject people, dirty people, ill fed, ill clothed people. They poison us morally and physically . . ." And that is the point: Undershaft *goes on.* Holmes stops at the fact of crime and "evildoers."

It is true that Holmes was never quite the same man after he fell over the Reichenbach Falls (although some of the stories are very fine indeed); to engage Doyle's real creative interest, he should have developed. For example, Doyle was always deeply concerned with the problem of life after death; he even dared to convert Professor Challenger into a believer in *The Land of Mist.* Yet because he had created Holmes as a skeptic, a "thinking machine," he was unable to introduce this concern into the stories and novels.* This might seem to be good sense, for we cannot imagine Holmes attending a séance—at least, not as a believer. But E. and H. Heron recognized the unexplored possibilities in their *Real Ghost Stories* (which began to appear in 1898). They created a psychic investigator called Flaxman Low, obviously based on Holmes, who probes into hauntings and suchlike. Low is as cool and intellectual as Holmes, but he takes for granted that ghosts exist, and investigates psychic phenomena on that assumption. In my own opinion, these are by far the most successful of Holmes's literary progeny (with the possible exception of a couple of stories by Jacques Futrelle).

I suggest this as only one of the possible directions in which Holmes could have been developed. But the truth is that if Holmes had been a real human being, he would have developed in other ways. After the Reichenbach episode, Doyle set out to develop him into a universal man, but his imagination failed him. He was too much absorbed in his make-believe world of history—which was not remotely like the reality of the Middle Ages—to attempt to make Holmes a real man in a real modern world. A man with so much interest in crime would have developed an interest in the sociological causes of crime, in the psychology of crime, in the causes of modern man's alienation. Doyle himself investigated a strange case of an animal-disemboweler—the Great Wyrely mystery —but only because an innocent man was accused; he obviously dismissed this sadistic Ripper as an unpleasant madman, without asking himself what could have motivated such a man. The real Holmes would have *wanted* to know. He would also have wanted to know what turns a mathematical genius into a Napoleon of crime. His literary works would not have ended with a monograph on beekeeping or the Chaldean roots of the Cornish language; he would have devoted his retirement to an enormous work on the part played by the sociology of crime in the decline of the West.

In short, Doyle failed to think his creation through to its logical conclusion, thereby demonstrating that he was not the intellectual equal of Sherlock Holmes. But then, perhaps that is just as well. We might draw a lesson from the case of Bernard Shaw. Like Doyle, Shaw made his impact by touching a nerve in the evolu-

---

* See Martin Gardner's article in this connection—*Ed.*

tionary consciousness of his age. Although three years Doyle's
senior, he achieved fame a great deal later, in the 1905 season of
plays at the Court Theatre. Shaw's leading characters have an air
of ruthless logic that reminds us of Holmes. When someone tells
King Magnus that he would like to be able to say "Off with their
heads," Magnus replies, "Many men would hardly miss their
heads, there is so little in them." That sounds as if it might have
been said by Holmes as he scraped away on his violin or filled his
hypodermic with a seven percent solution.

Shaw's concern with the superman was more conscious than
Doyle's; in fact, he wrote a play called *Man and Superman* in
which he formulated the notion that the aim of life is increased
consciousness. He developed the idea for two decades, and in *Back
to Methuselah* it is embodied in his "Ancients," human beings of
some remote future epoch, whose final hope is to become independent of the body and to achieve eternal life. Their ultimate
purpose is to develop into a "whirlpool of pure intellect." Shaw's
contemporaries rejected the idea with a shudder; they might admire intellect, but they didn't really like it. In a dispute about
the sinking of the *Titanic,* Doyle accused Shaw of heartlessness,
and most people (including Shaw's biographer Hesketh Pearson)
were inclined to agree with him.

Doyle, on the other hand, never made the mistake of trying to
think things through to their conclusion. In *The Sign of Four,*
Holmes quotes the German romantic, Richter, and comments:
"He makes one curious but profound remark. It is that the chief
proof of man's real greatness lies in the perception of his own
smallness. It argues, you see, a power of comparison and appreciation which is in itself a proof of nobility." This is a view you might
expect of Holmes in his early esthetic period. Yet in spite of his
belief in the powers of the intellect, Holmes only becomes more
pessimistic with the passage of years. His last appearance is in
"The Retired Colourman," in which we find him telling Watson:
"Is not all life pathetic and futile? Is not his story a microcosm of
the whole? We reach. We grasp. And what is left in our hands at
the end? A shadow. Or worse than a shadow—misery." This kind
of sentiment reassures the reader, like Shakespeare's speeches on
the futility of human existence. It convinces him that, even if
Holmes *is* an intellectual superman, the superiority is only skin-

deep; basically, he is as helpless and defeated as the rest of us. Unlike Shaw, Doyle was a master of protective coloring. The result is that, while Shaw's reputation has suffered a steep decline since his death, Doyle—and Holmes—is as popular as ever. Human beings love to admire a superman; but they greatly prefer a flawed superman.

Notes
on the Contributors

✗

FRANK ALFRED DUNBAR ALLEN has mixed, but happily compatible, loyalties: a pharmacist who likes (and, as his brilliant article shows, is good at) writing, and who was born into the world of the theater.

Frank Allen's father was in theatrical management, and when Frank was born in 1911 he had as godfather the then most distinguished ornament of the British stage, in both acting and management and, of course, production: the late Sir Henry Beerbohm Tree.

Educated at the second oldest grammar school in Wales, Frank Allen proceeded to follow in Dr. Watson's footsteps, to the University of London—not, however, to study medicine, but to enter the School of Pharmacy. He is now a Fellow of the Pharmaceutical Society of Great Britain, and Area Pharmaceutical Officer to a large eastern metropolitan area of the British Health Authority. Besides his Sherlockian and other writings, Frank Allen is a regular monthly contributor to the *Pharmaceutical Journal,* which has had (and not only from Frank Allen) its fair share of Sherlockiana.

He is this year's (1975) Chairman of the Sherlock Holmes Society of London, and at the Savage Club, now housed in the splendid eighteenth-century mansion built by the Adam Brothers for the Marquesses of Lansdowne, Allen meets both literati and people of the theater.

A man of immense energy and a multiplicity of interests, his sports include shooting, fishing, sailing, and rock climbing; while his hobbies include the truly Sherlockian one of beekeeping. He also rears bantams and collects old mineral-water bottles, antique fairy-lights, and—shades of Colonel Moran!—pneumatic weapons.

⚜

ISAAC ASIMOV needs no introduction as one of the most deservedly popular writers in the world—for his books have been translated into what it is the fashion to call "most civilized languages"; and his peculiar talent it is to be able to catch and hold the entranced interest of a readership extending from adolescence to advanced age.

No success is easy—or even possible—to explain, but it might be plausibly suggested that Isaac Asimov's world best-seller success may be due in great part to his ability, not merely to tell a story with all a born storyteller's magic, but to explain, as he goes, the facts on which he builds the solid structure of plot. He is very much the hermeneutic—the explainer—as well as the narrator of "a tale which holdeth children from play, and old men from the chimney-corner." Readers of those science-fact articles of his which for long have graced the pages of *Fantasy & Science Fiction* magazine will have seen the perfect examples of his skill in the exposition of fact, explained with a speculation at once sober and soaring.

Like some other notable contributors to this anthology, Isaac Asimov is a product of the Old World, come to become a part of, and add a luster to, the New. Born in Russia on 2 January 1920—historically, a time which marks the nadir of Russian prosperity—he was brought to the United States at the age of three and became a United States citizen five years later.

He is both a New Yorker and a New Englander, majoring in chemistry and obtaining his B.S. in 1939, his M.A. in 1941, and his Ph.D. in 1948. In the following year he joined the faculty of Boston University School of Medicine, and, though he has not actually taught since 1958, is the university's Associate Professor of Biochemistry.

By his first marriage, Dr. Asimov has two children; his second wife is a psychiatrist, and they live in New York.

"I sold my first story in 1938, published my first book in 1950, and, as of now, have published 160 books, with about a dozen more in press."

⚜

JACQUES BARZUN is classified in American reference books as an educator; in Britain, I think, and in France also, he would be described as a man of letters. It is true that his whole professional career has been passed as a university professor, but, though his influence at Columbia University has been undeniably powerful—"Delightful task! to rear the tender thought, to teach the young idea how to shoot; to pour the fresh instruction o'er the mind . . ."—the influence of his books has, one may feel, been greater.

Professor Barzun, born in France and educated at the Lycée Janson de Sailly, Paris, is the perfect example of the expatriate who has not changed one nationality for another, but happily added another to that into which he was born. He is at once a learned, polished Frenchman and a learned, polished citizen of the United States—which he became, officially, in 1933.

Born at Créteil, France, on 30 November 1907, Jacques Barzun accompanied his father, then on a diplomatic mission, to the United States. That was in 1920 and—to adapt a saying attributed to numerous figures outstanding in French history, young Jacques might have then said, "J'y suis, j'y resterai!"—from that time, he settled in, as they say, to the American way of life, graduating B.A. at Columbia in 1927, and progressing regularly through his degrees until his Ph.D. in 1932.

Joining the teaching staff of Columbia in 1927 as a lecturer, he rose through the professorial ranks until, in 1958, he became Dean of Faculties and Provost, a post that he held until 1967, when his official retirement was postponed *sine die* by the conferment of the rare honor of University Professor, a post from which, like those of field marshals and admirals of the fleet in Britain, one never retires.

Commanding an equal elegance and authority, whether he writes in French or English, he has an impressive list of books to his credit, ranging from *Teacher in America* (1945) to *God's Country and Mine* (1954); from *Pleasures of Music* (1951) to *Nouvelles Lettres de Berlioz* (1970).

As a man of letters, his range of subjects is impressively wide—far too wide, indeed, to be more than hinted at here.

But, if one may look for a linking theme to unite all this impressive diversity into a creative whole, one may reasonably suggest that Professor Barzun is deeply interested in man (*The French Race* [1932/ 1966];* *Race, A Study in Superstition* [1937/1965]; *Of Human Freedom* [1939/1964]), and thus, not only man's activities, but, more, man's two principal justifications for having reached the *sapiens* classification: man's art (*The Energies of Art; Music in American Life; On*

---

* The double dates indicate that of the first edition, and that of the reprint and/or revision.

Writing, Editing and Publishing, etc.) and man's endless inquisitiveness and what it has produced: *The Modern Researcher* (with Henry F. Graff), *Science: The Glorious Entertainment,* and—of special appeal to our readers—*The Delights of Detection* and *A Catalogue of Crime* (with Wendell H. Taylor). It is also relevant that his latest book, *Simple and Direct,* is "A Rhetoric for Writers."

In 1960, Professor Barzun was named Seth Low Professor of History, and received an appointment as Extraordinary Fellow of Churchill College, University of Cambridge, both appointments being concurrent with his teaching and administrative duties at Columbia. At present, Jacques Barzun, who never, as he told the Editor, stopped teaching during his administrative tenure, is offering two courses in his field of cultural history.

He is a member of the American Historical Association, the National Institute of Arts and Letters (of which he was president, 1972–75), and the American Academy of Arts and Sciences.

He is a Fellow of the Royal Society of Arts and a corresponding member of the Massachusetts Historical Society and of the Académie Delphinale, Grenoble. A director of the Council for Basic Education (Washington) and the Peabody Institute of Music and Art (Washington), he is also a member of the following clubs: The Century (New York), the Author's Club, and The Athenaeum (London). He is married and lives in New York.

ᖶ

JACQUES BERGIER, like another of our distinguished contributors, was born in Russia on 8 August 1912, at Odessa, that ancient, beautiful and busy port on the Black Sea. He was educated in France at the Lycée St. Louis, the Sorbonne, and the Institut de Chimie de Paris.

Dangerous as comparisons may often be, it is tempting to find resemblances, other than that of a shared country of origin, between Jacques Bergier and Isaac Asimov, though the first went on to become a physicist; the other, a biochemist.

Rather is it in what passionately interests both that the principal resemblance is to be found: a search for answers to cosmic questions in the widest and most scientific consideration of present events; in the thrilled survey of the past, and in a boldly imaginative extrapolation of the future. If Asimov's creative thinking has led him to imagine vast cosmic empires, millennia and light-years away, and Jacques Bergier sees, always with wonder and never with fear, the emergence of Homo superior from Homo sapiens, the fact to remember is that the creative work of both springs from a lively, irrepressible, and unquenchable interest in life in all its myriad forms. There is nothing—literally nothing —which does not interest and stimulate these two remarkable men.

Jacques Bergier is both a practical physicist and a practical author. In his first capacity, he achieved, in collaboration with Vladimir Gavreau and Alfred Eskenazi, some remarkable achievements in servomechanisms, especially as adapted to the automatic control of machine tools and guided missiles.

With the famous André Helbronner, he achieved the first synthesis of a natural radioactive element: the synthesis, in 1937, of polonium from bismuth and heavy hydrogen; and, still in the same collaboration, the first synthesis of a heavy atomic nucleus: the synthesis of gold from tungsten and boron (1938). Still working with Helbronner, Jacques Bergier, in the immediate pre-World War II days, conducted successful scientific experiments which bring us, in the mere naming of them, startlingly into the nuclear age; the most striking example: work with André Helbronner on the employment of heavy water for the slowing-down of neutrons, and on the concept of the heavy-water generator (1939).

With the coming of World War II, Jacques Bergier went into the dangerous and vitally important activities of the Resistance, work which earned him the thanks of the Allied governments, the Order of the Legion of Honor (military), and many other decorations. Field Marshal Bernard Montgomery signed the Special Certificate of Service to the United Nations, and France has paid this author-physicist—who has known the rigors of the concentration camps—the unique honor of naming a street in the city of Lyons after him.

He has continued to work at his scientific experiments—electronic refrigeration of nuclear reactors (1951), the subcritical nuclear reactor (1955), the documentation computer, ORDOC (1971)—even as he has built up an enviable international literary reputation with books which range from *Marvels of Modern Chemistry* to *Plasma, Fourth State of Matter;* from *Scientific Espionage* to *New Mysteries of Archaeology;* from directing the preparation of *The International Encyclopaedia of Science and Technology* to *The Encyclopaedia of the Unexplained*—some thirty books, written alone or in collaboration, which touch on every aspect of the normal and paranormal. Perhaps the best-known work so far is his collaboration with Louis Pauwels: *Le Matin des Magiciens* (variously, in English, *The Dawn of Magic* or *The Morning of the Magicians*), which has topped a million copies sold in France and has been a best-seller in most other Western countries. Jacques Bergier is, in the opinion of the writer, the greatest living authority on science fiction. He edited the Laffont reprint series of the

famous Arsène Lupin stories. He is very much an admirer of Holmes—
as his unusual presentation of the Master shows.

✂

S. TUPPER BIGELOW is one of the trio of Canadian contributors to this
anthology—the other two being Donald A. Redmond and Alan Bradley.
With a most impressive professional legal background—he has been
a magistrate, a Queen's Counsel and a judge of the Ontario Provincial
Court for over thirty years—he has shown himself, by his many articles
in *The Sherlock Holmes Journal* (London) and *The Baker Street
Journal* (New York), to be one of the most assiduous and successful
delvers into the hidden wealth of fact or supportable hypothesis beneath the too-often sketchily detailed Watsonian record.

He is—one would say, "naturally!"—an Investitured member of the
Baker Street Irregulars, "having," as he writes, "been designated with
the Irregular cognomen of 'The Five Orange Pips.' " The Judge received his Irregular Shilling as far back as 1959.

In the note on Donald A. Redmond (*This Is Not Our Sherlock!*),
reference is made to the fact that Mr. Redmond edited a work of the
Judge's: *Bigelow on Holmes*. This masterly compilation, into which
learning and industry have gone in equal amounts, is an Index of
Canonical Scholarship. This work alone would serve to establish, in
the firmest possible way, Judge Tupper Bigelow's claim to Irregular
pre-eminence.

The reader's attention is called to the characteristic modesty with
which Judge Bigelow begins his article; and some may find another
example of a common Sherlockian paradox in the meticulous detail in
which the Judge presents his analysis of the cases written by a man
who, on his own confession, had "never been nervous about details."

All Sherlockians look up to the Judge, not so much as a Father Figure—no one so young and vigorous could ever be quite *that*—but as
one of the great authorities, answering among Sherlockians to the position that the "Power Masters" must have occupied in that *fin de
siècle* Tibet to which Holmes went in search of arcane knowledge. And
this respect in which the Judge is held by all Sherlockians is no generalized respect: none hold him in higher honor than the lawyers among
the faithful. Observe, for instance, that Mr. Andrew Fusco's fine article
mentions, in its bibliography, a Bigelow classic article which appeared
in a *Baker Street Journal* of 1958: "Sherlock Holmes and Misprision
of Felony."

But it is in the learned study of words—their meanings, their sub-
meanings, their parameanings: the whole semantic gamut—that Judge

Tupper Bigelow has entered most respectedly into the Canon of Sherlockian Exegesis. In 1959 appeared his *An Irregular Anglo-American Glossary of More or Less Unfamiliar Words, Terms and Phrases in the Sherlock Holmes Saga* (Toronto: Castalotte & Zamba, 1959). The late William Baring-Gould calls this "an invaluable reference book for the American student unversed in British speech mannerisms." Invaluable is correct, but the word essential should be added, and all readers of this anthology who have not studied this masterly examination of speech patterns both sides of the Atlantic should get it at once—especially after they shall have read Professor Jacques Barzun's article in this same collection.

𝕄

ALAN BRADLEY is one of our three Canadian contributors; born in Toronto, "but lived most of my life in a small Ontario town, Cobourg" —a name that will evoke an instant response in every Sherlockian breast, especially after reading Dr. Hoffmann's article on page 175.

After leaving school, Mr. Bradley entered radio broadcasting as an operator/technician, extending his professional involvement to television in 1959.

For eight years, he was chief engineer of a television station in eastern Ontario; then, having come to Saskatoon (as Mr. Bradley expresses it) by way of the Ryerson Polytechnical Institute, he has spent the last seven years as Director of Television Engineering at the University of Saskatchewan. The Editor takes some pardonable pride in the fact that, though he certainly did not make Mr. Bradley a Sherlockian— least of all a Sherlockian scholar—the Editor did "regularize" Mr. Bradley's Holmesian inclinations by arranging to make him a free and accepted Baker Street Irregular. That this is no empty honor, Mr. Bradley's contributions to *The Baker Street Journal* will make clear.

We said above that Mr. Bradley was both a Sherlockian and a Sherlockian scholar—by which, one supposes, one means that the scholarship centers, not so much about the character and adventures of Sherlock (which are written down, for all time, in the Canon), as in the time and the character of that time in which Sherlock Holmes (as they say in dictionaries of biography) *floruit*. In our correspondence with Mr. Bradley, we have been impressed with his addiction to and knowledge of the ephemeral literature of Holmes's day: "unimportant" stuff that Holmes must have read in passing, and which, save to the occasional scholar, is forgotten matter to the average reader of today. Always conscious of the fact that Sir Arthur Conan Doyle began his serious attempt to earn a living by his pen with contributions to the boys' magazines of the late seventies and early eighties, Mr. Bradley (helped by his Anglophile nostalgia, of course) is as ardent a collector as reader of what, in the Austria of Dr. Krejci-Graf's childhood (see his article on page 240) , the adults called *Shundhefte:* the Penny Bloods or Penny Dreadfuls of British childhood. One wonders, looking back, what brought such *Trivialliteratur* into such indignant and world-wide contempt. There was nothing improper; there was no bad spelling; there was rarely (if ever) a grammatical solecism; they upheld the universally respected moral qualities of honor, self-respect, honesty, and so on. Why were they the object, on the part of the adults, of such condemnation?

Mr. Bradley thinks them—as we do—wholly admirable; and he is now planning a book to pay them the long overdue credit they deserve. Many years ago, we lived in a Kensington mansion converted into flats; on the first floor lived the editor of one of these boys' journals—by no means the most expensive or approved. To see with what dignity the silk-hatted and frock-coated editor entered the lift; to see the veneration with which the porter took him up to the first floor . . . Well, the ephemeral background of Sherlock Holmes's professional summer deserves to be recalled and acknowledged—and who better (as he proves in his strange little story on page 57) than Mr. Alan Bradley, Baker Street Irregular?

※

PETER COOPER writes on Holmesian chemistry and toxicology with an authority that is unchallenged. His two books on the subjects of poison and poisoning—*Poisoning by Drugs and Chemicals* (3rd ed. London: Lloyd Luke, 1974) and *Adverse Effects of Drugs* (London: Lloyd Luke, 1973)—are the acknowledged standard textbooks in their highly specialized field. Their titles are sufficiently descriptive of their important contents: but it should be made clear that the word drugs in the title of the latter book refers to therapeutic drugs—that is, those drugs commonly prescribed in normal medical practice.

Peter Cooper, after a mixed classical and scientific education, took up pharmaceutical chemistry and became a Fellow of both the Pharmaceutical Society of Great Britain (FPS) and the Chemical Society (FCS); societies as pleasantly housed as any others in the world: the former in ancient Bloomsbury Square, the latter in Burlington House, Piccadilly, home of both the Royal Academy and the Society of Antiquaries.

Mr. Cooper has had dealings with drugs in the context of hospital practice for a good quarter-century, and his interest in this direction crystallized (if we may use the word) in toxicology, and this led to the writing of his two books and many articles. At the present time, Mr. Cooper shares his attention between part-time hospital pharmacy and full-time scientific journalism as a regular contributor to the influential *Pharmaceutical Journal* (London) .

His interests—apart from Holmesian research and criticism—include the history of drugs, folklore, botany (particularly of the cryptogamic plants), music, stagecraft, and archaeology. He is married and has two daughters.

"So far as I am able to judge," Mr. Cooper writes, commenting on the Editor's praise of his article, "most Holmesian criticism is on a fairly high level, and I should be sorry to do anything to reduce it. The only second-rate material emanates from the opposition, and I suspect it is inspired by the successors of Moriarty!"

We—the world—first encountered Sherlock Holmes as he dizzied in the euphoria of an analytical chemist in a moment of triumph. Now, almost a century later, an expert modern chemist and toxicologist takes a long, searching look at the Holmesian chemical triumphs.

§

PHILIP JOHN MORGAN DALTON is unique in this association of dedicated Sherlockian commentators and exegetes, in that he is the only one of that distinguished company who is on the staff of New Scotland Yard (or Scotland Yard, as all but the police and reference books call it), which he joined in 1974.

Born in June 1923 and educated at Ewell Castle, Surrey—site of a palace of Queen Elizabeth I of England—Dalton entered full-time journalism as an editorial trainee under the late Viscount Kemsley, a then leading newspaper and magazine proprietor. That was in 1940, the first full year of World War II, when he was just seventeen.

Two years later, in 1942, Dalton entered the Royal Navy. He saw service until 1946, when he rejoined Kemsley Newspapers, remaining with them until 1952.

For the next twenty years, he developed his skills as an editor of specialized journals: *Good Motoring, London Electricity, Factory Management, Factory Equipment News*—skills which served both him and *Sherlockismus* well when, at various times, he worked as co-editor of the *Journal* of the Sherlock Holmes Society of London, a respected society of which Dalton became a founder-member in 1951 (one year after the foundation of *Sherlock Holmes Klubben i Danmark,* the Danish Baker Street Irregulars).

Philip Dalton is one of the stalwarts of the Sherlock Holmes movement (if that be the right word) in Britain. A founder-member of the

Sherlock Holmes Society, he has served as its Honorary Secretary, its Chairman, and now, its Honorary Treasurer. There can be no more dedicated worker in the cause of "keeping the memory of the Master green."

Between the ending of his twenty years' stint as an editor and his joining Scotland Yard's Press Division, Dalton had a brief experience in public relations. That he has not forgotten any of his writing skills, nor his ability to use the material of everyday experience, are facts pleasantly evident in his *very* Sherlockian contribution to this anthology.

⚔

QUENTIN DOWNES, solver, in this anthology, of the classic Sherlockian "Carfax Puzzle," is a citizen of the Irish Republic and a member of an old Limerick family, among whose distinguished members were Lord Downes of Aghaville, Lord Chief Justice of the Common Pleas in Ireland (Sherlockians should note that he lived at *Merville, Dublin!*); Major General Sir Ulysses de Burgh, to whom the title of Lord Downes came by Special Remainder; and the late Lord Seaton.

Journalist, book reviewer, drama critic, and special features reporter (he was the first to indicate whither the defecting British diplomats, Burgess and Maclean, had flown), Quentin Downes has worked on the *Manchester Daily Despatch, Sheffield Telegraph, Empire News, Daily Sketch, Sunday Graphic,* and other well-known British newspapers. He is the author of numerous short stories and articles, as well as radio and stage scripts; and is the author of three detective novels: *No Smoke, No Flame; Heads I Win;* and *They Hadn't a Clue.* Under the pen name of Martin Fiala, he wrote the best-selling *9:15 to Freedom,* the true account of a daring escape from Communist Czechoslovakia, of which the dramatized version was presented no fewer than nine times on BBC's network.

Quentin Downes describes himself as a "generalized puzzle-solver, rather than a dyed-in-the-wool Sherlockian, which makes me as much interested in Doyle as in Sherlock Holmes. I've always been interested in the use of the name 'Carfax' by novelists—of whom Conan Doyle is only one example. It's strange that, immediately after Conan Doyle had used it in 'The Disappearance of Lady Frances Carfax' in the *Strand Magazine* in April 1911, Hugh Walpole picked it up for the name of a shallow cad—Monty Carfax—in his superb novel, *The Duchess of Wrexe.* Walpole's novel was published by Martin Secker early in 1914, but Walpole had begun it in 1912—the year after Doyle had used the name. In Walpole's case, I think that the allusion *was* to the Oxford Carfax. The famous *Mitre* is only a yard or two away, and Walpole would naturally associate a boozy addlepate like his Monty with the pubs around the Carfax at Oxford—several more than there are today."

Using his recollections of service overseas and at home in World War II, Downes plans what he calls "research in depth into what Holmes was doing, undercover, *after* the unmasking of Von Bork in 1914."

※

ANDREW G. FUSCO, one of the two lawyers contributing to this anthology, is a practicing attorney in Morgantown, West Virginia, and a part-time instructor at the West Virginia University Law Center—which makes him one of two contributors from that respected university.

Mr. Fusco is a dedicated Sherlockian: an Investitured member of the Baker Street Irregulars of New York, with the title of "Athelney Jones"; and Commissionnaire of the Scion of the Four of Morgantown, one of the older scion (i.e., descendant) societies, founded around 1950.

Before he set up in practice as a Morgantown attorney, Mr. Fusco worked for some eight years as a newspaper writer and editor, and still does some free-lance work, mostly book reviews and writings on Sherlockian subjects. His work has appeared in the *Baker Street Journal,* and besides the brilliant contribution to this anthology, he has this year seen an article appear in a major American publication.

When he lectures on Sherlockian subjects, his loyalty to the Master goes down well with his audiences; but an overzealous attempt to further the cause domestically was not successful. On the birth of his twin sons—now aged about three—he suggested that "we call them Sherlock and Mycroft; or Thaddeus and Bartholomew (after the Sholto's). But my wife, Carol, sensible girl that she is, absolutely refused." One feels that such unusual names might have been a troublesome burden for children to bear—especially at school.

Their collie dog, however, could not protest when he was registered at the American Kennel Club as Thorneycroft Huxtable Ladd. This lightheartedness is reflected throughout Mr. Fusco's writings, but never at the expense of sound law or accurate Sherlockian reasoning.

※

JOHN GARDNER is the English author of that name, but in the variety of his formative employments, he might well pass for American—it is rarely that the English writer, even of best-selling thrillers, can claim such diverse experiences.

It is now just over ten years since John Gardner became a full-time author, but, between that qualitative jump and his coming down, a graduate, from St. John's College, Cambridge, he had been a stage magician, an officer in the Royal Marines, a journalist and drama critic. All these occupations have been laid under tribute to provide the background for his writings, but notably so in the case of his series of what he calls "comedy spy-thrillers," featuring the outrageous Boysie Oakes—the most convincing, as well as most popular, anti-hero in modern fiction.

Gardner would be the last to claim that he had invented the anti-hero, but he could well claim to have invented the anti-hero who does actually achieve something—often quite a brilliant something—albeit through half-witted misunderstanding or sheer incomprehension, and almost always by ludicrous accident. In creating Boysie Oakes, the lecherous, shifty, lying, cowardly all-round commando-trained super-killer, John Gardner has created one of the most satisfyingly individual and complete fictional characters of our day. (It has been pointed out that there is much of Falstaff in Boysie Oakes, and that even Falstaff saw some actual fighting; but the descent of Oakes from Falstaff may be maintained only if one may easily imagine Falstaff making scientifically monitored love to a Russian girl in an out-of-control spacecraft.)

It was inevitable that the man who gained both a European reputation by charting the dynamics of an asteroid—what may be called "one of nature's spacecraft"—and a criminal notoriety by organizing London villainy should have attracted the attention of the creator of Boysie Oakes. Two novels on the evil genius Professor James Moriarty, archfoe of Sherlock Holmes and of all that was decent in late-Victorian London, have already appeared: *The Return of Moriarty* was published in 1974 and was warmly received both in Britain and in the United States. The second volume of a planned trilogy concerning "the Napoleon of crime"—*The Revenge of Moriarty*—followed in 1975, and Gardner is at work on the third: three important volumes in a rapidly developing extension of the original Sherlockian exegesis, which is now coming to include a parallel corpus of facts or (at any rate) reasonable speculations about the lesser characters of the Sherlockian saga. Gardner's "further adventures of James Moriarty" brilliantly and satisfyingly complement such "further adventures" as those of Watson and Holmes (in that order) to be read in Nicholas Meyer's *The Seven Percent Solution*.

⋈

MARTIN GARDNER—no relation to the other contributing author of the same surname—has a link with yet another contributor, John Bennett Shaw, in that both were born in Tulsa, Oklahoma (oddly enough, within a year of each other).

Martin Gardner is probably best known to the periodical-reading public through his monthly column on "recreational mathematics" in *Scientific American,* a publication that Holmes must have seen and read, even though it is not mentioned in the Watsonian account. As regards the book-reading public, Mr. Gardner is famous as the kind-but-firm iconoclast whose destructive talent in exposing and correcting error is saved from all suspicion of riding a hobby and emotional prejudice by arguments imaginatively based on reason and coldly based on diligently gathered facts. (If there be an afterlife, one would always expect to find Mr. Gardner deep in friendly conversation with Sir Thomas Browne.)

Of his many books, one might justly select as the most popular—as well as the most representative (not always the case with authors' work) —*The Annotated Alice; The Ambidextrous Universe; The Flight of Peter Fromm,* a recent novel; and that work of his best known to the British, *Fads and Fallacies in the Name of Science.*

Born in 1914, Mr. Gardner graduated in 1936 from the University of Chicago, where he majored in philosophy—although, as he tells us, he was "hooked on Sherlock Holmes" in his early teens, adding that he has been rereading the Canon ever since.

Sherlockians owe Mr. Gardner for an invaluable contribution—not his own—to the corpus of responsible Sherlockian exegesis. It was he who introduced his friend the late (and greatly lamented) William Baring-Gould to New York publisher Clarkson N. Potter, "with the happy result that all Sherlockians know."

Mr. Gardner has been a full-time writer since the end of World War II, during which he served on a destroyer escort of the United States Navy.

Like another of our contributors, the Irishman Quentin Downes, Mr. Gardner is interested in both Sherlock Holmes *and* Conan Doyle (whether or not we call Doyle creator or Agent). In the article that Mr. Gardner has written especially for this anthology, he explores, for the first time in our knowledge, the differences—often seemingly irreconcilable—between Conan Doyle and Sherlock Holmes, choosing to concentrate on a credulity that Doyle permitted to himself but would never have allowed to Sherlock Holmes. In Samuel Rosenberg's article, the psychology of Conan Doyle as revealed through his writings is closely examined; in Mr. Gardner's, the psychologies of both Holmes and Doyle are analyzed, to point out (as we said, for the first time) the striking differences between them.

※

MICHAEL HARRISON was born at Milton, in the Hundred of Tolting-trow, Lathe of Aylesford, Kent, in the year in which man-carrying helicopter flight was first achieved simultaneously by Breguet and Cornu. Fifty years later, he wrote a long article in *Aeronautics* on this world-changing double event.

Intended for architecture, Michael Harrison was diverted into journalism, in which he has held every type of job, from reporter to columnist to drama critic to managing editor. From journalism he changed into advertising, and before his retirement was creative director of the technical and industrial division of one of Britain's largest advertising agencies.

During World War II, he saw service in the Middle East and North Africa, with the Royal Engineers, and on his return entered the Codes and Cyphers Section (No. 8) of British Military Intelligence.

His first book, a novel, was published in 1934 and was a literary-award-winning success; since then, he has published over sixty books, though, after the publication of his last novel, *A Hansom to St. James's,* in 1954, all have been nonfiction.

Following the publication of his now classic *In the Footsteps of Sherlock Holmes* (London, 1958; New York, 1960), Harrison has written and broadcast much on the subject of the Master. His later writings include two more full-length works on Holmes, *The London of Sherlock Holmes* and *The World of Sherlock Holmes* (in both British and American editions); and two monographs, *A Study in Surmise* and *Theatrical Mr. Holmes,* and he revised and updated his *In the Footsteps of Sherlock Holmes* for republication in 1971. Many others of his books have been published in the United States, including the controversial *Clarence,* a life of the unhappy elder son of the Prince of Wales (afterward King Edward VII). In *Clarence,* Harrison clearly identifies "Jack the Ripper" as the Duke of Clarence's insane tutor.

Michael Harrison is a member of both the Baker Street Irregulars of New York and the Sherlock Holmes Society of London, the former having, "in the recognition of his services in keeping the memory of the Master green," given him the award of "The Irregular Shilling," with the Titular Investiture of "The Camberwell Poisoning Case" (1964). He is now at work on a fourth Sherlockian full-length book.

BANESH HOFFMANN, as has been mentioned in the preface, has a relationship to this anthology different from that of all other contributors save that of the Editor: Dr. Hoffmann was one of the two "onlie begetters" of this Sherlockian collection.

His claims to the regard of Sherlockians generally are, however, based on sound work done prior to this anthologizing: more than a decade ago Dr. Hoffmann contributed a classic to the literature of Sherlockian Higher Criticism with his *Sherlock, Shakespeare and the Bomb,* in which unique product of the deepest learning and the lightest humor Dr. Hoffmann proves conclusively that Shakespeare not only foresaw but perfectly understood quantum theory and relativity: two aspects of scientific hermeneutics that Dr. Hoffmann has made specially his own. He is a member of the Baker Street Irregulars, and in 1963 received the Irregular Shilling with the Titular Investiture "The Dynamics of an Asteroid."

To the world outside of the relatively (no pun!) narrow limits of *Sherlockismus,* Dr. Hoffmann's fame is based on his several papers and books—not all of them scientific, but all of them popular—of which *The Strange Story of the Quantum* (1947; rev. ed., 1959) and *Albert Einstein: Creator & Rebel* (1972) may stand as characteristically brilliant examples of the author's imagination and literary skill.

The typical vigor of a thoroughly independent mind is amply—some have thought startlingly—demonstrated in his now famous (in some more ossified circles, notorious) *The Tyranny of Testing* (1964), the most devastatingly destructive-constructive attack on traditional methods of educational testing that has ever been written. No murmur of pigeons, suddenly finding a cat in their midst, put up such a cry of distress as did the traditional testers when Dr. Hoffmann's book (backed up by continent-wide personal lectures) erupted in their complacent, through vested interest, midst.

"There is no escaping the testers," wrote Dr. Hoffmann, "with their electrical scoring machines. . . . They tell admissions officers how many points' worth of college aptitude we possess. They classify us *en masse* in the army. They screen us when we apply for jobs." Dr. Hoffmann states and proves that these tests, though sanctified by uncritical acceptance over the generations, "reward superficiality, ignore creativity, and penalize the person with a probing, subtle mind"—such a mind, indeed, as Dr. Hoffmann so brilliantly described in his popular portrait of Einstein.

Banesh Hoffmann, like another of our American contributors, was born in England, attending one of its most famous schools, St. Paul's, and one of its most famous colleges, Merton, Oxford, where he took a First in Mathematics in 1929. He took his Ph.D. at Princeton in 1932, and there collaborated with O. Veblen on research in connection with relativity theory.

It was as a member of the Institute for Advanced Study at Princeton that he worked with Einstein and L. Infeld on a fundamental research paper, *The Gravitational Equations and the Problem of Motion,* a paper destined to become as classic as that of Moriarty's—but, fortunately, still in print!

Now Professor of Mathematics at Queen's College, New York, of which he became a Fellow in 1937, Dr. Hoffmann has worked mainly in the field of theoretical physics. In 1959 he was invited to do research work in relativity at King's College, University of London, and he has lectured at many universities and professional institutes in both America and Europe. British readers will recall Dr. Hoffmann's appearance on BBC television in 1965, the tenth anniversary of Einstein's death. In this program, Dr. Hoffmann explained Einstein's theories of relativity in laymen's terms—the first time that a simple explanation of these "mathematico-philosophical mysteries" had been given on TV and still the last time that it has been given so well.

※

ANTHONY DOUGLAS HOWLETT is yet another member of what must be the most tolerant profession of all: that of the law. Tolerant? Indeed! One might even say all-forgiving, since it is among the lawyers that we find the most ardent Sherlockians, and we all know what Sherlock thought of the law—even though (out of some regard, doubtless, for his friend Watson's established professional standing) he refrained from too prejudiced an evaluation of lawyers.

A barrister-at-law, a lieutenant commander in the Royal Naval Reserve, and a founder-member (1951) of the Sherlock Holmes Society of London, Commander Howlett is an LL.B. and an M.A. of Cambridge University. He was Chairman of the Sherlock Holmes Society from 1960 to 1963, and is a member of that eminent Society's Council.

But it is as the Society's—indeed, as Sherlockdom's—film expert that Anthony Howlett has established a unique reputation throughout the literally world-wide following of the Master. Although still only fifty years of age, Mr. Howlett has specialized for some thirty-five years in the deep study of Holmes stage plays and films, in obtaining copies of old films of Holmesian and allied interest, and in presenting them annually at the Society's film series for the past twenty-three years.

Deriving from and supporting his role as "Sherlockian Archaeologist Extraordinary" is Commander Howlett's authorship of numerous articles on the film and stage aspects of Holmesiana, both in the strictly Sherlockian press and outside.

To date, Commander Howlett has made more than thirty television and radio broadcasts on his chosen subject, in almost all the European countries: England, Belgium, France, Germany, Holland, Italy,

Sweden, and Switzerland—and he has also been featured in several documentary films about Holmes.

"Although bearing no resemblance whatsoever to Sherlock Holmes," he writes, "I once had the brazen effrontery to impersonate him for six out of the eight days of the Sherlock Holmes Society's Pilgrimage to Switzerland in 1968, and fought Professor Moriarty four times on the very edge of the Reichenbach Falls. Lord Gore-Booth, much more appropriately, starred as Mr. Holmes for the main two days of the ceremonies."

In the article that Commander Howlett has written for this anthology—an article that has been growing in length and importance since it first appeared, under the joint authorship of Anthony Howlett and his friend Michael Pointer, twenty-one years ago—the archival experience and discovery of some thirty-five years is here offered for the instruction and pleasure of, not only all Sherlockians, but also those many others who share the present ever-growing interest in the theater and cinema of the past.

❦

KARL KREJCI-GRAF is not the most senior of the Sherlockians represented in this collection, but he is among the most senior, having been born in Gmünd, Lower Austria (a small town, he tells us, of some 5,000 inhabitants), in the year 1898—the year in which, if we may accept the Baring-Gould chronology, Sherlock Holmes was involved in the ludicrous affair of the two Coptic patriarchs. "I know nostalgia," writes Dr. Krejci-Graf; "I knew it when I was a youth, attending the local *Gymnasium* (high school); forgot it during my travels; but now it is strong again." This nostalgia it is which not only takes Dr. Krejci-Graf back to his home town every year, but also deepens his interest in, and increases his enjoyment of, the vanished world of Sherlock Holmes.

Dr. Krejci-Graf has known that world of fogs and hansoms; stable, interchangeable, gold-based currencies; inexpensive, available-to-all luxury and taken-for-granted order and freedom. Indeed, that world had not vanished when, at the age of seven, in 1905, he first made acquaintance with the magic of the Holmes tales, in the (German) Lutz edition, published in Leipzig. He liked, and still likes, the early stories, but "I was disappointed by the stories written after 1908—*The Valley of Fear, The Case Book of Sherlock Holmes* and *His Last Bow.*"

He took his first lessons at the Gmünd primary school, and from there went on to the *Gymnasium* at Budweis (now Ceske Budejovice, Bohemia) "until my parents were told to take me away. I then went to Krems, where again I was in trouble . . ."

But by now it was 1915, and Karl Krejci-Graf was seventeen, and World War I, in which the Austrian Empire was to collapse and vanish, was now in its first full year. He volunteered for the Austrian Army, was passed for service, and was posted to the 49th k.u.k. (*Royal and Imperial*) Regiment of Infantry, whose first commander had been one of the "Wild Geese": the Irish expatriate Major O'Brien—the commander whose Austrians prevented Napoleon from crossing the Danube on the eve of Aspern, and so caused the Corsican to lose that important battle.

Dr. Krejci-Graf served throughout the long and bitter war, from Empire to Republic. He was wounded twice, and "collected," as he says, "all the medals available to soldiers of the Common Army."

The army had taught him the value of discipline: there was to be no more trouble at educational establishments. He studied geology in Austria, Finland and Germany, taking the degrees of Ph.D. Vindob. (*Vienna*) and Dr. habil. Berol. (*Berlin*). Though he returns to his home town each year, he has lived abroad for fifty years, prospecting for ores, coal, and oil throughout the 25,000-mile stretch of the Northern Hemisphere. Today, at the age of seventy-eight, he is a professor at the Geologisches Institut of Frankfort-on-Main.

As a boy and youth, Dr. Krejci-Graf read the German versions of the British schoolboy's Penny Dreadfuls—especially the imitations (he does not like the use of the word "plagiarism" in this connection) which merely used the name Sherlock Holmes, and supplied the (almost always incredible) plots. Some are to be found in C. G. Kayser's *Bücherlexikon,* 1907–1910: *Detektiv Sherlock Holmes und seine weltberühmten Abenteuer* (Detective Sherlock Holmes and His World-Renowned Adventures). What Karl Krecji-Graf could never have foreseen was that this ephemeral and unconsidered juvenile reading would one day make him a world authority on this curious aspect of *Weltsherlockismus*—an abstruse and recondite branch of knowledge of which some idea may be gathered from his article which is Part II of *This Is Not Our Sherlock!*

Dr. Krejci-Graf has contributed to both the (London) *Sherlock Holmes Journal* and the (New York) *Baker Street Journal.* For his services to the cause, he was awarded, in 1967, the Irregular Shilling and given the Titular Investiture as "Baron Gruner, the Austrian."

☙

HENRY LAURITZEN's fame as artist and author goes far beyond his native Denmark, where, at Silkeborg, he was born in 1908. In his own country, he is perhaps best known as one of Denmark's wittiest (and not always kindest!) cartoonists, but his range of work is so wide—from modern advertising to the serious illustration of his own and others' books—that his work, either as artist or writer, is as hard to classify as the man himself.

His first, most striking characteristic is a lively and insatiable interest in his world—an interest to which his apparently inexhaustible energy makes its fullest contribution.

Though his regular assignments as an artist provide him with the fullest of full days' duties, he can yet find time and energy to run the affairs of *Sherlock Holmes Klubben i Danmark* (The Danish Baker Street Irregulars), an extremely healthy and continually expanding organization which, in 1975, celebrated its Silver Jubilee. Lauritzen is not only the President of the Danish Irregulars, but also the editor-illustrator of their bright and thriving magazine, *Sherlockiana*.

Yet, as though all this did not provide full occupation for his diverse and brilliant talents, Hr. Lauritzen is also a committee member of the Danish Jockey Club, in which official position he is the club's handicapper for the racecourse at Billund and his home town of Aalborg.

In this capacity he organizes that most Sherlockian of all races (also known in the United States): the Silver Blaze Sweepstake, of which the thirteenth was run at Aalborg on 31 May 1975.

A dedicated Sherlockian for many years, Lauritzen is a member of the Baker Street Irregulars of New York, with the fitting Investitured Title of "The Royal Family of Scandinavia"—who, it may be remembered, gave the young Holmes his first royal commission.

As a writer, his talents are no less diverse; his range no less wide. A historian *par excellence* of the detective and of the detective novel, Lauritzen is also the recorder and interpreter of less specialized aspects of history, with a taste for, and a most demonstrable skill in, the synoptic study or biography. A random choice of titles (roughly translated) will sufficiently indicate the range of his interests: *A Close Look at the Great Sleuths; Conan Doyle and Napoleon; The Wit and Wisdom of P. G. Wodehouse; The Humor of Mark Twain; The Humor of Charles Dickens; My Friend the Bookmaker*—and very many more.

Invited to contribute a Sherlockian essay to this collection, Lauritzen preferred to pay his tribute to The Commissionnaire in artistic rather than literary form. Nothing could have pleased the Editor more: there is no shortage of first-class writers, but first-class *Sherlockian* artists are not so easily come by.

⚑

NICHOLAS MEYER is nearly the youngest of our contributors, but in his case youth is certainly not to be equated with literary inexperience. The outstanding success of his Sherlockian thriller, *The Seven Percent*

Solution (New York: Dutton, 1974; London: Hodder & Stoughton, 1974), was no fluke: there is plenty of solid literary know-how behind that assured achievement.

A New Yorker by birth, Mr. Meyer was thirty on Christmas Eve of 1975. His mother, now dead, was a concert pianist; his father is a practicing psychoanalyst, living and working in New York City. It cannot be detracting from Mr. Meyer's achievement in *The Seven Percent Solution* to see, in his father's profession, that subtle influence which inclined Nicholas Meyer to give that Sherlockian thriller the character and work of Sigmund Freud as its *point d'appui;* and, again, the theme of his contribution to this anthology.

It is likely that *Seven Percent* is the most successful Sherlockian work since Conan Doyle laid down his Sherlockian pen fifty years ago. The book was nominated as a Literary Guild Alternate and as a Mystery Guild Selection, and has been, at the time of this writing, on the *New York Times* best-seller lists for almost a year, with sales to date topping 150,000 (a tribute both to Mr. Meyer and to the perennial fascination of the Master!).

As we wrote, casting was taking place for the film version, which began in Europe in September 1975. All the players had not yet been chosen, but the distinguished cast at that point included Nicol Williamson as Holmes and Alan Arkin as Freud, with strong support from such well-known stage and film stars as Orson Welles, Laurence Olivier, Jeanne Moreau, Vanessa Redgrave, and Joel Grey. The film was made by Universal Pictures, produced and directed by Herbert Ross; Nicholas Meyer did the screenplay.

Nicholas Meyer was educated at the Fieldston School, Riverdale, New York, and at the University of Iowa. His literary background includes work as publicist for the film *Love Story* for Paramount Pictures, and as editor of Warner Brothers Story Department, New York City. His books now include *The Love Story Story* (Avon, 1971)—based on his experiences with Paramount; and *Target Practice* (New York: Harcourt Brace; London: Hodder & Stoughton—both 1974), which was nominated for an Edgar Award of the Mystery Writers of America for the best detective novel of the year. Mr. Meyer also wrote the American television versions of *Judge Dee* and *Monastery Murders* (both based on the late Robert van Gulick's novel), and this program also earned Mr. Meyer another Edgar nomination, this time—29 December 1974—for the best mystery teleplay of the year.

When we asked Mr. Meyer about work in progress, he told us that he was now at work on *Please Stand By!* a two-hour television play based on Orson Welles's famous (or notorious—depending how one reacted to the original shock) "Martian" broadcast; a sequel to *Seven Percent* (as yet unnamed), and *Amazon!*, "action adventure spectacular feature film for Warner Brothers, set in South America, 1906."

We wish, for all these current and future literary ventures, a success not incomparable with that which has greeted *The Seven Percent Solution!*

✖

DAVID JOHN TWYMAN PEARSON is another of our expatriate contributors; two of the others are Jacques Barzun and Banesh Hoffmann. Born 13 April 1941 at Woodchurch, Kent, England—"My earliest recollections are of American soldiers (my sister married one) and 'doodle-bugs' " [the German V2 "flying bomb" of 1944]—Mr. Pearson came to the United States in 1949 to live with his grandparents, who adopted him. He lives today in Hope, Arkansas, with his grandmother.

He lists music among his interests—"both listening and performing" —as one might expect from an Anglo-American who, as a boy of. thirteen, toured the United States with the Apollo Boys' Choir of Palm Beach, Florida.

A graduate of Phillips University, Enid, Oklahoma (1962), with a B.A. in Religion and Theater Arts, and of Henderson State College, Arkadelphia, Arkansas (1972), with an MSE in English, Mr. Pearson has been an ordained minister of the Christian Churches (Disciples of Christ) since 1963, and a public school teacher since 1967. ("Look at those big, isolated clumps of buildings . . ." "The board-schools." "Lighthouses, my boy! Beacons of the future! Capsules with hundreds of bright little seeds in each, out of which will spring the wiser, better England of the future." There is no doubt that Holmes approved of the public schools, in the American sense, and, by inference, of those who taught in them.)

Teaching history, geography and elementary economics, Mr. Pearson is Chairman of the Social Science Department at Hopewell Middle School, Hope, Arkansas; but, as with a very great number of American graduates, his occupational experience has been both varied and extensive: "I have also worked as a peach-picker, a department-store clerk and window-trimmer, an advertising salesman and a linotype operator and pressman."

Since some of the most persuasive masters of the English language, from Dickens to Chesterton; Marryat to Priestley, have sung the glories of the English pub, it is perhaps not astonishing that Mr. Pearson— "I am an incurable Anglophile to this day!"—should define his ambitions as: "To become a professor of English and a free-lance writer;

to find agreeable work in England (or to import my own pub into the U.S.!)."

On the more serious side, nothing could be more fitting than that an ordained minister should have presented, as his contribution to this very wide-ranging anthology, his careful, completely objective and always charitable analysis of Holmes's religious beliefs. That, as Mr. Pearson points out, Holmes frequently mentioned the fact—or, at least, the acceptable possibility—of a Great Architect of the Universe, with the perhaps corollary theory of a posthumous system of rewards and punishments, are matters well known to all Sherlockians. Where Mr. Pearson, viewing these matters from both a Sherlockian's and a minister's interest, breaks new ground is in not so much listing Holmes's religious utterances—that has already been done, long since—as in trying to discover exactly what Holmes means when he talks of God. Few articles more relevant to the author and to the Master are to be found in this anthology.

𝕏

DONALD A. REDMOND is pre-eminent among Sherlockian scholars—*primus inter pares,* as one used to say before it became fashionable to know not even the sketchiest Latin. Not for nothing is his Investitured Title (conferred, with his Irregular Shilling, in 1969) "Good Old Index."

Donald Redmond is Chief Librarian at Queen's University, Kingston, Ontario—one of the three Canadian contributors to this anthology, and the only professional librarian of the trio.

A graduate of the universities of Mount Allison, McGill, and Illinois, Mr. Redmond has held library administrative positions in the United States, Canada, Ceylon, and Turkey—a breadth of practical experience which is clearly reflected in the breadth (no less than in the depth) of his scholarship, Sherlockian and otherwise.

A member of the Baker Street Irregulars in the United States and of the Sherlock Holmes Society in Britain, he has written numerous articles in Holmesian periodicals, besides having edited a number of indexes essential to the Sherlockian scholar. These include a cumulative index to the *Baker Street Journal;* a checklist of the Arthur Conan Doyle Collection of the Metropolitan Toronto Central Library; and *Bigelow on Holmes,* an index of Canonical Scholarship originally compiled by Judge S. Tupper Bigelow, QC (who also contributes to this anthology), and published by the Toronto Library.

Sherlockian friends of Donald Redmond most appreciate those products of the "small change" of his lively scholarship: the light-hearted but still factually valuable Christmas cards, in which he explores some hitherto taken for granted aspect of the Sherlockian Canon. One particularly happy example of this highly specialized scholarship was that card which dealt with the least explicable details of Holmes's encounter with "the speckled band" at Stoke Moran—and, particularly, with a close look at Holmes's ability to distinguish the genus of a venomous creature seen, in one sudden startled *coup d'oeil*, by the dim light of the sort of Victorian candle that the mean Dr. Grimesby Roylott would have provided. "Did you ever try," Mr. Redmond asks, "whipping the end of a dangling rope with a lithe lath? It does anything except hang docilely still, Newton's Laws still being very effective. . . ." But it is in such questions, and the immense treasures of speculation that they reveal, that the joy of Sherlockian scholarship lies.

A far less speculative aspect of this scholarship led Mr. Redmond to the consideration of the German imitations of Holmes, "a selected edition of which was published in 1973, and which are very little known (not at all?) in English."

This consideration brought together two established Sherlockians—with the result that we are able to present Mr. Redmond's article and Dr. Krejci-Graf's comments as one learned commentary on the improbable adventures of Holmes and his *Famulus,* Harry Taxon, as seen through the imaginative eyes of German pulp-writers working for the German schoolboy market in those happier days before World War I.

❧

SAMUEL ROSENBERG certainly set the deductional cat among the Sherlockian pigeons when he published his *Naked Is the Best Disguise: The Death and Resurrection of Sherlock Holmes* (New York: Bobbs-Merrill, 1974). As one eminent certificated Sherlockian wrote to the Editor: "Rosenberg . . . unfortunately, will be laughed at excessively by a number of Sherlockians who should know better." The comfortable sales of this work of unprecedented novelty make it clear that there are still tens of thousands—presumably, many of them Sherlockians or Sherlockianly orientated—to whom Mr. Rosenberg's novel theories have made strong intellectual and emotional appeal. In recent years, the interest in Sir Arthur Conan Doyle as a parallel image or even *Doppelgänger* in relation to Sherlock Holmes has been steadily growing; and the tracing of the origins of the names and ideas to be found in the Canon has been an occupation (perhaps even a preoccupation) of the Editor's for decades. But it is not so much the trend to which Mr. Rosenberg's book belongs which marks it out for comment, as the conclusions to which he has come from a careful study of the evidence of Doyle's innermost sentiments and compulsions hidden away "in parable" in the sayings and actions of Sherlock Holmes.

Whether for good or ill—and Sherlockians of the more traditional type will find it only for ill—Mr. Rosenberg's book, *facile princeps* in a new and compelling fashion, has established the necessity of considering Holmes and his literary creator as one entity, never to be put asunder. The Editor recalls that, some twenty years ago, he was invited by the Dickens Fellowship to give that estimable body of novelist worshipers a lecture on their hero. The lecture, given by one who felt himself not inferior to the Dickens Fellows in admiration for the great novelist, expatiated on the courage of Dickens, who, dying of heart disease and further handicapped by a cerebral hemorrhage; and burdened, moreover, with the necessity of enduring the petulant demands of a greedy mistress nearly forty years his junior, kept himself going with alcohol. The lecture continued and ended in a hostile silence; the lecturer got, as his reward for a heartfelt praise of Dickens, what the actors call (at any rate, in England) the bird. Recently, while doing some research in the headquarters of the Dickens Fellowship, the Editor mentioned this disagreeable experience to the secretary. "Oh," said she, going far further in tolerance than even the Editor had come, "we think differently now. Poor chap, *surely he deserved a little pleasure in his life* . . . someone to understand him." It was the howled-down "humanizers" of Dickens who had brought about this tolerant attitude; and Sherlockians, like Dickensians, will come to accept the Rosenberg-type hermeneutics, I dare say, as a matter of course . . . in the not very distant future. In the meanwhile, he is—and will so remain for some time—the *enfant terrible* of Sherlockian scholarship.

For a prober into the innermost being of Doyle-Holmes, Mr. Rosenberg is remarkably and modestly reticent about himself.

"Samuel Rosenberg has been a playwright, stage manager, play reader, in the New York theater. In other incarnations he has been a photographer for the U.S. Government, the United Nations, and leading magazines. He has also been a collector of graphics, an artist, and a literary consultant for several motion-picture companies. He has served as a university teacher and lecturer. For some years he worked as a producer, director, writer, cinematographer for the American Broadcasting Company, and for various documentary film companies.

"Since 1967, Rosenberg has given most of his time to the writing of investigative books and essays about such 'real' and 'fictional' figures as Herman Melville, St. Nicholas, Mary Shelley, Perseus, Dr. Albert Schweitzer, Lot's Wife, James Joyce, Medusa, and others.

"Currently, he is writing an intensive literary detective investigation of certain episodes in the life of Dr. Sigmund Freud, of whom he is very fond."

※

JOHN BENNETT SHAW bears one of the most apt of Irregular titles: "The Hans Sloane of his Age," for Mr. Shaw, in a society where the collection of Sherlockian items is an occupational and pandemic disease, has one of the biggest—if not the biggest—of such collections. Of himself he writes: "Avocation: collecting and lecturing upon the Cult of Sherlock Holmes." Insofar as he has given some three hundred personal lectures and radio and TV talks on this subject, one might feel that vocation, rather than avocation, is the more precise definition of Mr. Shaw's all-absorbing occupation.

Born at Tulsa, Oklahoma, in 1913, Mr. Shaw is a graduate of the University of Notre Dame. Like many others of our contributors, he did graduate work at Columbia University, and took his M.A. degree at the University of Tulsa, his home city. He lectured in American Literature at this same university, went on (like that famous man of American letters, Raymond Chandler) to manage an oil well; ran, successively, a retail book-and-record shop and a funeral business. (*De mortuis,* rather than *de Moriartio* . . .)

He has been active as a library trustee—one of the several in the Baker Street Irregulars—for Tulsa City-County, the State Library of Oklahoma and the University of Notre Dame, while he has also held office in the American Library Association and in several regional associations. An active (and the only) layman on the national Catholic Liturgical Board, he has also served as what he describes as "a sort of ecumenical and PR officer for the Roman Catholic diocese of Oklahoma."

This dedicated Sherlockian of quite startling energies is a member of the Baker Street Irregulars, of the Sherlock Holmes Society of London, and of a dozen or so associated societies. Like his great original, Sir Hans Sloane, whose collection of "curiosities" bequeathed to the nation formed the basis of the British Museum's famed reliquary wealth, John Bennett Shaw, "The Hans Sloane of his Age," exhibits all that restless, constructive curiosity—with the willingness to travel immense distances to "see a New Marvell"—that the original Sir Hans displayed. Great as are the average American distances, John Bennett Shaw takes them in his ever-probing stride: ". . . next month I shall speak on Holmes at Tulsa and spend the night in Muskogee. . . . The Symposium on Holmes at Fort Collins was great. . . ." Jung, with his theories on coincidences, would have found it only right and proper that John Bennett Shaw should have lived to the north of *Moriarty* in a house "which is on the SE edge of Santa Fe, on the upper side of the plateau, just below the mountains; like many people do not believe, but in one mile from my house is wilderness, and, seventeen miles on, NO roads at all—only horse and helicopter. Great!"

✄

NICHOLAS RATHBONE UTECHIN is by far the youngest contributor to this anthology; that a span of sixty years divides his age from that of the oldest shows the enormous vitality of the Sherlock Holmes addiction (is that the right word?). But is there any other cult, hobby, obsession—call it what you will—that exerts its appeal, its compulsion, as equally on the young as on the old? But this is what *Sherlockismus* does—for, at twenty-three, Mr. Utechin explains the fact that he has received the Irregular Shilling and a Titular Investiture ("The Ancient British Barrow") by explaining that "I don't think I did anything remarkable to get the Irregular Shilling: just a steady flow of reasonably intelligent papers to the *Baker Street Journal*, the *Sherlock Holmes Journal* and *Shades of Sherlock* over seven years. . . ." So that it was at the age of sixteen that Mr. Utechin began to contribute toward the vast corpus of Sherlockiana.

A third cousin twice removed of the late Basil Rathbone—". . . a name not wholly unknown in Sherlockian folklore; my middle name is Rathbone: my grandfather shared the same grandfather with Basil . . . can you follow?!"—Nicholas Utechin was born in Oxford in 1952, studied modern history at the local university, and came down with a degree in his chosen subject. "Most of my time at Oxford, however, was spent being President of the Oxford University Broadcasting Society and doing programs for the BBC local station . . . together with attending various sporting dinners—of sports which I rarely participated in, but of which I knew the secretaries!"

On leaving the university (he still lives in Oxford, by the way) he went straight into broadcasting, becoming a newscaster and program director at London Broadcasting (the independent London radio service). Among his many interests—apart from his devotion to Sherlock Holmes—he lists the laying down of vintage port and claret, studying the films of D. W. Griffith and Lillian Gish, watching and playing cricket and squash rackets, following the fortunes of the Oxford United Football Club ("2nd Division stalwarts—no more, no less"), and "an avid follower of *baseball*."

"It may not mean a lot to you, but I was present in Montreal when

Henry Aaron of the Atlanta Braves hit home run No. 704—and I roared with the best of them!

"I've published papers on SH on both sides of the Atlantic; I have also been known to write songs and poetry . . . and am engaged at the moment in coauthoring a novel on Sherlock Holmes."

That Nicholas Utechin profited by reading modern history at Oxford is apparent from the research, no less than the literary brilliance, which has gone into his presentation of one of the more noted of Sherlockian villains.

❦

EDWARD VAN LIERE is our senior contributor; a veteran of World War I, and born at a time when Sherlock Holmes was at his most active; in vigorous pursuit of the truth, and the incidental pursuit of that undying fame that he now enjoys.

Dean Emeritus of the School of Medicine at the University of West Virginia, Dr. Van Liere's work on—if not exactly his interest in—the matter of Holmes and Watson has been almost entirely peripatetic: his entertaining essays on both have been written when he was on trains or airplanes, in motels and hotels, more often than not when Dr. Van Liere was traveling on business in connection with the development of his university's new Medical Center.

A midwesterner, Dr. Van Liere was born in Kenosha, Wisconsin, at whose university he took his degrees of M.A. and M.S., proceeding to Harvard for his M.D., and to Chicago for his Ph.D. He returned to the University of Wisconsin to teach zoology; taught physiology at the universities of Chicago and South Dakota; and—World War I being over—became professor of physiology at the University of West Virginia in 1921. He has also served as an expert consultant to the United States Surgeon-General, in relation to the general basic science course of the U.S. Army Medical Department Research and Graduate School.

In the more than half-century since he joined the professorial staff at West Virginia, Dr. Van Liere's reputation has passed far beyond the limits of his native country. As well as being a Fellow of the American College of Physicians and a member of the American Physiological Society, the Society for Experimental Biology, the American Medical Association, and the West Virginia and Monongahela County Medical Societies, Dr. Van Liere is also an Affiliate of the Royal Society of Medicine—founded in London in 1805, the year of Trafalgar. He is a member of Phi Beta Kappa and Sigma Xi.

A frequent contributor to medical and biological journals, Dr. Van

Liere is the author of the classic *Anoxia: Its Effect on the Body*
(University of Chicago Press, 1942). Sherlockians will recall that Miss
Morstan (and Watson, too, if it comes to that) presented the disturbing
syndromes of this momentary lack of the normal oxygen supply. But
Sherlockians all over the world will be more grateful to Dr. Van Liere
(Irregularly cognominated "The Priory School") for his completely
delightful *A Doctor Enjoys Sherlock Holmes* (New York: The Vantage
Press, 1960), a collection of Sherlockian essays whose learning and
charm reminded your Editor of those two incomparable essayists of a
generation ago, E. V. Knox and H. V. Morton.

Few Sherlockians are not, by the same token, historians—or, perhaps,
nostalgists who like to take a high magnification telescope to their
view of the past. In Dr. Van Liere's case, the backward glance encom-
passes western Americana—especially the lore of the Southwest.

To his careful observation of the saga's biologic plots, Dr. Van Liere
has brought both medical knowledge and Sherlockian understanding.

ALAN WATKINS is a Welsh journalist and author whose forthright and
persuasively argued views have brought him to the front ranks of
British political and social commentators.

Born in 1933 and educated at the Amman Valley Grammar School,
Ammanford (Carmarthenshire, Wales), and Queen's College, Cambridge, Mr. Watkins is one of the three lawyers among our contributors, being called to the bar of Lincoln's Inn in 1957 at the early age
of twenty-five.

Whether it was a taste for research which took him to the London
School of Economics as a research assistant in 1959, or whether his
two years at the LSE gave him a taste for research, we do not know;
but from the LSE Mr. Watkins joined the editorial staff of the (London) *Sunday Express* in 1959, staying there for five years. He then
became the political correspondent of *The Spectator*, one of Britain's
most influential weeklies, moving, three years later, to what most
British people regard as the other most influential weekly, *The New
Statesman*, for which he still writes.

He was political columnist on the (London) *Sunday Mirror* from
1968 to 1969, and at the time of this writing he is one of the most
respected columnists on the (London) *Evening Standard*. His books
include *The Liberal Dilemma* (1966) and, with Andrew Alexander—
political editor of *The Daily Mail*—*The Making of the Prime Minister*
(1970).

With such politico-economic experience and consciousness, it was inevitable that Alan Watkins's Sherlockian fantasy should involve the Master Sleuth in the half-witted, sullen malignancy of bureaucratic management.

Witty though the lighthearted presentation of Sherlock's involvement may be, as here portrayed by Mr. Watkins, his choice of subject is a long-overdue reminder that there is a serious lacuna in the Watsonian record: Holmes's frustration at the hands of the bureaucrats. Perhaps Watson took this frustration—the immovable object overcoming the irresistible force—as so inevitable, so much to be taken for granted, that he never thought to mention it, as he—and anyone else— would never think of describing how one opens a door. But that many a Sherlockian act died in the thinking, many a Sherlockian resolve came to nothing, many a Sherlockian enterprise was stifled at conception, we may be sure, because then, even as now, bureaucracy stood firm against imagination and enterprise. Mr. Watkins has done well to remind us of that fact.

※

COLIN WILSON woke to fame with his brilliant first book, *The Outsider,* a study of the human being through the ages who is not so much out of step with his fellows as outside the normal pattern. This fascinating study, which securely established Wilson's international reputation as a creative philosopher, has been followed by some thirty books—all varied in subject, but linked to the central theme of what Wilson has named "Faculty X."

Those who know Wilson personally, and not merely through his seductively readable books, find that his most impressive quality is that of honest self-appraisal. Therefore, if one needs to find a descriptive phrase about Wilson and his writings, then go for it to Wilson himself. The first sentence of the Preface to his best-selling *The Occult: A History* (Random House, 1971) provides the needed and completely comprehensive phrase: "A single obsessional idea runs through all my work: the paradoxical nature of freedom."

It is this single obsessional idea that has linked all the work of a prolific output of two decades: science fiction; studies of detection, espionage and in-depth psychology; analyses of the criminal and his motivations; a fictional life of a compulsive murderer; and a true biography of the important psychoanalyst, Maslow. These in addition to a number of novels—different, yet each within the group gathered about Wilson's single obsessional idea. Already he is a considerable literary force in both Britain and America, and it is to his unusual merging of the reporter with the philosopher that Wilson may look for that authoritative position in Letters that he must surely come to in the end.

For Wilson not only writes about murderers and poltergeists, Freud and Strindberg, Jack the Ripper and Gilles de Rais; he investigates, personally, as much as possible. Before he wrote a series of articles on Jack the Ripper, he familiarized himself with his grim subject by probing into the darkest alleys and courts of Whitechapel. He attends inquests; he has spoken to every available witness, from the policeman on the beat to the nosey neighbor half-hidden behind the dingy lace curtains; from the dim-memoried passerby to the coroner in his office.

Colin Wilson is a student of literature, and though widely read to an almost incredible degree, he has taken that study further, by seeking out the men and women who actually *make* the literature which so fascinates him. There is hardly a writer of repute in Britain, the Continent, or the United States whom he has not met.

He lives in a house in Cornwall so crammed with books that, as one visitor remarked, "it seems almost more books than house." To this multiple study of Sherlock Holmes, Wilson brings, as always, a new illumination.